WALT WHITMAN AS MAN, POET, AND LEGEND

WITH

A CHECK LIST OF WHITMAN PUBLICATIONS

WALT WHITMAN

AS

MAN, POET, AND LEGEND

By Gay Wilson Allen

WITH

A CHECK LIST OF
WHITMAN
PUBLICATIONS 1945-1960

By Evie Allison Allen

SOUTHERN ILLINOIS UNIVERSITY PRESS

CARBONDALE

ACKNOWLEDGMENTS: *The illustration on page 2 and on the jacket is taken from* Walt Whitman Sangen Orn Meg Selv Av *Leaves of Grass. Oversettelse og innledning ved Per Arneberg Tegninger av Kai Fjell. Reproduced with the permission of* H. Ascheboug & Co., *Oslo, Norway. The illustration of Whitman's revision of "A Riddle Song" on page 26 is from the collection of Charles E. Feinberg and is reproduced with Mr. Feinberg's kind permission.*

To The Memory Of

FREDERIK SCHYBERG

1905-1950

PREFACE

THE FIRST IDEA for this book was a collection of my Whitman studies tucked away in various scholarly and literary periodicals, where they are not inaccessible to the diligent searcher but nevertheless likely to be overlooked—such as "The 'Long Journey' Motif" essay. But once I started assembling the pieces, the experience that I have had so many times before began repeating itself: I never return to Whitman without an expansion of my angle of vision.

Some of the studies seemed too technical to interest anyone but the dedicated specialist; or the ideas and information had been amplified in subsequent publications. Thus I discarded my first scholarly publication on Whitman, a paper in the pre-World War II *Revue Anglo-Américaine* called "Biblical Analogies for Walt Whitman's Prosody." (I still treasure the note of acceptance from the late Charles Cestre, who then edited the *RA-A.*) Pushed back into the file for similar reason was "The Reception of Walt Whitman in Scandinavia," printed in *The Papers of the Bibliographical Society of America* (see Check List).

Then I began to feel the need for filling in gaps— or, more accurately, for completing studies left unfinished. As a result this volume contains more unpublished than reprinted work. One essay, "Mutations in Whitman's Art," was written for and accepted by the late review called *Noonday*, but darkness eclipsed that estimable magazine before the essay could be printed.

"Translations of Whitman since World War II" appeared without the present adaptations and considerable additions as a "mass-review" in *Comparative Literature*. I once intended to end my biography of Whitman, *The Solitary Singer*, with a chapter on the poet's posthumous fame; but in "The Legend" section I have completely rewritten and somewhat redirected that unpublished chapter.

The Check List is my wife's contribution; she has studied Whitman with me for the past thirty years and has been especially helpful in my comparative studies—most of all in the Scandinavian and German languages where her linguistic abilities considerably excel my own. We also enjoyed together the discovery of Frederik Schyberg, whose book on Whitman first aroused my interest in the critical comparison of texts and the study of literary parallels for critical comprehension. Unfortunately, Dr. Schyberg died before we could meet him in person, but we have *skoaled* most delightfully with his friends in Copenhagen during summer *lyse Naetter* ("light nights").

In looking back over my thirty years of writing about Whitman, I feel grateful especially for two blessings it has brought. One is the friends I have made, both in this country and foreign lands, through my publications. In America they are too numerous to list, but I must name that friend of scholars and prince of all Whitman collectors, Charles E. Feinberg. In France there is Roger Asselineau; in Germany (by correspondence), Hans Reisiger; in Sweden, Frederic Fleisher; in Israel, Simon Halkin and Sholom Kahn; in Japan, Shigetaka Naganuma, Sabura Ota, Arata Mituoka, Yoshinoro Yoshitake, Ichiro Nishizaki, Haruo Shimizu, William Moore, and others; in India, V. K. Chari and O. K. Nambiar; in New Zealand (by correspondence), Mrs. J. W. Stewart.

The second blessing shows, I hope, in the present volume. I have not published so many essays and books on Whitman because I changed my opinion, or because one study cancelled another. I am surprised myself to see how little my various contributions contradict each other. I continued writing on Whitman because each publication seemed to call for another. Truly Whitman is large and contains multitudes of problems for scholars and critics.

My *Walt Whitman Handbook* is now in some respects out of date, and it also contains typographical errors that are a constant embarrassment. But it was reprinted in 1957 without my having an opportunity to revise and correct it. Perhaps for the present this book will supply the need for a revision of the *Handbook*. The bibliographies in the *Handbook* are the parts most in need of up-dating, and the Check List in the present volume should take care of that deficiency. Of course the critical interpretations (as in "Mutations in Whitman's Art") go considerably beyond those in the *Handbook*.

Part III contains some letters—most of them published for the first time—by men who helped to create the twentieth-century image of Whitman. Though they are perhaps more valuable for the light they throw on the correspondents themselves rather than the poet who puzzled and baffled them, these letters are important documents in the history of Whitman's posthumous fame. All of these letters except one are in the Slocum Library of Ohio Wesleyan University, and I am indebted to the Director of the Library, J. H. Lancaster, for permission to publish them.

I wish to thank the officials of the Library of Congress for permission to reprint "The Man"; the New American Library and the former editors of *New World Writing* for "Cosmos-Inspired"; the editor of the *Journal of English and Germanic Philology* for "The 'Long Journey' Motif"; and the editor of *Comparative Literature* for a portion of "Translations of Whitman since World War II." In addition, I am grateful to Lawrence Ferlinghetti, publisher of City Lights Books in San Francisco, for permission to quote several lines from Allen Ginsberg's "A Supermarket in California"; and *New Directions* for a quotation and translation from Lorca's famous "Ode to Walt Whitman."

The Norwegian artist, Kai Fjell, has kindly consented to the reproduction of his symbolical drawing of Whitman, and Mr. Charles E. Feinberg to the illustration of an interesting manuscript in his collection, Whitman's work-sheet of "A Riddle Song."

Oradell, N. J.   G. W. A.

CONTENTS

PREFACE   vii

I. Walt Whitman as Man, Poet, and Legend

ONE: The Man   3

TWO: The Poet

    1 Cosmos Inspired   27

    2 Mutations in Whitman's Art   46

    3 The "Long Journey" Motif   62

    4 Translations of Whitman Since
       World War II   83

THREE: The Legend

    1 Whitman's Image in the Twentieth
       Century   101

    2 Some Letters Concerning Whitman   154

II. A Check List of Whitman Publications, 1945–1960

BIBLIOGRAPHY   179

EDITIONS AND SELECTIONS BY YEAR
   OF PUBLICATION   182

UNCOLLECTED WRITINGS   185

TRANSLATIONS   189

BOOKS ABOUT WHITMAN   196

ARTICLES ON WHITMAN   207

THESES ON WHITMAN   240

WHITMAN IN ART   242

NOTES   245

I

WALT WHITMAN
AS
MAN, POET, AND LEGEND

ONE

The Man

I am the man, I suffer'd,
I was there . . .

IT IS DIFFICULT to say anything accurately and critically on Whitman the man without considering his art and his thought, for what made him a great poet—great enough to have the first centennial of his masterpiece observed throughout his native country and even in many foreign lands—was the remarkable intensity and depth of his life of the mind and the imagination.

We often think of a man's physical life as his *real* existence, and regard his subjective life as shadowy, illusive, unsubstantial. And so it may be. But Walt Whitman's aesthetic and spiritual life was so real to him that he often himself confused the physical and the psychological realms of his experience—or at least wrote and spoke of them in such a way as to cause his readers and biographers to confuse them. One of his greatest literary ambitions was to make his poems seem so real that the reader would forget he was reading a book.

. . . this is no book,
Who touches this touches a man.

.   .   .   .   .   .

A lecture delivered at the Library of Congress in 1955 under the auspices of the Gertrude Clarke Whittall Poetry and Literature Fund and published by the Library, together with lectures by Mark Van Doren and David Daiches, as Walt Whitman: Man, Poet, Philosopher.

It is I you hold and who holds you,
I spring from the pages into your arms.
"SO LONG!"

As a consequence of such poetic statements, Whitman's
first biographers assumed that the book and the man
were one: if you would know Walt Whitman, they said,
read *Leaves of Grass*. Or they reversed the order, and
said that one could not understand *Leaves of Grass*
without knowing its author.

Later biographers and critics of Whitman, however,
were to discover that the poet himself had made it difficult to understand the author of *Leaves of Grass*. Jean
Catel, the late French biographer, argued that Whitman deliberately created myths about himself, a view
elaborated a few years later by the Danish critic,
Frederik Schyberg. Henry Seidel Canby, one of our
best American biographers, found two Whitmans, the
person known to his family and friends and the symbolical self of his poems. Malcolm Cowley[1] went a step
further and wrote of three Whitmans. I would say that
if one searched thoroughly for the man behind the first
person pronoun in "Song of Myself" and other major
lyrics in *Leaves of Grass*, he could find as many as five
or six personalities; for although the lyric is the most
personal form of poetic art, it is also a kind of drama,
and the "I" can assume many roles—as it does even in
Leaves of Grass.

Sometimes the first person pronoun of Whitman's
poems is himself, the physical man, and sometimes it
is a dramatization of his fantasy self—or selves. This
is not to imply that he was a split personality in the
sense that a psychiatrist might use this term. He did
write in an early notebook, "I cannot understand the
mystery, but I am always conscious of myself as two
—as my soul and I: and I reckon it is the same with
all men and women." And in his poems written in old

age his consciousness became a trinity of self, fancy, and soul, which is to say, biological organism, creative faculty, and metaphysical essence. But this does not prove the poet a schizophrenic. Quite the contrary, for he devoted his life to cultivating the health and unity of this trinity, and his successes and failures—for he was mortal and therefore fallible—constitute his biography.

The 1855 edition of *Leaves of Grass* was Whitman's first contribution toward a mythical biography. To appreciate this fact we must understand the intense American nationalism of the period. In all sections of the country, politicians, authors, and newspaper editors were demanding that native writers free themselves from Europe, the past, and especially from British literature. In 1837 Emerson orated: "Our day of dependence, our long apprenticeship to the learning of other lands, draws to a close . . . We have listened too long to the courtly muses of Europe." The almost unanimous demand was for both a democratic and a new literature in conformity with American experience and the nation's unexploited natural resources. In 1849 James Russell Lowell rhymed of the "goddess of freedom":

> She loses her fresh country charm when she takes
> Any mirror except her own rivers and lakes.

His advice to American authors was:

> Forget Europe wholly, your veins throb with blood,
> To which the dull current in hers is but mud.

Longfellow preferred universality to nationalism, but one of the characters in his novel *Kavanagh* stated the literary creed which was to be echoed time and again in the first *Leaves of Grass*: ". . . we want a national literature commensurate with your mountains and riv-

ers, —commensurate with Niagara, and the Allegha-
nies, and the Great Lakes! . . . we want a national
literature altogether shaggy and unshorn, that shall
shake the earth, like a herd of buffaloes thundering on
the prairies!"

In his 1855 preface Whitman declared with the
same patriotic fervor: "Here are the roughs and
beards and space and ruggedness and nonchalance that
the soul loves." His ideal poet, which he was striving
with supreme effort to become, must "incarnate" (his
own term) the "largeness" of nature and the nation.
It is not surprising, therefore, that the first person
pronoun of Whitman's poems possesses a mythical
strength and vitality, and in appearance and personality is shaggy and unshorn like an untamed buffalo
of the Western plains. For frontispiece in his book he
used a photograph of himself in work clothes, in nonchalant pose, with hat cocked at a rakish angle, as if
to illustrate a line in his leading poem, later called
"Song of Myself": "I cock my hat as I please indoors
or out." And in this same poem he described himself as,

Walt Whitman, an American, one of the roughs, a
    kosmos,
Disorderly fleshy and sensual . . . eating drinking and
    breeding,
No sentimentalist . . . no stander above men and women
    or apart from them . . . no more modest than im-
    modest.
    .   .   .   .
Divine am I inside and out, and I make holy whatever I
    touch or am touched from;
The scent of these arm-pits is aroma finer than prayer,
This head is more than churches or bibles or creeds.
    .   .   .   .

I dote on myself . . . there is that lot of me, and all so
    luscious,
Each moment and whatever happens thrills me with joy.

Here it is difficult to separate the flesh-and-blood
man from the symbolical personality of the poem. Walt
Whitman was large, strong, ruddy, and disorderly in
appearance, though the appearance—bearded face,
tousled hair, shirt open at the throat exposing a colored undershirt—he studiously cultivated after 1855
in corroboration of his role as the voice of nature in a
broad, untamed continent. One of his major endow-
ments as a poet was his remarkably acute sensitivity
to touch, hearing, sight, but in reality he was no hedonist, as his later life was to prove. And his auto-
intoxication was at least in part vicarious, for one of
the most influential beliefs which he had inherited from
Romantic philosophy was the doctrine that man is a
part of God and that it is proper to worship the Divinity innate or immanent in humanity—a dangerous
theology, many thoughtful people would say today,
but Whitman shared it with Goethe, Heine, Emerson,
and other great men of the Romantic movement.

In at least one detail this mythical personality of
Whitman's poems was strikingly at variance with the
man whom his family and daily associates knew. In
some of his self-written reviews he interpreted his symbolical virility and arrogance as "rowdyish," but
everyone who knew him testified to his quiet, gentle,
courteous nature. He was abundantly endowed with
Dutch stubbornness, and he was a hard man to swerve
from a resolute decision, but "rowdy" he certainly
never was. Most of his literary personality, however,
was merely an extension—a magnification—of his own
character and disposition.

The "sensualism" in Whitman's poems to which his contemporaries objected most strongly was sexual emotion. And his claim that he presented his own "flesh and form, undraped" made him more culpable in their eyes. This is still one of the thorniest problems in the biography of the poet because reality and symbolism are so subtly interfused. In "Song of Myself" *touch*, quivering the poet "to a new identity," symbolizes "the procreant urge of the world." But he does not always adhere to this lofty purpose. In some passages the imagery is unmistakably auto-erotic, and at times the poet has a puzzling sense of guilt: He calls his senses "traitors" and cries out that "on all sides prurient provokers are stiffening my limbs."

This is hardly the time and place for a detailed analysis of Whitman's sex pathology, but I can say, in brief, that the poet of the early editions of *Leaves of Grass* evidently experienced a profound emotional turbulence, possibly to a considerable extent on the subconscious level. From this turbulence, sexual imagery floated up into the fantasy in which the poems took their form. When he could gain control of all his faculties, Whitman fused these images into symbols of love—vicarious paternal love, comradeship and love of country, and sometimes religious adoration. When the perturbation was too great for him, his imagery remained simply erotic, untransformed into universal symbols. This is a subject which I have dealt with in my biography;[2] it is too involved for further comment here.

It is important to realize, however, that Walt Whitman did not gain control over his emotions without great struggle, indeed, a lifelong struggle. Had he been a simple hedonist, there would have been no struggle. He would have yielded impulsively to his appetites and dissipated his energies. But few men on record have more carefully guarded their health, more assiduously cultivated their art, or striven more energetically to save their souls; and thereby more successfully turned their weaknesses into strength.

Whitman was the poet of comradeship, perhaps above all else, but his notebooks show that he was a lonely man who never found the ideal comrade in life, and finally, in old age, sought for him in God. But Whitman's unsatisfied yearning for love and comradeship enabled him to render truly heroic service to the Union during the Civil War by his voluntary hospital ministrations. His sympathy and affection for the soldiers was so intense that some recent critics have doubted its normality. That his compassion was exceptional in its depth and extension, there can be no doubt, and this is Walt Whitman's most distinguishing characteristic as a man. He was capable of intimate friendship with simple, ignorant men like Peter Doyle, the Washington street-car conductor and former soldier in the Confederate Army. But what seems to have attracted him to Doyle was the young man's need for fatherly affection and guidance. Whitman had formerly shown the same compassion in New York for men in prison, for omnibus drivers in the city hospital, and for anyone in trouble. He manifested his compassionate nature toward the members of his own family. He was his mother's chief dependence, and from his early manhood until her death it was to him that she always turned for affection, understanding, and financial assistance. Her youngest son, Edward, was crippled and feeble-minded, perhaps the result of an attack of scarlet fever in infancy. As he grew up, some of his brothers and sisters found him repulsive and resented his dependency, but Walt cheerfully sacrificed his own comfort to provide for him.

Walt's sister Hannah made an unfortunate mar-

riage and became increasingly neurotic and sorry for
herself, but Walt's sympathy never wavered. In fact,
the more she suffered the more he seemed to love her.
Two of his brothers ruined their lives by dissipation.
Although Walt never found them personally congenial,
he did not criticize them in his letters, as his favorite
brother, Jeff, did, but quietly rendered what aid he
could. His older brother, Jesse, went insane and had to
be committed to an asylum. It was Walt who took him
to the hospital and made the arrangement, meanwhile
comforting his mother in her grief. Andrew became a
drunkard and married a disreputable woman. All her
in-laws except Walt detested her and evidently showed
their resentment in many ways. Walt sent her kind
messages and small sums of money at Christmas time,
even after Andrew's horrible death from a throat disease, possibly cancer. This was after the Civil War,
when Walt was employed in Washington as a Government clerk at a modest salary. During most of this time
Mrs. Whitman was living in Brooklyn with her son
Jeff and his wife, Martha. There was often friction between Mrs. Whitman and her daughter-in-law, and
again it was Walt who tried in his letters to soothe
ruffled emotions and to urge tolerance.

Whitman had always been accustomed to living on a
very modest scale. In addition to sharing his meager
salary with his mother and other members of the family
when they were in need, he also used it to buy little
gifts for the wounded men who lingered on in the
Washington hospitals for several years after the end
of the war, and his small but dependable income enabled him to print successive editions of his poems,
which publishers still refused to accept. It was necessary, therefore, for him to live as economically as possible. During his ten years' residence in the national
capital he lived in a manner described by a British

journalist and member of Parliament, Justin Mc-
Carthy,[3] who visited him in the winter of 1870:

Through the kindness of a friend in Washington I made
the acquaintance of Walt Whitman. I was naturally anx-
ious to meet the poet whose name and fame were beginning
just then to be subjects of keen debate in English literary
circles. Walt Whitman was then living in the most unpre-
tentious sort of way. He was lodged in a room like a garret, up several flights of stairs in a thickly populated
building. I had heard in America two very distinct descriptions given of Walt Whitman. One was that of a man
who by his very nature was absolutely indifferent to public opinion and the conventional appearances, a man who
as long as he had a roof to cover him, a truckle bed to
sleep in, a basin and ewer wherewithal to wash, any sort
of homely food to eat, and a desk to write upon, could be
happy in himself and let the world go on its way unheeded.
The other description was that of a man who went in for
being a penniless poet, who made up for the part and acted
it, and was more concerned to display his poverty than
Dives or Jim Fisk would have been to show off his wealth.
Even as I stood in Walt Whitman's room for the first
time and looked at the stately figure of the iron-grey poet
himself, I could not keep out of my mind a whimsical sort
of an idea that if I were asked then and there to decide at
once as to the comparative accuracy of the two descriptions I should be a little puzzled as to the answer that I
ought to give. For, certainly, if one were getting up the
part of a poverty-stricken poet proud of his poverty and
parading it defiantly before the eyes of all stray comers,
it must be owned that the theatrical business could not be
better arranged. There was the humble bed, there was the
poor washstand, there were two or three rickety chairs,
there was the shelf with the cut loaf of bread, there was
the staggery writing-desk, and there were leaves of paper

strewn over the desk and table. Anyone in the least acquainted with the ways of the theatre would only have to
see the curtain rise on such a scene in order to know that
the poverty-stricken poet was about to be "discovered."
But then, on the other hand, it was surely more reasonable
to take the whole scene in its natural sense as the home
of one who was simply poor and was not in the least
ashamed of his poverty.

Thus I read the story of Walt Whitman's room the moment I had looked into the eyes of the good old poet himself. If ever sincerity and candor shone from the face of
a man, these qualities shone from the face of Walt Whitman. There was an unmistakable dignity about the man
despite his poor garb and his utterly careless way of life.
He had a fine presence with his broad rugged forehead
and his iron-grey hair, giving the idea of premature old
age. There was a simple dignity in his manner which
marked him out as one of nature's gentlemen.

The "keen debate" over Whitman in Great Britain
to which this English visitor refers was the result, at
least in part, of Whitman's dismissal from his clerkship in the Department of the Interior in the summer
of 1865. At that time there was no Civil Service Law
to protect Government employees, and soon after
James Harlan became Secretary of the Interior he began, as the newspapers of the time said, to "clean
house"—an action, one must agree, not unique in
American politics. Whitman was only one of many who
were dismissed without warning or explanation, but
when his friends protested, the Secretary said he
would not have in his employ the author of *Leaves of
Grass*, which he appeared to regard as an obscene book.
Whitman's friend, J. Hubley Ashton, an Assistant Attorney General, promptly got him transferred to the
Attorney General's office, and a few months later an-

other equally loyal friend, William Douglas O'Connor, published an impassioned defence and eulogy called *The Good Gray Poet*.

This pamphlet was the first contribution toward the hagiography of Walt Whitman. Although much of O'Connor's praise was deserved, he gave the impression that his subject was more than human: "a man of striking masculine beauty . . . powerful and venerable in appearance; large, calm, superbly formed; oftenest clad in the careless, rough, and always picturesque costume of the common people . . . head, majestic, large, Homeric, and set upon his strong shoulders with the grandeur of ancient sculpture . . ."[4] Except for the heroic overtones, this description was in truth fairly accurate. Whitman's calmness was perhaps deceptive, for his notebooks prove that in secret he worried over his failure to win literary success and tortured himself with self-analysis, but in outward appearance he did have a majestic poise, as McCarthy observed. O'Connor, however, intended to give the impression that Whitman was more god than man, for two years later he published a story called "The Carpenter,"[5] in which he cast Whitman in the role of a modern Christ, who performed a miracle on Christmas Eve.

The person superficially acquainted with Walt Whitman's life is likely to find O'Connor's *The Good Gray Poet* too miraculous to believe, and to be somewhat alienated by the poet's tolerance, if not actual encouragement, of such adulation. But there was at least some basis for belief in Whitman's remarkable healing powers. After the war hundreds of soldiers wrote him grateful letters for the kindness, encouragement, and affection which he had shown them during the hours of their agony and despair. The *Drum-Taps* poem called "The Wound Dresser" shows the poet's discovery of his true nature after he had visited the

battlefield and become acquainted with the wounded
soldiers:

(Arous'd and angry, I'd thought to beat the alarum, and
    urge relentless war,
But soon my fingers fail'd me, my face droop'd and I
    resign'd myself,
To sit by the wounded and soothe them, or silently watch
    the dead;)

.   .   .   .

The hurt and wounded I pacify with soothing hand,
I sit by the restless all the dark night, some are so young,
Some suffer so much, I recall the experience sweet and sad,
(Many a soldier's loving arms about this neck have
    cross'd and rested,
Many a soldier's kiss dwells on these bearded lips.)

What especially set Walt Whitman apart from
other men was the breadth of his sympathy and love.
A typical example during the war years is a letter
which he wrote to a young man in the hospital, Lewis
Kirk Brown, in 1863. He addressed this letter to
"Dear son and comrade, and all my dear comrades in
the hospital." After specifying numerous men by name
and ward to whom he wished to send his "love," Whitman finally wrote:

Lewy I would like you to give my love to a young man
named Burns in Ward I, and to all the boys in Ward I.—
and indeed in every ward, from A to K inclusive, and all
through the hospital, as I find I cannot particularize
without being tedious—so I send my love sincerely to each
and all, for every sick and wounded soldier is dear to me
as a son or brother, and furthermore every man that
wears the union uniform and sticks to it like a man, is to
me a dear comrade . . .[6]

A recent critic says regarding this letter, "One cannot
believe that Whitman *really* 'loved'—in any ordinary

acceptance of the term—'all the boys' equally and 'sincerely' . . .'" But however abnormal—or supernormal —this trait may seem, nearly everyone who knew Whitman intimately has testified to its existence in the poet's character and personality. And it was this trait that convinced some of his friends that he was truly a saint.

Saintliness, however, implies asceticism, and this Whitman always rejected, at least in theory, for of course he did practice frugality and self-denial, as we have seen, in order to stretch his always inadequate income. But from the 1855 *Leaves of Grass* until the so-called "death-bed" edition of 1892, Whitman consistently presented himself as the "caresser of life." As time passed he toned down his symbolical sensuality, but he continued to praise the life of the senses and the joy of physical existence. As Dr. Bucke stated, *Leaves of Grass* "represents a man whose ordinary every-day relationship with Nature is such that to him mere existence is happiness."[8] In this mood he wrote in "Song of Myself":

I think I could turn and live with animals, they are so
    placid and self-contained,
I stand and look at them long and long.

How much of this was Romantic theory and how much the poet's own innate disposition it is a little difficult to say, but he certainly wanted to be known as a "natural pagan." George Santayana called him a "barbarian," a man who regards "his passions as their own excuse for being . . . who merely feels and acts, valuing in his life its force and its filling, but being careless of its purpose and its form." There are many passages in Whitman's writings that do express this doctrine, but Santayana did not read Whitman sufficiently to discover that this idea, and its application in personal conduct, was balanced by a contrary theory of "prudence":

All that a person does, says, thinks, is of consequence,
Not a move can a man or woman make, that affects him
    or her in a day, month, any part of the direct lifetime,
    or the hour of death,
But the same affects him or her onward afterward through
    the indirect lifetime.

.   .   .   .

Not one word or deed, . . .
But has results beyond death as really as before death.
                   "SONG OF PRUDENCE"

Even the phrenologists[9] found Whitman long on "prudence"; and if ever a man was cautious, aware of the consequence of his acts, and deliberate in creating a record for posterity to remember and profit by, it was Walt Whitman.

This very thoughtfulness, in fact, presents another biographical paradox. Whitman desired so earnestly to live the life of his ideal poet that he seemed at times too self-consciously to parade his personality, both on the street and in his poems. He anonymously reviewed his first *Leaves of Grass*, and he persisted until near the end of his life in supplying newspapers with self-written interviews and little squibs about himself, such as this item which appeared in the New York *Times* on October 1, 1868:

With the bright, crispy Autumn weather, WALT WHITMAN again makes his appearance on the sidewalks of Broadway. His large, massive personality,—his grave and prophetic, yet free and manly, appearance,—his *insouciance* of manner and movement,—his easy and negligent, yet clean and wholesome dress,—go to make up a figure and an individuality that attracts the attention and interest of every passer-by.

Although such practices have exposed Whitman to the charge of having cultivated and exploited his personal idiosyncrasies for the sake of publicity, we find abundant evidence in his private notebooks that he strove assiduously to form his actual character and personality on the pattern of his literary ideal. He was acutely aware of his imperfections and strove manfully to overcome them. As late as 1870 he set down an "Outline sketch of a superb calm character," calmness evidently being a trait which he felt he especially needed at that time. One example of his ideal was "Merlin strong & wise & beautiful" at the age of one hundred. In an undated diary notation he wrote:

The idea of personality, that which belongs to each person as himself, or herself, and that you [i. e. anyone] may so heighten your personality by temperance, by a clean and powerful physique, by chastity, by elevating the mind through lofty discussions and meditations and themes, and by self-esteem and divine love, that you can hardly go into a room—or along the street, but an atmosphere of command and fascination shall exhale out of you upon all you meet—[10]

Here also the poet thinks of creating an impression, but the personality will exhale "an atmosphere of command and fascination" because both mind and body have been purified by clean living and lofty meditation. Pleasing manners and an attractive appearance will then harmonize with an inward state of grace and spiritual health.

Whitman wanted not only to be loved but to generate love. In the preface to one of his old-age books, *Two Rivulets*, he confessed one of his strongest motives in writing his poems:

I . . . sent out LEAVES OF GRASS to arouse and set flowing in men's and women's hearts, young and old, (my present and future readers,) endless streams of living, pulsating love and friendship, directly from them to myself, now and ever. To this terrible, irrepressible yearning, (surely more or less down underneath in most human souls,)—this never-satisfied appetite for sympathy, and this boundless offering of sympathy—this universal democratic comradeship—this old, eternal, yet ever-new interchange of adhesiveness, so fitly emblematic of America—I have given in that book, undisguisedly, declaredly, the openest expression.

Many passages in Whitman's poems were such eloquent pleas for love that some of his contemporary readers took their meaning literally. One of these was a woman named Susan Smith, of Hartford, Conn., who wrote him after reading the third edition of *Leaves of Grass* (1860) that she loved him and wanted to bear his child:

Know Walt Whitman that thou hast a child for me! A noble beautiful perfect manchild. I charge you my love not to give it to another woman. The world demands it! It is not for you and me, *is our child*, but for the world. . . . Thine the pleasure my love. Mine the sweet burden and pain. Mine the sacrifice. Mine to have the stinging rebuke, the shame. I am willing. My motives are pure and holy. Our boy my love! Do you not already love him? He must be begotten on a mountain top, in the open air. Not in *lust*, not in mere gratification of sensual passion, but in holy ennobling pure strong deep glorious passionate broad universal love. I charge you to prepare my love.

I love you, I love you, come, come. Write.

Many years later Whitman showed this letter to his friend Horace Traubel. He had written "insane asylum" across the envelope, and Traubel asked him why. This dialogue ensued:

"Isn't it crazy?"

"No: it's Leaves of Grass."

"What do you mean?"

"Why—it sounds like somebody who's taking you at your word."

"I've had more than one notion of the letter: I suppose the fact that certain things are unexpected, unusual, makes it hard to get them in their proper perspective: the process of adjustment is a severe one."

"You should have been the last man in the world to write 'insane' on that envelope. . . . You might as well write 'insane' across Children of Adam and the Song of Myself."

"Many people do."

"Yes, . . . they do—but you don't."

"I suppose you are right."[11]

It was not unlikely that Whitman was correct in his suspicion of the woman's sanity, but the interesting thing about this incident is the poet's normal, healthy reaction. Nine years later Mrs. Gilchrist, widow of the biographer of Blake, a refined, educated woman, respected friend of Tennyson and the Rossettis, repeated this episode on a more dramatic scale. In reading Whitman's poems, especially the "Children of Adam" and "Calamus" groups, she felt vicariously embraced by the "strong divine soul" of the poet. "I never before dreamed what love meant," she wrote him, "nor what life meant. Never was alive before—no words but those of 'new birth' can hint the meaning of what then happened to me." Without ever having seen the man, she proposed marriage to him. Whitman held her off as kindly as he could, but he finally wrote her bluntly: "Let me warn you about myself and yourself also. You must not construct such an unauthorized and imaginary figure and call it W. W., and so devotedly invest your loving nature in it. The actual W. W. is a very plain personage and entirely unworthy such devotion."[12]

But despite such honest warning, she persisted in her infatuation, and after he suffered a paralytic stroke she came to America with the intention of taking care of him, doubtless as his wife. It is one of the most remarkable one-sided love affairs in literary history. But it is no less remarkable for the strength of character that it revealed in Whitman. Mrs. Gilchrist made her pilgrimage when Whitman was pathetically in need of sympathy, companionship, and financial assistance. Soon after his first paralytic stroke his mother died, an emotional shock from which he never entirely recovered. He regained partial use of his paralyzed left side, but he was forced to give up his government clerkship and live with his brother George in Camden, N. J. Though he was devoted to his brother and sister-in-law, he had interests which they could not understand and he became so lonely and discouraged that at times he longed for death. Mrs. Gilchrist could have made life easy for him, and he found her society congenial and stimulating. But he could not feel the same affection for her that he aroused in her. Besides, he was extremely independent and was determined to maintain as much personal freedom as sickness and old age would permit.

It was terribly ironic that the poet who had celebrated in song what he believed to be his sound heredity and enormous vitality should spend the last nineteen years of his life as a half-paralytic and semi-invalid. He needed truly heroic spiritual resources to endure such a fate, but when the need was greatest, he had these resources. Probably the most difficult year of his life was the year following his mother's death. During this time he wrote one of the great poems of his old age, the "Prayer of Columbus." By his own confession he identified himself with the "batter'd, wreck'd old man" stranded on the Island of Jamaica in 1503,

ill, neglected, when "death seemed daily imminent."
But Columbus did not lose faith in God, and his prayer
in this poem was Whitman's own prayer:

> My hands, my limbs grow nerveless,
> My brain feels rack'd, bewilder'd,
> Let the old timbers part, I will not part,
> I will cling fast to Thee, O God,
>   though the waves buffet me,
> Thee, Thee at least I know.

Like Columbus, too, Whitman had attempted to sail
unexplored seas, and he felt in 1874 that he was as un-
recognized for his discoveries as Columbus in 1503.
He had published five editions of his poems, yet the
literary value of his work was recognized only by a
score or two of people in Europe and a considerably
smaller number in America. It seemed like a pitifully
small band of admirers for two decades of effort. He
had not lost hope, however, that the prophetic vision
of the explorer in "Prayer of Columbus" might still
be his own:

> And these things I see suddenly, what mean they?
> As if some miracle, some hand divine unseal'd my eyes,
> Shadowy vast shapes smile through the air and sky,
> And on distant waves sail countless ships,
> And anthems in new tongues I hear saluting me.

As if in answer to the prayer which he shared with
the old man in his poem, Whitman's health began to
improve. He had the good fortune to make the acquaintance of the Staffords, who lived on a farm beside
Timbēr Creek, ten or fifteen miles from Camden.
There during the next three years he recovered sufficient use of his limbs to be able to make a long trip
to the West in 1879, going as far as Denver, followed
by a trip to Canada a few months later. The scenery

and the people in general were all that he had dreamed
they would be, though he confessed that he was disap-
pointed with the women in Kansas City and Denver.
He recorded disapprovingly: "They are 'intellectual'
and fashionable, but dyspeptic-looking and generally
doll-like; their ambition evidently is to copy their Eastern sisters. Something far different and in advance
must appear, to tally and complete the superb masculinity of the West, and maintain and continue it." In
view of Whitman's lifelong romanticizing of Western
character, it is rather amusing that in the spring of
1881, while giving a lecture on Lincoln in Boston, he
noticed his ideal women in his audience: "many *fine-
looking gray-hair'd* women . . . healthy and wifely
and motherly, and wonderfully charming and beautiful."[13]

Wifely, motherly women always appealed to Walt
Whitman, and a considerable number of them became
his loyal friends and ardent admirers. One of these was
Susan Stafford, who understood his psychology perhaps better than any other friend of his and helped him
to regain faith in his ultimate recovery from his illness.
Near the end of Whitman's life she gave her impressions of him to an English visitor who had come to
America just to see the poet and gather information
about him.

Let me quote a paragraph of the account:

She said that at times he used to be like a volcano, and
then very quiet. Not angry—she scarcely knew how to
express herself, but he seemed to love everything and
everybody. He *could* be angry: she had seen him more angry than anyone she knew, but it soon passed away. He
used to be angry when his papers were disturbed; but she
did not mind that at all, and in a few minutes he would
burst into song again. She let him have his own way as

a rule, and she knew intuitively what he wanted or disliked; but she insisted on straightening up his papers. She
thought it was a thing that had to be done. He didn't like
to be disturbed when out alone, and she used to tell the
children that if they saw him in some secluded place they
were not to go near him. Once when Mrs. Gilchrist came
to see him he was very angry. Of course he was glad to
see her, but he would have liked it better if she had come
another day.[14]

The capricious temperament experienced by Mrs.
Stafford could have been the result of the poet's illness
and premature aging, but his character and personality had always been paradoxical. Whitman's official
biographer, Dr. R. M. Bucke, another friend of this
period who literally worshipped him, talked with "a
distant relative of the poet," a portrait painter (unidentified), who insisted that Walt had always had a
"double nature."

Dr. Bucke himself had not seen this duality, but he
reported this man's opinion:

[He] tells me that Walt Whitman, in the elements of his
character, had deepest sternness and hauteur, not easily
aroused, but coming forth at times, and then well understood by those who know him best as something not to be
trifled with. . . . His theory is, in almost his own words,
that there are two natures in Walt Whitman. The one is
of immense suavity, self-control, a mysticism like the oc-
casional fits of Socrates, and a pervading Christ-like benevolence, tenderness, and sympathy. . . . But these
qualities, though he has enthroned them, and for many
years governed his life by them, are duplicated by far
sterner ones. No doubt he has mastered the latter, but he
has them.[15]

Another witness, Edward Carpenter, who came over

twice from England to visit Whitman, the second time
in 1884, reported a similar observation:

I am impressed more than ever with W.'s contradictory,
self-willed, tenacious, obstinate character, strong and even
extreme moods, united with infinite tenderness, wistful
love, and studied tolerance; also great caution (he says:
the "phrenologists always say that caution is my chief
characteristic—did you know that?") and a certain art-
fulness, combined with keen, penetrating, and determined
candour; the wild-hawk look still there, "untamable, untranslatable," yet with that wonderful tenderness at
bottom.[16]

Carpenter came to the conclusion that there was "a
great tragic element" in Whitman's nature, which
"possibly prevented him ever being quite what is called
'happy in love affairs.' . . . He celebrates in his
poems the fluid, all-solvent disposition, but often was
himself less the river than the rock." This, in my opinion, was the most profound deduction that any of the
men who knew Whitman in life ever printed in their
reminiscences of him—"less the river than the rock."
I have called my own biography of Whitman *The
Solitary Singer*, not only because the poet himself
used this metaphor (as in "Starting from Paumanok"
in the line, "Solitary, singing in the West, I strike up
for a New World," and in describing the mockingbird
in "Out of the Cradle" which the poet says projects
him, "O solitary me . . ."), but also because Whitman had to fight his own battles with very little assistance from anyone. Almost singlehandedly he fought
for the literary freedoms which later poets were to enjoy. But the hardest fight was with himself, to bring
harmony out of the chaos of his emotions, and lasting
peace between his body and soul. How well he succeeded all who knew him in his final years have testified.

After visiting Whitman in 1885, Edmund Gosse went away with his "heart full of affection for this beautiful old man":

I felt that the experience of the day was embalmed by something that a great poet had written long ago, but I could not find what it was till we started once more to cross the frosty Delaware [it was January]; then it came to me, and I knew that when Shelley spoke of

> Peace within and calm around,
> And that content, surpassing wealth,
> The sage in meditation found,
> And walk'd with inward glory crown'd,

he had been prophesying of Walt Whitman, nor shall I ever read those lines again without thinking of the old rhapsodist in his empty room, glorified by patience and philosophy.[17]

John Burroughs visited his old friend while the poet lay on his deathbed and thought that he had "never seen his face so beautiful. There was no breaking-down of the features, or the least sign of decrepitude, such as we usually note in old men. The expression was full of pathos, but it was as grand as that of a god. I could not think of him as near death, he looked so unconquered."[18]

Indeed, Walt Whitman was not conquered by death. Half a century ago Bliss Perry[19] declared that no other American poet then seemed "more sure to be read, by the fit persons, after one hundred or five hundred years." At the end of the first centennial of *Leaves of Grass* this judgment seemed even more prophetically inspired than it did in 1905, and the poet, to quote Perry once more, is "somewhere among the immortals," and there is no reason to think that he will not remain there.

A Riddle Song

By Walt Whitman

That which eludes this verse & every verse,

profoundest bard!

And yet is here and here,

in thought in every

life, Throughout

the world,

Yet real & palpable, every day,

to every land; thro'life,

Which you and I pursuing

ever, ever miss;

Not love, nor fame,

Nor gain, nor happiness,

nor wealth.

Unseen; unform'd in mortal

sight or eye, cunningest mind;

heard by sharpest ear

on mental subtlety,

The Poet

---

*Finally shall come the
poet worthy that name . . .*

1

COSMOS INSPIRED

"THERE HAVE BEEN," says Lazare Saminsky, "three periods of music in Western culture, the classical, the romantic, and the 'cosmos-inspired.'" For the third period he cites Wagner's *Parsifal*, Scriabin's *Poems of Ecstasy*, and Dubussy's *Nocturnes* and *La Mer*, and mentions Whitman's poetry as a parallel in literature, quoting with approval William James's comment that, "The only sentiments Walt Whitman allowed himself to express were of the expansive order —a passionate and mystical ontological emotion suffuses his words."[1] Whether the last phase of Western music should be called "cosmos-inspired" I do not know, but the association of Whitman's name with this classification is particularly significant because no other nineteenth- or twentieth-century poet in the English language has had so many of his poems set to music or had so many full-scale symphonies based on them, and he was, without a doubt, "cosmos-inspired." The particular musi-

cians to whom he has appealed and the kind of appeal
he has had for them also throws light not only on
what William James calls Whitman's "sentiments" but
likewise on the form and structure of his poetry.

In the first quarter of the twentieth century it was
the British musicians who were most attracted to
Whitman, notably Frederick Delius, Ralph Vaughan
Williams, and Gustav Holst. Then in the second
quarter of the century the Americans discovered him:
John Alden Carpenter, Percy Grainger, Ernest Bloch,
Charles Wood, Norman Lockwood, Charles E. Ives,
Howard Hanson, George Kleinsinger, Elie Siegmei-
ster, and Roy Harris. Probably the most famous of all
Whitman music is Paul Hindemith's symphony, with
choral arrangements, *When Lilacs Last in the Door-
yard Bloom'd.* (Hindemith composed this work in
Germany, but he has since become an American citizen.)

These composers have found congenial both Whitman's ideas (or "sentiments") and "organic" form.
Holst, for example, according to his biographer, discovered in 1917 that, "Of all that could be said about
death, those words of Whitman's [in 'When Lilacs Last
in the Dooryard Bloom'd'] came nearest to his own
feelings on the subject."[2] Apparently he was already
working on his *Ode to Death* when he read Whitman's
invocation, "Come lovely and soothing death!," but as
soon as he read the passage he knew that he had found
the right poem for his inspiration. It was thus the
sharing of Whitman's emotions and attitudes toward
death that aided the composer in his musical interpretation and development of his subject.

Delius, too, had a similar experience: ". . . one
could never foresee precisely what the finished work
would be like . . . [which] shaped itself according to
the laws of its own inner being. . . . Take *Sea-Drift*

. . . the shape of it was taken out of my hands, so to speak, as I worked, and was bred easily and effortlessly of the nature and sequence of my musical ideas, and the nature and sequence of the particular poetical ideas of Whitman that appealed to me."[3]

The testimony of Holst and Delius is corroborated by Carpenter's experiences in writing still another composition based in part on the group of poems in *Leaves of Grass* which Whitman called "Sea-Drift." In 1915 Carpenter felt his "first acute Whitman excitement," and for some time "studied the problem of setting to music in vocal form excerpts from some of the *Sea-Drift* poems," but could not bring his experiments to any satisfactory conclusion. In 1935, while living in a village on the shores of the blue Mediterranean, he "took up the old problem again, and abandoned any attempt to make a literal setting of Whitman's verses in a vocal work. I tried to make a complete orchestral record of the imprint *upon me* of these poems." His finished composition represents, he says, "an effort to transcribe my impressions derived from these magnificent poems."[4]

The literary critic is likely to dismiss the effects of Whitman's poems on these composers as merely the fancies of impressionable musicians, but they contain implications of considerable importance to the student of Whitman's art. It is no accident that he has appealed more to musicians than to poets. Nor is it primarily the result of Whitman's interest in music. His fondness for Italian opera and his belief that "except for the opera" he could never have written his poems is well known, but the relationship goes deeper than this. As early as his 1855 Preface Whitman stated his ambition to "indicate the path between reality and the soul," and in the "program" poem[5] called "Shut Not Your Doors to Me, Proud Libraries" he declared,

"The words of my book nothing, the drift of it every thing." This was his lifelong intention, as reiterated in 1888: "I seek less to state or display any theme or thought, and more to bring you, reader, into the atmosphere of the theme or thought—there to pursue your own flight."

Several years earlier (1881) in an essay entitled "The Poetry of the Future," Whitman had called this poetic method "the free expression of emotion," which meant, he explained, "to arouse and initiate, more than to define or finish." This statement has sometimes been taken as the poet's excuse for his crudity or impatience with structure, and perhaps unconsciously or half-consciously it was an apology, but it had deeper implications. "Like all modern tendencies," Whitman wrote, "it has direct or indirect reference continually to the reader, to you or me, to the central identity of everything, the mighty Ego. . . . Character, a feature far above style or polish—a feature not absent at any time, but now first brought to the fore—gives predominant stamp to advancing poetry. Its born sister, music, already responds to the same influences. 'The music of the present, Wagner's, Gounod's, even the later Verdi's, all tends toward this free expression of poetic emotion, and demands a vocalism totally unlike that required for Rossini's splendid roulades, or Bellini's suave melodies.' "

Where Whitman first encountered this theory, or whether he discovered it himself before he read it in someone else's words, has not been determined, but in this same essay he quoted Sainte-Beuve:

Formerly, during the period term'd classic, . . . when literature was govern'd by recognized rules, he was consider'd the best poet who had composed the most perfect work, the most beautiful poem, the most intelligible, the

most agreeable to read, the most complete in every respect,
—the Aeneid, the Gerusalemme, a fine tragedy. To-day,
something else is wanted. For us the greatest poet is he
who in his works most stimulates the reader's imagination
and reflection, who excites him the most himself to poetize.
The greatest poet is not he who has done the best; it is he
who suggests the most; he, not all of whose meaning is at
first obvious, and who leaves you much to desire, to explain, to study, much to complete in your turn.[6]

It is interesting that in this theory Whitman was
anticipating the Symbolist movement in France, which
had scarcely begun in 1881, when he first published his
essay. As P. Mansell Jones, the Welsh student of
Whitman and French literature, has pointed out, the
Sainte-Beuve passage quoted by Whitman is a "prototype of the Symbolist argument."[7] However, whether
or not there was literary influence one way or the
other, or both ways, "on both sides of the Atlantic," to
quote Jones again, "it seems to have been distinctly realized that poetry was akin to music and that the essential power of each was to suggest."

With this thought in mind, it is not surprising that
a recent study by A. G. Lehmann illuminates Whitman's poetic method. A French symbolist remarked
apropos Mallarmé's *L'Après-midi d'un faune*, "*Desi-
reux d'exprimer un sujet par la musique des mots, il
devait adopter d'abord un sujet musical, c'est-à-dire,
un état émotionnel de l'âme, ensemble homogène et
complex.*"[8] Lehmann's comment on this is that "the
emotional state" is "the musical subject." Mallarmé,
of course, speaks of the "emotional state of the soul,"
but in *La Musique et les lettres* he calls the horror of
the forest the essential theme and not the description of
trees and branches. It would be as difficult to define
"l'âme" as Whitman's use of the "soul," for with both

poets the term covers a wide range of subjective connotations; but whether metaphysical essence or levels
of consciousness, we need not determine in the present
discussion. The subject of *L'Après-midi d'un faune* is
not the time, place, or the faun, but the musings of the
faun, and the interior music is objectified for the
reader or hearer by symbolical images and sounds.

This is precisely Whitman's own attitude toward the
music of his poems, as in "To Soar in Freedom and in
Fullness of Power":

> I have not so much emulated the birds that muscially
>   sing,
> I have abandon'd myself to flights, broad circles.
> The hawk, the seagull, have far more possess'd me than
>   the canary or mocking-bird.
> I have not felt to warble and trill, however sweetly,
> I have felt to soar in freedom and in the fullness of
>   power, joy, volition.

Of course, Whitman is here defending his special kind
of music and implying that the more formal poets
merely "warble and trill." But it is technically true
that he never attempted in his bird songs (e.g., "Out of
the Cradle . . ." and "When Lilacs Last . . .") to
imitate the sounds of birds. In fact, in general he gives
subjective rather than literal descriptions. Many of his
individual images are remarkably clear and exact, but
he seldom gives extended descriptions, as Longfellow
does in *Hiawatha* or Whittier in *Snow-Bound*. Whitman's subject, like Mallarmé's, is "an emotional state"
or a "state of the soul," *his* soul, but a state which he
wishes to communicate—or evoke—in his reader.

In his 1855 Preface Whitman declared: "The poetic
quality is not marshalled in rhyme or uniformity, or
abstract addresses to things, nor in melancholy com-

plaints or good precepts, but is the life of these and
much else, and is in the soul." For this reason "the
greatest poet brings the spirit of any or all events and
passions and scenes and persons . . . to bear on your
individual character as you hear or read." Thus Whitman wanted his "expression" to be "transcendent and
new. It is to be indirect and not descriptive or epic."

But Whitman's aesthetics was no "art for art's sake"
theory.[9] In fact, he professed scorn for beauty alone,
and searched always for some profound truth residing
in or emanating from external form, surface appearance, or "show," to use his favorite term (usually in
the plural). As an "ontological" poet, Whitman believed poetry to be a variety of knowledge, and he
exercised his poetic faculties not to create beauty but
to recover and propagate wisdom—"recover" because
he held the Platonic notion that truth is eternal and
existed before the world was created. "The poets of the
kosmos advance through all interpositions and cover-
ings and turmoils and stratagems to first principles,"
he says in his 1855 Preface, and elaborates the doctrine in "Song of Myself," where it is called "truth":

> All truths wait in all things,
>
> .   .   .   .   .
>
> To me the converging objects of the universe
>   perpetually flow,
> All are written to me, and I must get what the
>   writing means.

In "A Song of the Rolling Earth" this becomes "the
unspoken meanings of the earth," and in the same year
(1856) Whitman calls it "wisdom" in "Song of the
Open Road":

> Here is the test of wisdom,
>
> .   .   .   .   .

> Wisdom is of the soul, is not susceptible of proof,
>   is its own proof,
>
> .   .   .   .
>
> Is the certainty of the reality and immortality of
>   things, and the excellence of things;
> Something there is in the float of the sight of things
>   that provokes it out of the soul.

The spiritual world in which Whitman believes is, of
course, invisible, but like Emerson, Carlyle, and other
"transcendentalists," he accepts the natural world as
one vast analogy of the spiritual. This was one of the
basic concepts of Romantic philosophy, which Heine
had defined several decades earlier:

God . . . manifests Himself in plants, which lead, without consciousness, a cosmic-magnetic life. He manifests
Himself in animals, which in their sensual dream-life feel
their existence more or less dimly. But supremely, He
manifests Himself in man, who both feels and thinks, who
can distinguish his individual existence from objective nature, and whose reason even entertains the ideas that assume phenomenal existence in the world of appearances.
In man the Deity attains self-consciousness, and this
self-consciousness in turn reveals itself through man.
However, this does not eventuate in the individual or
through the individual, but in and through man as a col-
lective existence, so that each man embraces and manifests
only a part of the Divine Universe; all men, however, col-
lectively embrace and represent the Divine Universe as
an idea and as a reality. Every people, possibly, has the
mission to recognize and realize a definite phase or part of
this Divine Universe, to comprehend a series of phenomena
and to manifest a series of ideas and to transmit the result to future peoples, who have a similar mission. God,
therefore, is the real hero of world history, the latter is
His perpetual thought, His perpetual act, His word, His

deed, and of all humanity, one may rightly say! It is the incarnation of God![10]

Although this is the basis of Whitman's philosophy, we find some modifications of Heine's definition in Whitman's poetic adaptation. The American poet, too, as in "A Song for Occupations," declares that "Objects gross and the unseen soul are one," asserts in "Crossing Brooklyn Ferry" (1856 version) that "We realize the soul only by you, you faithful solids and fluids," and asks and answers in "Starting from Paumanok":

> Was somebody asking to see the soul?
> See, your own shape and countenance, persons,
>   substances, beasts, the trees, the running
>   rivers, the rocks and sands.
>
> .   .   .   .
>
> Behold, the body includes and is the meaning, the
>   main concern, and includes and is the soul;
> Whoever you are, how superb and how divine is
>   your body, or any part of it!

Here the poet uses "soul" and not "God," but he declares elsewhere, in "Song of Myself," that he hears and beholds "God in every object,"

> In the faces of men and women I see God, and in
>   my own face in the glass,
> I find letters from God dropt in the street, and
>   every one is sign'd by God's name, . . .

but he is "not curious about God." Why not? Partly because he is so confident God is everywhere that he need not search for Him, but partly also because he believes that "nothing, not God, is greater to one than one's self is." This is the contribution of the "poet of democracy." He worships not God but the Divinity in-

nate in each individual self, and thus in "Song of Myself" he can even worship himself:

> Divine am I inside and out, and I make holy
>   whatever I touch or am touch'd from,
> The scent of these arm-pits aroma finer than prayer,
> This head more than churches, bibles, and all
>   the creeds.

This pride and arrogance of selfhood shocked many
of Whitman's contemporaries, and some thoughtful
minds of the twentieth century blame the social and political crisis of the present day on man's self-worship.
Whether good or bad, it was Walt Whitman's religion, a secular religion, which he expected to replace
the institutional religion of priests and creeds—and
the source of the poetic role which he played in *Leaves
of Grass*.

Whitman delineated his poetic role most clearly—
or at least most vividly—in the preface to his first edition of *Leaves of Grass*, and it was both cosmological
and national. Cosmologically, the poet that Whitman
wanted to be was the "one complete lover" of the known
universe, i.e. of the natural order of existence, and out
of his love for the physical world he could intuit the
spiritual world which gives life and existence to the
physical. This love and intuition enabled the poet to
acquire the "wisdom" which we have already noticed,
wisdom which defies adequate translation into words,
but in passage after passage Whitman reveals his conviction that in the eternal scheme of creation each part,
regardless of how seemingly trivial, is equally important and equally immortal. In fact, he believes that
there is no actual termination of existence of any kind
—no death—only change. What is called "death,"
therefore, is no more to be feared than birth, for both
are merely stages in the everlasting cycles of life.

Consequently Whitman's poems are filled with symbols of resurrection, from fish eggs to sprouting grass and Adam propagating the human race.

> I believe a leaf of grass is no less than the
>   journey-work of the stars,
> And the pismire is equally perfect, and a grain
>   of sand, and the egg of the wren,
> And the tree-toad is a chef-d'oeuvre for the
>   highest,
> And the running blackberry would adorn the
>   parlors of heaven, . . .
> > "SONG OF MYSELF"

Whitman worships the human body not only because every man or woman is the son or daughter of God (one of the tenets in his "new" religion) but also because it ferries the seeds of life, so that each person bridges, potentially at least, past and future generations. The act of procreation he describes in the same poem as

> Parting track'd by arriving, perpetual payment of perpetual loan,
> Rich showering rain, and recompense richer afterward.
> Sprouts take and accumulate, stand by the curb prolific and vital,
> Landscapes projected masculine, full-sized and golden.

The poet, too, is a propagator, and Whitman often uses sexual imagery to describe his function, begetting a new race on women fit for conception. And this is not inconsistent with his role as cultural time-binder, conserving the knowledge and experience of past generations and by his imaginative intuition drawing upon the future, thereby making both past and future present and available to his readers:

Without effort, and without exposing in the least how it is done, the greatest poet brings the spirit of any or all

events and passions and scenes and persons, some more
and some less, to bear on your individual character as you
hear or read. To do this well is to compete with the laws
that pursue and follow Time. What is the purpose must
surely be there and the clue of it must be there—and the
faintest indication is the indication of the best, and then
becomes the clearest indication. Past and present and future are not disjoin'd but join'd. The greatest poet forms
the consistence of what is to be, from what has been and
is. He drags the dead out of their coffins and stands them
again on their feet. He says to the past, Rise and walk
before me that I may realize you. He learns the lesson—
he places himself where the future becomes the present.[11]

The poet capable of performing these miracles
would have to be "great" indeed, and Whitman calls
him not only a poet of the cosmos but himself a "kosmos" (Whitman's preferred spelling), that is, a symbolical microcosm of the macrocosm. By the magic of
sympathetic identification the symbolical "I" can
range back and forth in time and space, thus in a sense
annihilating time and space. Whitman's poems are suf-
fused with "cosmic emotion" when he images the evolutionary processes which have culminated in his own
birth and personal identity in the present physical
world—see section 44 of "Song of Myself."

All forces have been steadily employ'd to
complete and delight me,
Now on this spot I stand with my robust soul.

Here Whitman drew simultaneously upon both mysticism and contemporary science. As a mystic he in-
tuited "the kelson of the universe" to be love, and he
trusted the "Faithful and friendly . . . arms" of nature that had carried and guided him to the present
moment of human existence, but scientific theory (in

astronomy, biology, and geology, all of which he studied in books, lectures, and journalistic popularizations) enabled him in the same section to visualize his evolutionary origin:

My feet strike an apex of the apices of the stairs,[12]
On every step bunches of ages, and larger
    bunches between the steps,
All below duly travel'd, and still I mount and
    mount.

.   .   .   .

Cycles ferried my cradle, rowing and rowing
    like cheerful boatmen,
For room to me stars kept aside in their own
    rings,
They sent influences to look after what was to
    hold me.
Before I was born out of my mother generations
    guided me,
My embryo has never been torpid, nothing could
    overlay it.

Thus through the lyric "I" of "Song of Myself," speaking for the human race from its faint inception to its future culmination, Whitman can prophesy:

The past and present wilt—I have fill'd them,
    emptied them,
And proceed to fill my next fold of the future.

The cosmic poet and the national poet would seem logically to be at opposite extremes of the literary spectrum, but Whitman was more successful in fusing the two than might be expected; though when we consider the national temper of the American people in the 1850's his achievement is not so surprising. From the early Puritans the young nation had inherited the belief that God had ordained a special, fortunate des-

tiny for it. The Puritans intended the Theocratic
State of Massachusetts to be God's Own Government
on earth, and the successes of the American people in
their two wars with England had increased their confidence in a Providential destiny. After the acquisition
of the vast territories in the regions of Oregon and
California, just nine years before Whitman published
his first *Leaves of Grass*, the possibilities for future
growth and development fairly staggered their imagination. They shared William Cullen Bryant's vision of
the "Mother of a Mighty Race":

> Oh mother of a mighty race,
> Yet lovely in thy youthful grace!
> The elder dames, thy haughty peers,
> Admire and hate thy blooming years.
>
> .   .   .   .   .   .
>
> They know not, in their hate and pride,
> What virtues with thy children bide;
>
> .   .   .   .   .   .
>
> There's freedom at thy gates and rest
> For Earth's down-trodden and opprest,
> A shelter for the hunted head,
> For the starved laborer toil and bread,
>   Power, at thy bounds
> Stops and calls back his baffled hounds.

Despite the fact that slavery still existed in the
United States, Whitman continued to harbor this national dream, this idealistic hope in 1855. He was well
aware that slavery was a great evil, and in newspaper
editorials and articles, he had angrily denounced the
political corruption of all existing political parties in
the late 1840's and 1850's. In 1856, in a political tract
called "The Eighteenth Presidency!,"[13] he admitted
that, "At present, the personnel of the government of
these thirty millions, in executives and elsewhere, is

drawn from limber-tongued lawyers, very fluent but empty feeble old men, professional politicians" and rarely from "the solid body of the people." In this tract he even predicted a civil war if the slave-owners continued to dominate the national legislature and the judiciary. But he still had faith in the innate goodness of human nature and the common people.

When he wrote his Preface, Whitman was not narrowly provincial or chauvinistic. Although he believed that most nations had failed to provide a society worthy of humanity, he did not reject or undervalue their contributions:

America does not repel the past, or what it has produced under its forms, or amid other politics, or the idea of castes, or the old religions—accepts the lesson with calmness—is not impatient because the slough still sticks to opinions and manners and literature, while the life which served its requirements has passed into the new life of the new forms—perceives that the corpse is slowly borne from the eating and sleeping rooms of the house—perceives that it waits a little while in the door—that it was fittest for its days—that its action has descended to the stalwart and well-shaped heir who approaches—and that he shall be fittest for his days.[14]

The idea of building on the past Whitman never rejected, and his ideal nation was always something to be achieved in the future. He was never smugly complacent about present conditions. He did say in the 1855 Preface, "Here at last is something in the doings of man that corresponds with the broadcast doings of the day and night." But in the same paragraph he showed that what he meant was that nature had made unprecedented development possible: "One sees it must indeed own the riches of the summer and winter, and need never be bankrupt while corn grows from the ground, or the orchards drop apples, or the bays contain fish, or men beget children upon women." In the next paragraph Whitman stated his main theme: "The largeness of the nation, however, were monstrous without a corresponding largeness and generosity of the spirit of the citizen."

As late as 1874, in "Song of the Redwood-Tree," Whitman reasserted his belief that on the North American continent, with its abundant and unexhausted natural resources, a new society could arise "proportionate to Nature." But it was not material prosperity, mere wealth or power, or world-domination, that he expected:

> But more in you than these, lands of the
>   Western shore,
> (These but the means, the implements, the
>   standing-ground,)
> I see in you, certain to come, the promise of
>   thousands of years, till now deferr'd,
> Promis'd to be fulfill'd, our common kind, the
>   race.

This same thought Whitman had already treated in "Passage to India" (1868–71), in which he presented the functions of the poet as that of humanizing the discoveries and inventions of science:

> Then not your deeds only O voyagers, O
>   scientists and inventors, shall be justified,
> All these hearts as of fretted children shall be
>   sooth'd,
> All affection shall be fully responded to, the
>   secret shall be told,
> All these separations and gaps shall be taken
>   up and hook'd and link'd together,
> The whole earth, this cold, impassive, voiceless
>   earth, shall be completely justified,

Trinitas divine shall be gloriously accomplish'd
  and compacted by the true son of
  God, the poet,
(He shall indeed pass the straits and conquer
  the mountains,
He shall double the cape of Good Hope to
  some purpose,)
Nature and Man shall be disjoin'd and diffused
  no more,
The true son of God shall absolutely fuse them.

It is now abundantly obvious that Walt Whitman's greatest ambition was to be a moral leader, but he hoped to initiate and exert this leadership through his poems, and he ended his 1855 Preface with this test: "The proof of a poet is that his country absorbs him as affectionately as he has absorbed it." Judged by this standard, he failed dismally, as he himself admitted in 1888 in "A Backward Glance o'er Travel'd Roads." Except for a few American readers here and there, he first gained significant acceptance in England among the literary elite.

Today most literary historians and critics in the United States rank Whitman as the greatest poet America has yet produced, but it has taken a long time for him to win this recognition, and the victory is far from complete even yet. During the past decade or two the most fashionable poetic style in English and American literature has been close-textured, unimpassioned, hard, cold, and ironic. Whitman's emotional, expansive style has not appealed to the disciples of Ezra Pound and T. S. Eliot. Yet these two masters did not really reject Whitman, however difficult at times they found it to come to terms with him. As early as 1909 Pound recorded in an essay only recently published, "I think we have not yet paid enough attention to the de-

liberate artistry of the man, not in details but in the
large."[15] Pound thought himself to be "more in love
with beauty," but confessed "a lesser vitality," and
credited Whitman with being "The first great man to
write in the language of his people," even as Dante did.
In a poem called "A Pact," written in 1913, Pound declared: "I make a truce with you, Walt Whitman—/I
have detested you long enough." From time to time he
broke the truce, but Pound continued to believe that
"Whitman's faults are superficial, he does convey an
image of his time, he has written *histoire morale* as
Montaigne wrote the history of his epoch."

Eliot has made few public statements about Whitman, but in 1927 in reviewing Emory Holloway's biography he compared the American poet and Tennyson, and subsequently in an open letter he called Whitman "a great master of versification, though much less
reliable than Tennyson."[16] He did not care for Whitman's social, religious, or moral ideas, but said he deserved to be remembered as "a verse maker." Edith
Sitwell, however, in *The American Genius, an Anthology of Poetry and Some Prose* (1951), compares
Whitman to Blake, and reminds us that both poets
"were born at the time when their characteristics were
most needed": Blake during an age of stultifying ma-
terialism; Whitman "after a time of vague misty abstractions," and he made it his mission "to lead poetry
back to the 'divine original, concrete.' " This mission
he did not accomplish during his lifetime, but his influence continues to live, and will probably increase as
his poems become more widely read and understood.

The understanding is as important as the reading,
for no poet of his century has been more often carica-
tured and distorted, unintentionally by himself and his
friends as well as his enemies. Furthermore, Whitman
can be embarrassing even to his admirers. He not only

personified *the self* in himself, but actually exploited
his personality in a relentless, indiscriminate, and
sometimes almost unscrupulous manner. Such conduct
alienated most educated people of his own literary generation. Today the "genteel" authors whom the nineteenth-century readers admired, to the exclusion of
Whitman, are in low repute, but this reversal has not
sufficiently erased the public suspicion that a poet who
exploited his own eccentricities must have been a fake.

Some of Whitman's self-exploitation cannot be easily excused, and it is all the more regrettable because
he misjudged and distorted his own poems. He was not
strongest in his most personal poems, such as parts of
"Starting from Paumanok," or his sentimental pleas
to his reader to forget that he was holding a book instead of a human being who invited kisses and ca-
resses. Nor is Whitman strongest in his most doctri-
naire poems—those in which he preaches—states
general principles in abstract language instead of
appealing to the senses through vivid, concrete imagery. "Salut au Mond!" is almost as tiresome as the
doctrinal sections of "Starting from Paumanok," but
its final goal is a poetic expression of an ambition both
personal and cosmic:

> My spirit has pass'd in compassion and determination
>   around the whole earth,
> I have look'd for equals and lovers and found them
>   ready for me in all lands,
> I think some divine rapport has equalized me with
>   them.

This vision was "cosmic" because Whitman believed
it to be in harmony with the underlying structure of
the universe. Hart Crane, the aborted follower of
Whitman in the twentieth century, was right when he

declared that "He, better than any other, was able to coordinate those forces in America which seem most intractable, fusing them into a universal vision which takes on additional significance as time goes on."[17]

2

MUTATIONS IN WHITMAN'S ART

IN HIS PROVOCATIVE Introduction to the first popular reprint of Walt Whitman's first edition of *Leaves of Grass* (Viking Press, 1960), Malcolm Cowley not only claims that in this edition we have "Whitman at his best," but he also calls the first version of "Song of Myself" "perhaps his one completely realized work." That it is "one of the great poems of modern times" I heartily agree, but I am also convinced that a few other poems, of later composition, are also "completely realized."

The problem which this interpretation points up is the *difference* between Whitman's poems of various periods.[1] In addition to "Song of Myself," Cowley admires to a lesser extent the first published version of "The Sleepers," which he calls the "fantasia of the unconscious," as well as "To Think of Time," "I Sing the Body Electric," and "There Was a Child Went Forth." Whether these are *better* than "Crossing Brooklyn Ferry," "Out of the Cradle Endlessly Rocking," "When Lilacs Last in the Dooryard Bloom'd," "Passage to India," and several other major poems of the later editions is a question that can never be answered to everyone's satisfaction. But they are more radically different in content and technique than is generally recognized, and they should be judged in terms of these differences, which have never been adequately defined. This essay is intended as a beginning of such definition, and needs to be greatly extended.

Cowley is not the first to regret that Whitman continued until near the end of his life to tinker with his poems,[2] perennially changing titles, grouping and regrouping them, and rewriting and remotivating phrases, segments, even whole poems. Most critics will have to agree, too, that in the first edition we have Whitman at his freshest in vision and boldest in language, "Whitman transformed by a new experience, so that he wanders among familiar objects and finds that each of them has become a miracle." Without disputing the contention that "Song of Myself" is the product of a mystical experience (or experiences), one can say that it details in concrete imagery the objects and sensations experienced by an ecstatic observer of the physical world. It is this very concreteness, even in the long "catalogs," that makes the poem still seem so fresh and "modern."

It is almost impossible for the twentieth-century reader to understand the moral and esthetic revulsion experienced by most of Whitman's contemporary readers when they first encountered his undraped metaphors: "loveroot, silkthread, crotch and vine," for his private anatomy, and his insistence that "Copulation is no more rank to me than death is." A poet who "doted" on himself, "hankering, gross, mystical, nude," and "belched" his words out over "the roofs of the world," seemed to one contemporary reviewer[3] to know no more about poetry than a hog does about metaphysics. But today, having read many franker practitioners, most readers find nothing to shock them in such language, whether they like it or not. This sophistication, however, makes it necessary for the modern critic of Whitman to insist upon the marvelous accuracy and strength of his imagery in order that it may not be taken too casually for granted.

In none of his later poems does Whitman so acutely convey the felt experience. To take a very simple example from "Song of Myself":

> The big doors of the country-barn stand open and ready,
> The dried grass of the harvest-time loads the slow-drawn wagon,
> The clear light plays on the brown gray and green intertinged,
> The armfuls are packed to the sagging mow:
> I am there. . . .[4] I help . . . . I came stretched atop of the load,
> I felt its soft jolts . . . . one leg reclined on the other,
> I jump from the crossbeams, and seize the clover and timothy,
> And roll head over heels, and tangle my hair full of wisps.

The carpenter's foreplane dressing the plank "whistles its wild ascending lisp." And "The spinning-girl retreats and advances to the hum of the big wheel." The pilot of the ferry-boat "seizes the king-pin, he heaves down with a strong arm." In hundreds of sharply-focused images the poet inventories the domestic and national life of the period.

Whitman's almost pathological sympathy also enabled him to convey vicarious experience with remarkable intensity, and was the source of his numerous *metamorphoses*—another link with twentieth-century poetry.[5]

> I am the hounded slave . . . I wince at the bite of the dogs,
>
> .   .   .   .
>
> Agonies are one of my changes of garments;

> I do not ask the wounded person how he feels I
> myself become the wounded person,
> My hurt turns livid upon me as I lean on a cane and
> observe.
>   "SONG OF MYSELF"

Whitman's metamorphoses accomplish much more than the conventional, artificial nineteenth-century *personification,* such as the wandering clouds and babbling brooks of Wordsworth and Shelley. In "Song of Myself" the metamorphoses are of two kinds, two levels of association, the one social and the other cosmic, both functioning psychologically. On the social level the poet enters vicariously into the life of every man or woman he has known or can imagine. On the cosmic level he intuits his identity in the evolution of the stars, the origin of life, and the beauty of all elemental things. Thus as he "walks with the tender and growing night" he becomes the sensuous lover of the "Rich apple-blossomed earth!" The metaphor is extended with tactile and kinetic imagery. Later, in his cosmical metamorphosis he devours time and space, skirts sierras, covers continents with his palms, and, in a burst of acceleration and dilation, speeds "with tailed meteors . . . throwing fire balls like the rest"; finally he departs "as air," shaking his white locks "at the runaway sun," effusing his "flesh in eddies" and drifting "it in lacy jags." But the basic metamorphosis is not that of a personality magnified to the dimension of a comet or planet. It is rather the generative power and fecundity underlying and permeating the universe, symbolized in the poem by an "I" acutely sensitive to sexual "touch." This was to remain one of Whitman's favorite themes, but he never found more successful imagery for it than in this poem, in which the fecundating orgasm is described as

Parting tracked by arriving . . . . perpetual payment
  of the perpetual loan,
Rich showering rain, and recompense richer afterward.
Sprouts take and accumulate . . . . stand by the curb
  prolific and vital,
Landscapes projected masculine full-sized and golden.

The concepts of "Song of Myself" are so large that
the critics have never agreed very closely on what they
are, though most now think the poem is about *the self*
rather than *myself*.[6] And opinions as to the structure
and coherence are just as diverse. But the poet's iden-
tifications and metamorphoses obviously needed both
flexibility and expansion in form and language. He
could produce space empathy, for example, only by
piling image on top of image in a seemingly endless
procession. Thus the poem is long, loosely organized,
and repetitive. The marvel is that it does have aesthetic unity and the effect of completion. For many
readers it is without doubt Whitman at his best. But
the very nature and quality of "Song of Myself" make
it almost inevitable that Whitman can never duplicate
the performance. What else can he do except repeat
himself?

Of course he might elaborate some of the minor
themes or motifs in new poems. And that, or something
very like it, was what he did in the other eleven poems
of the 1855 edition—or more accurately, nine, for
"Europe . . ." and "A Boston Ballad" predated
"Song of Myself." One of the other poems, "To Think
of Time," resembles "Song of Myself" only superficially, being concerned with the pathos of human fini-
tude: "To think that the rivers will come to flow, and
the snow fall, and fruits ripen . . and act upon others as upon us now . . . . and yet not act upon us."
Still another, "A Child Went Forth," merely demon-

onstrates somewhat obviously the Wordsworthian doctrine that each of his experiences becomes a part of the child-man, though it has effective imagery. With one or two possible exceptions, the remaining poems of the first edition are not important.

The chief exception is "The Sleepers" (using the later title). It *can* be regarded, in Cowley's words, as a "fantasia of the unconscious," for the dream-imagery drifts, merges, and changes as in hypnagogic vision, and no doubt arose partially, at least, from the poet's secret longings, fears, perhaps even traumas. But closer inspection also reveals an order and structure indicating conscious planning, the kind of planning to be found henceforth in most of Whitman's longer poems. In fact, it is a turning point in his art, a turning to more conscious artistry—sometimes too self-conscious.

Though "The Sleepers" begins as a vision of the sleepers of the world, leveled by slumber and their equality in nature, it becomes an analogy of the transmigratory journey of the soul from its embowered garden of spirit to the physical world and back again to reinvigorating sleep in the womb of time, to await another avatar. "Night" is not so much death itself as the strength-restoring interval between death and birth, analogous to the physiological chemistry of sleep.

I will duly pass the day O my mother and duly return to
    you;
Not you will yield forth the dawn again more surely than
    you will yield forth me again,
Not the womb yields the babe in its time more surely than I
    shall be yielded from you in my time.

Even while Whitman was thus turning to a more deliberate, planned ordering of his symbols and structure, he was misleading his readers and himself by writing prefaces in which he asserted two ambitions that contradicted his practice. The first was a program of nationalism, which led to his playing the role, and finally being accepted as, *the* poet of American democracy. By his choice of imagery he did, as remarked earlier, mirror his experience, his times, and the life of nineteenth-century America. And to this extent he achieved his nationalistic program. But the larger themes of "Song of Myself," "The Sleepers," and indeed most of his poems, are universal: the nature of the *self* in relation to the cosmos and the meaning and purpose of birth and death. These huge themes he could present artistically only by suggesting analogies in nature, which tended, as he developed his art, toward literary designs approaching the structure and function of allegories.

Whitman's second contradictory ambition was to create an anti-art, or no-art; or at least to work by intuition and instinct rather than conscious artistry, which he regarded as artificial, trivial, and false. Like D. H. Lawrence later, he wanted to think with his hips and create with his blood. "All beauty," he said in his 1855 Preface, "comes from beautiful blood and a beautiful brain. If the greatnesses are in conjunction in a man or woman it is enough." At times he seemed to think of the poet as a passive agent of cosmic beauty and truth: "The greatest poet has less a marked style and is more the channel of thoughts and things without increase or diminution, and is the free channel of himself."

But whatever the strength and source of the poet's energy may be, a poem is a *thing*: it has size, shape, and structure. After "Song of Myself" Whitman reduced the size, controlled the shape to a greater extent, and fitted together the parts with painstaking care. His romantic fancy, in the 1855 Preface, that his poems could grow naturally like lilacs on a bush or melons on a vine can be disproved by a glance at almost any of his manuscripts, but this is not necessary to prove that they were shaped by conscious effort and measured judgment. We need only to examine the poems themselves to see and compare their "made" beauties.

The second edition of *Leaves of Grass* (1856) was evidently put together hastily, erratically, and arrogantly—under the double stimulation of Emerson's unexpected praise and in defiance of the public disapproval of the first edition.[7] But it contained one of Whitman's most expert aesthetic creations, first called "Sun-Down Poem" and later "Crossing Brooklyn Ferry." Taking a simple object, such as the ferry, and gradually shaping poetic and metaphysical symbolism out of its physical characteristics was not a new method in Whitman's art, for he had done that with the grass in "Song of Myself." But "Crossing Brooklyn Ferry" has a more balanced symmetry, development, and climax than any poem in the first edition. In one hundred and twenty-two lines he transforms his literary "ferry" into a vehicle for an aesthetic journey from the prosaic shores of Manhattan and Brooklyn to a vision of the eternal destination of the "soul." The physical objects of the East River become "beautiful ministers" to the psyche, each furnishing its part "toward eternity." Some of these "ministers" are the flood tide, the clouds, the sunset, the circling sea-gulls, the dark patches in the murky water, and the reflections of light on the "scallop-edg'd waves." To interpret the symbolical meaning of these out of context would make the poem sound mechanical and arbitrary; in context they seem altogether fitting and convincing. This is accomplished partly by letting the symbolical

meaning emerge gradually from the natural and literal
fact. The poet is describing one of his favorite daily
experiences, in which the movement is back and forth
across the not-very-wide river separating two cities.
But in the poem the forward movement is interrupted
by suspension and centrifugal movement, as in the
diverging "spokes of light" radiating from the poet's
reflection in the water. He merges his identity in the
crowd, feels in the "float" sustaining the ferry himself
and all humanity dissolved into the flood and ebb-tide
of eternity: the endless cycle of birth, death, and re-
birth.

The impalpable sustenance of me from all things at all
    hours of the day,
The simple, compact, well-join'd scheme, myself disinte-
    grated, everyone disintegrated yet part of the
    scheme, . . .

The sense of movement conveyed both by the pro-
gression of images and by the imperatives to the river
to "flow," "suspend," "expand," etc. carries the sympathetic reader to the completion of a vicarious experience with the poet, the abstract and concrete having
operated simultaneously to the speaker's conclusion:
"Great or small, you furnish your parts toward the
soul."

In form and structure the 1860 "Out of the Cradle
Endlessly Rocking" (first published in 1859 as "A
Child's Reminiscence") is similar to "Crossing Brooklyn Ferry" and most of the longer poems of 1855,
which employ a basic metaphor flowering into an un-
folding cluster of symbols. But the great difference is
that it includes a narrative, a simple story of two
mockingbirds observed by a boy of indefinite age. The
poet's retrospective identification with the bird which
he supposed to have lost its mate symbolizes his own

poetic awakening. To this point, the story is an allegory of the birth of a poet, whose theme is to be unsatisfied love. This is what the poet supposedly learned
from the bird, but despite the prominence of the bird
in the narrative, it is a secondary symbol in the poem.
The primary symbol is the ocean, "the cradle endlessly
rocking," the maternal principle, which reconciles the
boy-poet to the fact and meaning of death.

This poem is highly emotional, partly because of the
pathetic bird-story, and partly because of the lyrical
effect of the bird song, which Whitman presents in the
form of the aria in Italian opera. No attempt is made
to imitate the natural sounds of bird songs, the poet
aiming rather at the more subtle effect of the spirit of
the song.[8] The language is impassioned, exclamatory,
and—a new development in Whitman's art—musical
in the strict sense of the term.

> *Two together!*
> *Winds blow south, or winds blow north,*
> *Day come white, or night come black,*
> *Home, or rivers and mountains from home,*
> *Singing all time, minding no time,*
> *While we two keep together.*

This is a new rhythm for Whitman, with its cretics
(/ x /) and choriambs (/ x x /), its tone colors and
harmonies, its iterated and balanced sounds.

But Whitman far surpassed the music of this poem
in his great elegy, "When Lilacs Last in the Dooryard
Bloom'd." Here he used the whole key-board of his or-
gan, from the fortissimo "O powerful western fallen
star!" to the pianissimo (the voice of the poet's spirit
tallying "the song of the bird"):

Come lovely and soothing death,
Undulate round the world, serenely arriving, arriving,

In the day, in the night, to all, to each,
Sooner or later delicate death.

As with "Out of the Cradle," though with greater
skill and control, in "Lilacs" Whitman alternates the
recitative and aria (speaking and singing lines). In
both poems, too, he varies the music and the empathy-
producing space imagery by a syntactical device which
he perfected after his first two editions. In "Out of the
Cradle" this consists of an opening sentence of twenty-
two verses, in which subject and predicate are held in
suspense until the last three verses. The effect of this
suspended predication is greatly magnified by an accompanying rhetorical device which he had used as
early as "Song of Myself," the reiteration of the first
word or phrase of the line (a kind of psychic rhyme[9]),
but used more effectively here:

Out of the cradle endlessly rocking,
Out of the mocking-bird's throat, the musical shuttle,
Out of the Ninth-month midnight,
Over the sterile sands and the fields beyond, . . .

This is rudimentary, however, compared to the use
of the same device in "Lilacs," where it is employed
with marvelous success to transport the coffin through
the lanes and streets, across the broad land, over the
breast of the spring landscape. The various motifs—
symbolical, emotional, and musical—interweave in a
unity transcending variety, all conducing to an inevitable destination, the arrival of the coffin at the grave.
The verses continually vary in length, and so do the
number of verses in each section, each with its cooperat-
ing semantic and musical unit. One example of the symmetry without regularity is the manner in which rhetorical pattern and flowing imagery lead the reader to
feel the passing of the coffin through the land in Sec-

tions 5, 6, and 16, at the end of which the bier comes to rest with a falling cadence,

There in the fragrant pines and the cedars dusk and dim.

The "Lilac" poem is a good test of the reader's ability to recognize and appreciate the mutations in Whitman's art. The imagery is less concrete and startling than in "Song of Myself," and natural word-order is sometimes sacrificed for cadence: Whitman would not in the first edition have written "cedars dusk and dim." The lilac has vague "delicate-color'd blossoms" and almost too obviously symbolical "heart-shaped leaves." The bird is merely "gray-brown" and a "wondrous singer." The star is a "western orb sailing the heaven." "Orb" is almost poetic diction. Whitman's diction is now almost as generalized as the language of Longfellow or Tennyson, to whom he had drawn closer in poetic sensibility since writing his 1855 poems. But it is precisely the music—verbal harmonies—in combination with the symbolical imagery, the rhetoric, and the modulation of sound that constitutes the originality, power, and aesthetic poise of this poem. The sharp, clear imagery of "Song of Myself" would divert attention from, or even destroy, the mood and tone of this elegy. It is a nineteenth-century masterpiece, and the finest composition in his middle style that Whitman ever did, though he later used some of the same techniques in other good poems, such as "Prayer of Columbus," "Song of the Redwood-Tree," and "Passage to India."

The third major development in Whitman's art was the short poem. In the first edition there are no short poems, and no good ones in the second. But in the third (1860) we find many brief poems, some of which are excellent. This edition also gives a clue to the reason for Whitman's turning to the shorter form, and his

manuscript notes show plainly the model for his new
experiments in verse structure.

The best of these shorter poems are found in a group
which he calls "Calamus," a somewhat esoteric title derived from the calamus plant, of the Iris family, with
lance-shaped leaves, a phallic blossom, and pink, aro-
matic roots that thrive in bogs and marshes. The symbolism is indicated in the first poem of the group:

In paths untrodden,
In the growth by margins of pond-waters,
Escaped from the life that exhibits itself,
From all the standards hitherto published, . . .
.   .   .   .
Strong upon me the life that does not exhibit itself, yet
    contains all the rest

Resolved to sing no songs to-day but those of manly at-
    tachment . . .

The symbolism itself is not a new departure, for the
calamus plant is only another kind of grass. But the
tone, treatment, and poetic structure are a new departure for Whitman. In his manuscripts he refers to
these poems as "sonnets," and when we recall the similarity of the "manly attachment" theme present in
most of these poems to Shakespeare's sonnets to his
male friend, the connection is obvious. Of course an un-
rhymed poem without definite metre can only resemble
a sonnet in its length, concentration, and thematic
treatment, and this we do find in the best of these "Calamus" poems, such as the following:

When I heard at the close of the day how my name had
    been received with plaudits in the capitol, still it was
    not a happy night for me that followed;
And else, when I caroused, or when my plans were accom-
    plished, still I was not happy;

But the day when I rose at dawn from the bed of perfect
    health, refreshed, singing, inhaling the ripe breath of
    autumn,
When I saw the full moon in the west grow pale and dis-
    appear in the morning light,
When I wandered alone on the beach, and undressing,
    bathed, laughing with the cool waters, and saw the sun
    rise,
And when I thought how my dear friend my lover was on
    his way coming, O then I was happy,
O then each breath tasted sweeter, and all that day my
    food nourished me more, and the beautiful day passed
    well,
And the next came with equal joy, and with the next at
    evening came my friend,
And that night, while all was still, I heard the waters roll
    slowly continually up the shores,
I heard the hissing rustle of the liquid and sands, as di-
    rected to me, whispering, to congratulate me,
For the one I love most lay sleeping by me under the same
    cover in the cool night,
In the stillness, in the autumn moonbeams, his face was in-
    clined toward me,
And his arm lay lightly around my breast—And that
    night I was happy.

This poem, however, lacks the tight structure of a real
sonnet, and in this characteristic it is a transition to
Whitman's mastery of a compact form.

Another group in the 1860 edition, called "Enfans
d'Adam" (later "Children of Adam"), was written, as
Whitman's manuscripts show, to balance the "friendship for men" group with a cluster on the "amative
love of woman." Oddly enough, these do not show the
same influence of the traditional sonnet, being either
longer and more diffuse or shorter and more epigram-
matic, as in No. 14:

I am he that aches with love;
Does the earth gravitate? Does not all matter, aching,
  attract all matter?
So the body of me to all I meet, or that I know.

But in the first poem in this group Whitman
achieved a weight of connotation and an originality of
symbolical structure that anticipated the Symbolists at
the end of the century:

To the garden, the world, anew ascending,
Potent mates, daughters, sons, preluding,
The love, the life of their bodies, meaning and being,
Curious, here behold my resurrection, after slumber,
The revolving cycles, in their wide sweep, having brought
  me again,
Amorous, mature—all beautiful to me—all wondrous,
My limbs, and the quivering fire that ever plays through
  them, for reasons, most wondrous;
Existing, I peer and penetrate still,
Content with the present—content with the past,
By my side, or back of me, Eve following,
Or in front, and I following her just the same.

Since Charles Davis and I have already given a detailed explication of this poem in the Evergreen edition of *Whitman's Poems*, I will merely refer here to a
few of its accomplishments in language and structure.
Although the poem appears to be more regular than
Whitman's earlier poems, the whole approach is ob-
lique—in syntax, rhetoric, and statement. The thought
is of the world (human society) returning ("ascending") to the lost innocence of Eden, especially in sexual
matters. But this has not happened, nor is it prophe-
sied. The situation evoked is hypothetical—like the
poet's metaphorical "resurrection"—and both the syntax and the diction support the implied incompletion.
Many critics have thought the anacoluthon, as illus-

trated here, the result either of Whitman's ignorance or carelessness, but he used it so many times and so often with effectiveness that we must assume he used it deliberately. Another fine example of such use is in "The Dalliance of the Eagles" (1880). And of course many of the "Drum Taps" poems violate syntax in order to emphasize the immediacy, the retrospective *presentness* of scene and incident.

The point to be emphasized, however, is that in working on his shorter poems Whitman gave more attention to diction, word order, cadence, and finish. Perhaps his failures are as numerous as in his longer poems, but in "Sparkles from the Wheel," "To a Locomotive in Winter," and "A Noiseless Patient Spider," to mention only a few, he wrote some of his finest lyrics. The "Spider" poem, especially, shows superb mastery. The theme is solitude, and Whitman used the analogy of a spider sitting on a little promontory, surrounded by vacant space, as a parallel to his own human condition. Just as the spider throws out "filament, filament, filament, out of itself" (the repetitions convey the "tireless . . . unreeling"), so does his soul spin its gossamer thread into "measureless oceans of space." But I must quote the whole poem:

A noiseless patient spider,
I mark'd where on a little promontory it stood isolated,
Mark'd how to explore the vacant vast surrounding,
It launch'd forth filament, filament, filament, out of itself,
Ever unreeling them, ever tirelessly speeding them.

And you O my soul where you stand,
Surrounded, detached, in measureless oceans of space,
Ceaselessly musing, venturing, throwing, seeking the
    spheres to connect them,
Till the bridge you will need be form'd, till the ductile
    anchor hold,

Till the gossamer thread you fling catch somewhere, O my
  soul.

Notice the difference between "patient noiseless spider" and Whitman's emphatic, deliberately delayed
"noiseless patient spider." Throughout the poem the
words, the imagery, and the rhythm perfectly fit the
spider's action and the poet's almost desperate prayer
to "catch somewhere, O my soul." It is a pleading im-
perative, not a confident exclamation. "Here," as Mark
Van Doren has remarked,[10] "is solitude with a venge-
ance, in vacancy so vast that any soul at its center, trying to comprehend it, looks terribly minute."

The subject and the symbols remind us of Emily
Dickinson, and yet it is such a poem as she never wrote.
But to think of the comparison is to realize Whitman's
great diversity, for no one would ever think of compar-
ing "Song of Myself" to any example of Emily Dickinson's fragile, subtle art. This poem, no less than "Song
of Myself," has space empathy on a vast scale, but the
one is painted on a mile-long canvas and the other on
the gossamer thread of a spider. The two poems show
the vast range in the mutations of Walt Whitman's art.

3

THE "LONG JOURNEY" MOTIF

WALT WHITMAN's ambition to be the poetic
spokesman of America has been discussed so widely and
frequently, both by the poet himself and by his critics,
that his earlier, far more grandiose, plan to write a

Reprinted, with slight revisions, from The Journal of English and
Germanic Philology, XXXVIII (*January, 1939*), 76–95.

work of epic scope on the progress of the human race throughout the ages has been overlooked by the scholars and interpreters. Whether this work was to have been in prose or poetry is uncertain. One of the preparatory schemes, preserved by Dr. Bucke in *Notes and Fragments,* records the intention but not the method: "A volume—(dramatic machinery for localities, characters, etc.,) running in idea and description through the whole range of recorded time—Egyptian, Hindustanee, Assyrian, Greek, Roman, Alb, Gallic, Teutonic—and so on down to the present day."[1]

That Whitman ever planned to write a world history seems preposterous, though we know from the Bucke manuscripts that he industriously applied himself during the early fifties to studying the history of various races and periods. In a prose sketch for the poem, "Unnamed Lands," he remarked, "The best and most important part of history cannot be told." Apparently it was simply "the tumultuous procession" itself, as he called it, which appealed to his imagination. Further evidence that he was thinking of the subject as poetic material is found in a projected poem, never finished or published by Whitman himself, entitled in *Notes and Fragments,* "The March of the Human Race Across the Earth," which celebrates the "procession without halt."[2]

But general and vague as these phrases are, the frequent references in the manuscripts to "those stages all over the world . . . leaving their memories and inheritances in all the continents," and the awe and reverence with which the future poet stands "before the movements of the great soul of man in all lands and in every age," can leave no doubt of Whitman's serious intention to celebrate what Johannes V. Jensen, Whitman's Danish disciple, has, in our day, called *The Long Journey.*[3]

Why, then, did Whitman ever relinquish this ambitious subject? We might suppose that he found it too
big for him and his own preparation inadequate, but
actually he did not discard the theme: he merely transformed it. As he became more nationalistic he felt a
stronger desire to celebrate the American people, but
even his brash patriotism of 1855 and the '60's is based
at least in part on a special interpretation of the earlier history-of-the-race theme. The 1855 Preface begins, "America does not repel the past or what it has
produced . . ." He thinks of America as merely one
stage in the endless "procession," though this stage is
now his primary concern. But the "procession" idea is
always an underlying motif; the word itself constantly
recurs in Whitman's poems.[4] In fact, the theme of life
as a journey, and of the evolution of man and the universe as a journey, may well be called a major motif in
Leaves of Grass.[5]

Whitman's fascination with the idea of the "procession of races, swiftly marching and countermarching
over the fields of the earth," and of each stage in the
travel as "but temporary journeys,"[6] led him to the
mystical desire in "Song of the Open Road"

To know the universe itself as a road, as many roads,
    as roads for traveling souls
All parts away for the progress of souls,
All religions, all solid things, arts, governments—
    all that was or is apparent upon this globe or any globe,
    falls into niches and corners before the procession of
    souls along the grand roads of the universe.

    .   .   .   .

Forever alive, forever forward,
[All humanity] . . . I know not where they go,
But I know they go toward the best—toward something
    great.

Thus the journey motif includes a scientific theory, a metaphysics, a religious faith, and a personal philosophy; in fact, it provides a background for the various themes of *Leaves of Grass*—evolution, for example.

In one of those characteristic notes to himself which he wrote during the years of his poetic gestation, Whitman says, "put this section forward . . . that this earth is under a constant process of amelioration . . . that the processes of refinement and perfection of the earth are in steps, the least part of which involves trillions of years." In accord with the philosophical concept of "plenitude," Whitman believes in a cosmic evolution, an eternal process of "becoming,"[7] never reaching perfection but always ascending the scale of being:

This then is life,
Here is what has come to the surface after so many
    throes and convulsions,
                    "STARTING FROM PAUMANOK"

The arrogance of "Song of Myself" depends upon this faith proclaimed in the poem:

Before I was born out of my mother generations guided
    me,
My embryo has never been torpid, nothing could overlay
    it.
I am an acme of things accomplish'd and I [am] an en-
    closer of things to be.

Both before and after the appearance of Darwin's *Origin of Species* in 1859 Whitman's doctrine is almost uniformly consistent. "The law of promotion and transformation cannot be eluded."[8] The cause, the origin, the Demiurge, was perhaps always hazy in his own mind; in "A Thought of Columbus" he can only say,

A breath of Deity, as thence the bulging universe unfold-
   ing!
. . . the widest, farthest evolutions of the world and man.

But in "Song of the Universal" he has a religious conviction that,

> In this broad earth of ours,
> Amid the measureless grossness and the slag,
> Enclosed and safe within its central heart,
> Nestles the seed perfection.

Thus, in "Going Somewhere,"

"The world, the race, the soul—in space and time the uni-
   verses,
All bound as is befitting each—all surely going somewhere."

Cosmic evolution, therefore, the "float forever held
in solution," a divine flux of an Hegelian nature,[9] is
the fundamental philosophical background of Whitman's use of the "Long Journey" motif. But the theme
also has other immediate and personal applications.
Whitman has been accused of indifference to the past
and of ignorantly exalting Americans as the culmination of the ages. He does believe that they are a culmination, just as his own life is "an acme of things accomplish'd," but he does not mean a final culmination.
"Humanity . . . never at any time or under any circumstances arrives at its finality." Always, "I see the
road continued, and the journey ever continued."[10]
Only by understanding this motif can we fully comprehend Whitman's poems. For example, the real theme of
"Pioneers! O Pioneers!" is less the celebration of the
American pioneers than the journey itself; they are
merely a link in the chain[11] which extends from Europe
to America, and from America to Asia—the "Passage

to India," which also contains the "Passage to more than India." Other poems, such as "Birds of Passage," "Crossing Brooklyn Ferry," and, already mentioned, "Song of the Open Road" also give noble expression to the great journey theme.

Likewise Whitman's ideas on religion fall into niches of the vast scheme. Each religion "means exactly the state of development of the people [up to that time] . . . by-and-by they will pass on further."[12] Thus each age must have its own religion and this belief accounts for Whitman's desire to found a new religion for the modern age.[13]

Even the erotic poems are explained by this journey motif, for the very thought of the "countless germs waiting the due conjunction, the arousing touch"—in other words, waiting for the "arousing touch" to start them upon their lap of the journey—this thought is sufficient to convince Whitman of the sacredness of sex; and the conviction is strengthened by his belief that "all that was or is apparent upon this globe or any globe, falls into niches and corners before the procession of souls along the grand roads of the universe." Whether or not this doctrine is akin to the Leibnitzian belief that each soul in the "chain of being" migrates to other planes of existence, where it may attain higher perfection, at any rate the cycle of existence gives Whitman a great spiritual and imaginative stimulation.[14]

> Ages and ages returning at intervals,
> Undestroy'd, wandering, immortal,
> Lusty, phallic . . .
>> "AGES AND AGES"

And as with birth, so with death:

A minute, a touch and a drop of us can launch immortality . . .

and what we thought death is but life brought to a firmer parturition.

"SONG OF MYSELF"

The nobility and grandeur of death was not a theme which appealed to Whitman only in his old age; it was prominent even in the preparatory notes and fragments. It is part of the whole "Long Journey" motif, and it explains Whitman's constant insistence that there is no death. The process is ceaseless, restless, an eternal journey.[15]

I tramp a perpetual journey . . .

.   .   .   .

This day before dawn I ascended a hill and look'd at the
    crowded heaven,
And I said to my spirit *When we become the enfolders of*
    those orbs . . . shall we be fill'd and satisfied then?
And my spirit said *No, we but level that lift to pass and*
    continue beyond.

"SONG OF MYSELF"

Whitman's conception of his role as poet and prophet naturally involves this motif. Indeed, it is prominent to some extent in nearly all romantic poetry, as witnessed by Goethe, Nietzsche, Chateaubriand, Mme de Staël,[16] Wordsworth, Shelley, and others, but none of these used the theme in so varied and significant a way as Whitman did.

Afoot and light-hearted I take to the open road,
Healthy, free, the world before me,
The long brown path before me leading me wherever I
    choose.

"SONG OF THE OPEN ROAD"

There we have the obvious use of this motif by a nature poet. But though Whitman liked to swim, lie in the sun, and listen to the ocean, he was not a great hiker. He tramped with his imagination. "I tramp a perpetual journey," he announces, then adds,

Not I, not any one else, can travel that road for you,
You must travel it for yourself.
"SONG OF MYSELF"

Always the journey becomes allegorical, and it may signify life, the cosmic process, the task of the poet, or the search for the perfect "comrade"—sometimes identified with the reader:

> Camerado, I give you my hand!
> . . . will you come travel with me?
> "SONG OF THE OPEN ROAD"

That the exquisite scheme is for it, and the nebulous float
   is for it, and the cohering is for it!
And all preparation is for it—and identity is for it—
   and life and materials are altogether for it!
"TO THINK OF TIME"

But the poet can also identify himself with the cosmic journey, with time and space, or with the lives of other people. He can therefore wander at will over the universe, and through past and future ages. In his role as mystic poet he can even identify himself with Christ:

. . . we walk unheld, free, the whole earth over, journeying up and down till we make our ineffaceable mark
   upon time and the diverse eras,
Till we saturate time and eras, that the men and women of
   races, ages to come, may prove brethren and lovers as
   we are.
"TO HIM THAT WAS CRUCIFIED"

The journey motif is also the key to Whitman's style. His insistence that each person must travel the road for himself and his own individualistic nature would inevitably lead to the desire for independence in style. Late in life he summed it up in this manner:[17]

The objections to me are the objections made to all men who choose to go their own road—make their own choice of methods.

And there was Lincoln, too: see how he went his own lonely road, disregarding all the usual ways—refusing the guides, accepting no warnings: just keeping his appointment with himself every time.

This idiomatic use of the road metaphor is not significant in itself, but is more appropriate than may appear on the surface. Possibly Whitman himself never fully understood the psychology of his style—or the psychological necessity for his peculiar form—though he puzzled enough over it. But it is not a mere coincidence that he should have anticipated "expressionism" and the Dujardin "interior monologue." Long before Bergson's *Creative Evolution*[18] and William James's "stream of consciousness" theories had been formulated, Walt Whitman, by mystic pyschology and his pantheistic philosophy, felt the mysterious current of the living process coursing through the fibres of his sensitive organism, and he experienced the illusion of identity with the process itself, so that, at the height of his "cosmic consciousness," time and space ceased to exist for him. His thin thread of life connected him with all life, past and future, until all time became one eternal present.

Whitman himself, in a poem called "L. of G.'s Purport," defined his intention in these words:

Haughty this song, its words and scope,
To span vast realms of space and time,
Evolution—the cumulative—growths and generations.

The haughtiness need not detain us here, though we may note in passing that it grew out of the poet's consciousness of the relationship between man and nature

—nature, crude, virile, growing and traveling toward a higher goal. This aspect of Whitman's style has been sufficiently discussed since the beginning of his poetic career. But notice that the song also purports "to span vast realms of space and time," and to do so in order to express "evolution" and "cumulative . . . growths." In the 1855 Preface the "American poet" is to "incarnate" the geography of his country, from the Atlantic to the Pacific oceans: "He stretches with them north and south. . . . He spans between them also from east to west and reflects what is between them." Then in the poetic prose which was later arranged almost verbatim in the form of verse, "By Blue Ontario's Shore," a typical "catalog" passage enumerates in rapid succession examples of the flora, fauna, topography, and human occupations existing within these dimensions, given as they might be seen by an omniscient observer, or as Whitman says in the same Preface, "High up out of reach he [the poet] stands turning a concentrated light."[19] The obvious intention of Whitman is both symbolical and mystical, based on his sense of unity with the vast expanse of the North American continent and the mystic illusion of transcending time and space.

From "Song of Myself" to "Roaming in Thought" (1881) the central theme and the literary technique are the same. In "Song of Myself" the poet feels himself covering continents:

Space and Time! now I see it is true, what I guess'd
     at, . . .
My ties and ballasts leave me, my elbows rest in sea gaps,
I skirt sierras, my palms cover continents,
I am afoot with my vision.

In "Starting from Paumanok" he roams the continent, projecting himself backward in time and space

until he identifies his life with the continuity of the
race, and then has a vision of the "successions of men"
who constitute for him "an audience interminable." In
another poem the sleepers "flow hand in hand over the
whole earth from east to west" while the poet wanders
all night in his vision. In "Proud Music of the Storm"
he hears the sounds of all the world and of all history;
he is filled "with the voices of the universe."

As Furness says in the *Workshop* (p. 189), "There
is . . . evidence that Whitman made a conscious goal
of 'meditation, the devout ecstasy, the soaring flight.' "
In one of those notes to himself Whitman recorded his
formula:

Abstract yourself from this book; realize where you are at
present located, the point you stand that is now to you the
centre of all. Look up overhead, think of space stretching
out, think of all the unnumbered orbs wheeling safely
there, invisible to us by day, some visible by night; think
of the sun around which the earth revolves; the moon revolving round the earth, and accompanying it; think of
the different planets belonging to our system. Spend some
minutes faithfully in this exercise. Then again realize
yourself upon the earth, at the particular point you now
occupy. Which way stretches the north, and what country, seas, etc.? Which way the south? Which way the
east? Which way the west? Seize these firmly with your
mind, pass freely over immense distances. Turn your face
a moment thither. Fix definitely the direction and the idea
of the distances of separate sections of your own country,
also of England, the Mediterranean sea, Cape Horn, the
North Pole, and such like distinct places.[20]

Here we have the real explanation of Whitman's
catalogs, his association of ideas, his declamatory lists
of objects, scenes, and occupations extending not only
over the North American continent—and therefore

symbolical of the nation he celebrates—but even at times over the whole globe, as in "Salut au Monde!" in which he sees the Himalayas, Alps, Pyrenees, the Arctic, Japan, the Dardanelles, the Ganges, and the scenes and nations of the earth. His mystic flights are by no means confined to "journeys through these states," as often presumed. Sometimes his ecstasy defies not only mundane but even interstellar space, as here in "Song of Myself":

Hurrying with the . . . crowd . . .
Walking the old hills of Judæa . . .
Speeding through space, speeding through heaven and the
    stars,

.   .   .   .

Speeding with tail'd meteors, throwing fire-balls like the
    rest,
Carrying the crescent child that carries its own full
    mother in its belly,

.   .   .   .

I tread day and night such roads.

And in a later section of "Song of Myself":

I depart as air, I shake my white locks at the runaway
    sun,
I effuse my flesh in eddies, and drift it in lacy jags.

The problem of Whitman's style has often been approached as a special biographical mystery. But this style is not as peculiar or unique as the poet himself thought. It is the natural result of the journey motif, and can easily be paralleled in other poets who have handled the same theme from the same philosophical background. The last quotation above reminds us of Shelley's "West Wind," "Skylark," or "Cloud," all of which express ecstasy of motion. But only in rare pas-

sages does Whitman remind us of Shelley, though the
two poets had much in common.[21]

A more significant parallel is Hans Christian Andersen in his earlier works, *Walking Trip, Improvisator*,
and *Picture Book without Pictures*. Schyberg has already pointed out some of the similarities:

Anderson was a fanciful traveler, a real world vagabond
—and his "Salut au Monde!" is his first little book of
prose, *A Walking Trip from Holmen's Canal to the East
Point of Amager*, in which he first takes a thought-flight
out into the planets and over the whole earth.[22]

Andersen's latest biographer, Signe Toksvig, calls the
Walking Trip "a pre-Joycian experiment in free associations," and in one place Andersen himself used the
term "association of ideas" to describe one of his rever-
ies. Concerning his arrival at the quaint city of Ama-
gar, Andersen wrote:[23]

Truly here was the place for [my] thoughts to swarm.
Now it seemed to me that I walked on the Finnish Bay,
now in the Nova Scotian Arcadia. Now I wandered
through the Gobi Desert, to visit the Delhi Lama, now
through the Sahara, to find the source of the Niger River.
Now I followed the holy caravan to Mecca, and now stood
among the Eskimos on Hudson Bay.

Though Andersen's poetic fancy is more humorous
than Whitman's, and is at times motivated by such mechanical devices as airplanes (while the airplane was
still a romantic dream), his kaleidoscopic visions and
half-mystic sensations are expressed by a truly Whitmanesque technique. In *Walking Trip* (*Fodreise*,
p. 203) he sees the sleepers in the same manner that
Whitman does in his poem by this title.

The well-known *Picture Book without Pictures* is the
most Whitmanesque of Andersen's works, though again

the great similarity is in style. The stories are supposedly told by the moon, who each night recounts the scenes witnessed the night before on his journey around the globe. Many of the stories are episodic, but others pile image on top of image in the same catalog technique and space-defying manner that we find in *Leaves of Grass*. The scenes range from India to Germany, Greenland, Pompeii, Venice, the desert, the life and death of Christ, Chinese temples, to a sleeping inn in Denmark. The breadth of Whitman's cosmic vision is lacking, but the same kind of sympathetic identification of author and subject and desire to feel in one's own self the unity of the universe have resulted in similar images, associations, and technique of composition.

With Andersen, however, the "Journey" motif is important only as a trick of style. But the great Norwegian poet, Henrik Wergeland, eleven years older than Whitman, treated the theme in a manner not only comparable to *Leaves of Grass* but his epic actually supplements Whitman's poems, and several critics in England, Germany, and Denmark have compared the two poets, though without specifically mentioning the "Long Journey" motif.[24]

Although many of Wergeland's minor poems (such as one called "Myself") are comparable in theme or style to passages in *Leaves of Grass*, the important work is the great epic, *Creation, Man, and Messiah* (1845).[25] Wergeland's early erotic poetry developed into a Whitmanesque cosmic lyricism in his masterpiece. Both poets, inspired by similar philosophical and evolutionary doctrines, deliberately strove to create a new poetry and a new theology on the foundations of modern science (or their own concepts of the cosmic processes); but although Whitman frequently announced a new religion and, by implication, himself as its prophet, the outlines of his theology always re-

mained hazy. *Leaves of Grass* contains the materials of
a theology, but Whitman was never able to organize
them into a coherent structure. Wergeland, however,
in his *Creation* raised the structure which Whitman
needed, and, mainly from Oriental sources, even provided a mythology. The evolutionary process is personified by the two creative spirits, one working in
darkness and the other in light. After the birth of human beings, the doubting spirit enters man and the believing spirit enters woman. Whitman was forever com-
batting such "terrible doubts of appearances" (see
"Of the Terrible Doubt of Appearances") as those
raised by Phun-Abiriel, the Byronic spirit, and consequently the believing spirit, Ohebiel, is particularly
Whitmanesque—though together the two spirits sym-
bolize a conflict which existed in Whitman too. "See
from the teeming womb of Space again a new world
born: a last new mystery," exclaims Phun-Abiriel,
then asks skeptically, "Is God, then, in this lump?"
Ohebiel replies, "He has quickened this dank slime,"
and declaims almost in the words of Whitman:

Think, if thou knewest how grows a blade of grass,
Creation's key thou heldest in thy hand;
·   ·   ·   ·   ·   ·   ·
The gentle current, though of giant force,
Which tore thee on like the blind seed which yonder
Grows to a shoot and after to a palm.

To the question, "Can I not see my Father?" Ohebiel
replies: "Dost not see/Skirts of His raiment hanging
o'er the deep?" while Whitman uses the phrase "letters of God." And Wergeland's "The dewdrop hides
the key to all existence" is matched by Whitman's
"The gnat is explanation enough." Wergeland represents the most primitive forms of life as lying unconscious in the grass, sucking life's bosom.[26]

Though retaining, for dramatic purposes, much of the Biblical account, Wergeland's scenes in the Garden of Eden are truly Whitmanesque. Adam and Eve, symbols of the creative process, speak in the erotic images of Whitman's "Children of Adam." Adam:

Because I now embrace you I am bound
To the heart of life.

.   .   .   .

My blood seems to me right now to spout
Life into each grain of sand on earth . . .
O warmth of life! My loins seem to me like an arch,
Of sinking, trembling, bending warm clouds,
. . . which may burst with a benediction
Like a tepid rain.

Eve feels that her "whole body is the earth," and

From this vapor of love from our veins
Which flows together into a stream of life,
A rainbow of life stretches between our hearts—
  of life intertwined with life.[27]

The part of Wergeland's epic called *Man* accomplishes exactly what Whitman planned to do before he wrote *Leaves of Grass* (see first part of this essay), for *Mennesket* dramatizes the history of mankind, as perhaps Whitman had in mind when he was thinking of "A volume . . . dramatic machinery for localities, characters, etc . . . running in idea and description through the whole range of recorded time." Wergeland shows the evolution of the different religions, enumerates the various stages, and indicates the epochs of human life by means of cumulative images—primitive men, the hunters, the agriculturists, the growth of kingdoms, cities, etc., in all parts of the world throughout the ages. Wergeland, with his sound university training and his theological degree, was able to illumi-

nate the stages in a way that Whitman could never
have done; but he presents the varied scenes, occupations, and sweep of time in an impressionistic, kaleidoscopic, and even "catalog" style of "Salut au Monde!"
Like Whitman, Wergeland often makes a name or an
image stand for a complete predication. Gerhard Gran
said of him:

He thought in pictures, which bubbled in overwhelming
numbers out of his heart; he scarcely gave himself time to
choose; one picture pressed hard into another and took its
place in long parentheses, often making his poetry into a
wild-growing jungle thicket which requires patience to
penetrate.[28]

Gran probably had in mind such passages as these:

                        . . . with his scepter
He measured the earth into kingdoms, like
Thick-bellied elephants lying
With beetle-browed glances and snouts toward each other,
Ho, Hindustani, and China and Egypt!
Ho, Babylon and Medea and Bactria,
Assyria, Arabia, and Persia,
And Lydia and Scythia and Libya,
Ethiopia and Mexico and Peru! . . .
Behold Babylon built over the swamps,
Walking on the Euphrates with marble feet,

  .   .   .   .

Behold Nineveh cleaves the sky with copper towers!
And the Ganges is like Delhi's circumscribing
Elephantine tongue . . .
Behold the moon lies high on Peking's roofs
And stars scatter star light
On Samarkand's towers! Behold Persepolis,
A beautifully colored Caucasus of marble! . . .[29]

This aspect of Wergeland's style caused him to be
attacked by the critics in much the same manner that

Whitman was, and he also revolutionized Norwegian poetry much as Whitman influenced American poetry.[30] But the important point is that he developed this style in working out the theological side of the same "Long Journey" theme which we find in Whitman's poetry.

Wergeland's "journey" ends with the resurrection of the Messiah, ostensibly the Christ of the New Testament, but his role is in entire agreement with Whitman's own self-prophetic role, and the democratic and nationalistic[31] sentiments of both messiahs are in almost complete harmony. But this section of Wergeland's epic is of no special importance in the present discussion.

It remained for Johannes V. Jensen to climax the "Long Journey" theme, and both Wergeland's and Whitman's experiments were undoubtedly guiding influences: Wergeland because he is one of the greatest Scandinavian poets, and Whitman because Jensen, with his interest in world literature, has been a Whitman disciple in Denmark. In *The Wheel* (1905) Jensen translated long sections from *Leaves of Grass* and showed through his Whitmanesque hero and his falsely Whitmanesque villain the vital and the dangerous elements in Whitman's doctrines.[32] In this novel Jensen also advanced his "Long Journey" theory, to be developed later in a series of five novels, now called, in the English translation, *The Long Journey*. The theory is that the human race was born in the North, which was tropical before the glacial period. The emergence of the first glaciers drove many of the North dwellers South, and all lost their original homes. Thus these people began their restless wandering over the face of the earth, becoming more human, "realizing themselves," as they went. Finally in America they found a resting place, as the pioneers of the young nation. At

last their journey had come to an end. In the sequel
Jensen has somewhat expanded this theory, but the
work is essentially a dramatization of the struggle of
the human race in its long series of struggles and travels from the sub-human to the modern period. A great
novelist—as well as poet, dramatist, and critic—has
filled in the outline which Walt Whitman sketched between 1850–55. Of course Jensen developed the theme
primarily out of his own travels and anthropological
interests; but the ending of the story, and also some of
the lyrical passages, was almost certainly inspired by
Leaves of Grass—which retains, as we have seen, many
vestiges of Whitman's original history-of-the-race
scheme. But aside from these direct relationships, the
comparisons are illuminating in themselves, and show
the intrinsic importance of Whitman's journey motif.

  Christopher Columbus, the last book of Jensen's
Long Journey, is based entirely on the theme which
Whitman used in his poems, "Prayer of Columbus"
and "Thought of Columbus," and Jensen's whole portrait of Columbus is closely akin to Whitman's "Batter'd, wreck'd old man." To both Whitman and Jensen,
Columbus is but a symbol of the yearning of mankind,
a symbol of that urge which has propelled humanity
through the eternal journey. As Whitman says in "A
Thought of Columbus":

The mystery of mysteries, the crude and hurried ceaseless
    flame, spontaneous, bearing on itself.
    .   .   .   .

A breath of Deity, as thence the bulging universe unfold-
    ing!
    .   .   .   .

The eras of the soul incepting in an hour,
Haply the widest, farthest evolutions of the world and
    man.

It is in such a mood as this that Jensen imagines (p. 672) as in a mystic vision, "All the yearners and discoverers . . . the great names"—he too is fascinated by names—: "There they are, all the . . . travelers, pioneers, and mapmakers who gave their names to rivers and mountains . . ."

And Jensen has also written (p. 675) his "Pioneers! O Pioneers!":

Yes, life begun over again, in the person of a young settler's wife, who leaves the log-hut on the first warm day to sun her baby and sits with her fair hair uncovered in the sunshine; the blows of an axe reach her ears from the forest hard by, the strong man, carpenter, tiller of the soil and hunter in one: the family founded again in a wild spot, Canada, the depths of Minnesota or Dakota, where the Northern peasants find again their own weather and their seasons, and where the hard winters keep them strong of soul.

The well-defined characters and the narrative details of Jensen's *Long Journey* may lead us to suspect that he is more mundane, less concerned with "the journey work of the stars," than Whitman, but the last chapter of the work refutes such an accusation. A being in the form of Woman, symbol of life, leans out from Heaven over the beautiful blue rolling globe and (p. 677)

sees the immense extent of oceans and continents, countries and the realms and all the life there is in them, ships moving over the seas all round the ball, trains hastening across the continents from coast to coast, great cities shrouded in smoke, arteries of traffic peppered full of people, in every zone, from both Poles to the Equator, all the Earth's motley, teeming, fantastic circle of countries, peoples, animals, plants, and things, fixed and definite things, the sea blue, raw and wet the whole way round, the greensward green and not a spot anywhere on earth but it is directly in contact with space, every blade of grass stretching straight out into the Universe as far as it can reach.[33]

The rolling Earth [Cf. Whitman's "Song of the Rolling Earth"], what is it? . . . this phantom ship in eternity. . . . What is it carrying? why? whither? . . . the cosmic Being . . . is Life, the stem of Life beyond the æther, from which the germs have come to earth; true Life, the source of Love, of which we can know no more than longing teaches us.

And then Jensen asks the rhetorical question, which Whitman attempted to answer so often in *Leaves of Grass:* "Have the creatures of Earth, through a long process of life and change—approximate, faulty, abandoned and taken up again—been seeking a form for an eternal, intrinsic, unknown type existing on the other stars?"

In conclusion, the "Long Journey" motif is thus of the greatest importance in a study of the genesis of *Leaves of Grass,* in the interpretation of its message, and in understanding the psychology of Whitman's style. The theme, moreover, belongs to a nineteenth-century movement in world literature; and when studied against this background, both the content and the method of *Leaves of Grass* take on new and broader significance. The comparative method of study is likewise necessary in evaluating Whitman's contribution. Lacking historical training and weak in dramatic skill, Walt Whitman could not write a Wergeland epic or a Jensen saga; nevertheless, his mystic vision of the cosmic journey has been a major inspiration to world literature—influencing even Jensen himself, at least in spirit and method if not in actual content.

Whether or not this motif has aided Whitman in

gaining recognition as a world poet, he nevertheless shares with his Norwegian contemporary, Wergeland, a curious paradox, for which the world vision is largely responsible. Mr. Gathorne-Hardy says (p. xxxi), "It is true that Wergeland regarded himself, and was regarded, as above all else a national poet and prophet," but "Wergeland's nationalism . . . was tempered by an interest in contemporary movements, literary and political, which was really cosmopolitan, and he consequently takes his place naturally in the great poetic revolution or renaissance of his age." Certainly the same thing could be said of the American poet, Walt Whitman. And it is highly significant that the same motif is responsible for this paradox. Likewise, Jensen's use of the "Long Journey" shows to what extent Whitman succeeded in being "the poet of the future," for *The Long Journey* is a strictly modern work, though anticipated by Whitman's projected poem "The March of the Human Race Across the Earth," and the journey motif in *Leaves of Grass*. Thus through Wergeland, Whitman, and Jensen (and other nineteenth- and twentieth-century European writers who of necessity have been ignored in this essay), the "Long Journey" theme links the literature of two continents.

4

TRANSLATIONS OF WHITMAN
SINCE WORLD WAR II

WALT WHITMAN might be said to have become a world poet before he was recognized in his own coun-

Part of this essay was published as a mass review of Whitman translations in Comparative Literature, *I (summer, 1949), 272–77.*

try as a major author. Indeed, the praise and analysis
of his work by critics and scholars in England, Germany, France, and Denmark contributed greatly to the
eventual growth of his reputation in the United States.[1]
Since World War II the translation of his poems (and
occasionally some prose) has greatly increased in
France and Japan, though major translations, along
with critical studies, have also appeared in other countries (see Check List).

Hélène Bokanowski's small book of selected translations, published in a limited edition of 600 copies, is a
symptom of a new trend in Whitman criticism, not limited to France. She begins her short introduction by
referring to *"Feuilles d'herbe"* as *"ce monument puis-
sant et totémique."* (Even American critics write more
and more frequently of the "symbolical Whitman.")
She has translated only some short poems and piquant
extracts from "Song of Myself," "Song of the Open
Road," "Song of the Rolling Earth," the Lincoln
poems, and a few others, with the English text facing
the French. She is interested, not in Whitman's role as
prophet and leader of a new humanity, but in his lyrical expression and his historical importance: *"Bien da-
vantage qu'un apôtre de la démocratie, il faut con-
sidérer Walt Whitman comme un visionnaire. Sa
réceptivité exceptionnelle exprime fortement la vision
métaphysique de son époque, le développement gigan-
tesque et brutal de son pays, de cette terre neuve en
gestation, les complexités d'un tempérament sensuel et
hybride."*

Leaves of Grass has not been easy for French translators. Léon Bazalgette's complete version of the book
(editions of 1909, 1914, and 1922) was, in the opinion
of André Gide and other competent judges, too facile
and "prettified." In protest against Bazalgette's first
two editions, Gide, Jules Laforgue, and Louis Fabulet

published some translations of their own in *Œuvres choises, poèmes et proses* (1918), and until recently this was still the most satisfactory book of Whitman selections in French.

Anyone who reads even one foreign language knows that the connotations of poetic language are almost untranslatable, and Whitman's baroque diction, with its *"mélange"* of colloquialisms, hybrids, and esoteric symbolism, is enough to balk the most skilled translator. And Hélène Bokanowski is at times far from skilled. She renders

> Mine is no callous shell,

as

> *Point n'est creuse ma coquille*

Bazalgette's plodding

> *Mon enveloppe n'est pas une dure coquille,*

is at least more accurate. In "Song of the Open Road" she misses the allusion to "charging" an electrical battery when the poet declares of the "efflux of the soul,"

Now it flows unto us, we are rightly charged.
A présent qu'il nous inonde, nous sommes en bonnes mains.

In the more difficult lines in section 28 of "Song of Myself" she perhaps might be pardoned for failing to get all the implications in the poet's betrayal by his "fellow-senses":

> Treacherous tip of me reaching and crowding to help
>   them . . .
> They bribed to swap off with touch and go and graze
>   at the edges of me . . .
> *Je suis trahi par ce qu'il y a de plus extrême en moi*
>   *qui progresse et se rassemble afin de leur venir en*
>   *aide . . .*

*Ils ont usé de corruption afin de me posséder par ce
contact et puis effleurent tout ce qui touche à mes
limites . . .*

In "When Lilacs Last in the Dooryard Bloom'd" she
fails to convey the symbolism of "heart-shaped leaves"
in *"feuilles lancéolées"* (Bazalgette has *"dessinées
comme un cœur"*), but aptly uses *"ramille"* for
"sprig" instead of Bazalgette's more general *"branch-
ette."* Possibly these examples indicate not only some
of the limitations of this translation but also Walt
Whitman's lack of affinity for the French language,
despite his fondness for French words.

Paul Jamati's book, with its long *étude* and generous
sampling of the major sections of *Leaves of Grass*,
amounts practically to a new French biography and
anthology of Whitman's poems. The selections range
all the way from the opening "One's-Self I Sing" of
Leaves of Grass to the closing "So Long"[2] (which loses
its colloquial flavor in "Adieu"). The anthology is composed of new translations by Marcelle Sibon and Paul
Jamati, and a reprinting of some of Léon Bazalgette's,
especially eight sections of his *"Chant de moi-même."*
Both the virtues and shortcomings of Bazalgette's famous *Feuilles d'herbe* are apparent throughout the
book, including, uncorrected, even some of the faulty
translations.[3]

Bazalgette is unmistakably M. Jamati's master, for
his influence permeates the whole book, and not least in
the critical part. Rejecting all the discoveries and
psychological insights of Catel, and apparently un-
aware of the researches of Mrs. Molinoff on Whitman's
family background, Jamati returns to a glorification of
Bazalgette's saintly poet prophet. He is acquainted
with Catel's point of view, but exclaims *"O psychana-
lyse, que de ravages!"* Consequently, he sees in the

"Calamus" poems nothing but the social themes that the poet attached to them after he had gained control of the emotions that gestated them.

However, Jamati's essay is not simply a rehash of Bazalgette's two studies of Whitman. Something new has been added, something that may be portentous. Admitting that Whitman and his disciples built up a legend, he looks upon all discussions of the poet's sex pathology as a deliberate *"contre-légende"* perpetrated by antidemocratic critics. Afraid to attack democracy directly, they attack the most famous poet of democracy: *"Il est plus simple et plus efficace de discréditer l'adversaire en le convaincant d'imposture. Or l'adversaire, c'est Whitman. Et c'est ainsi que se développe, en face d'une légende, qu'il faut en effet détruire, une contre-légende, aussi mensongère, donc aussi nocive, qu'il faudra détruire à son tour."*

Jamati's charges are not entirely hysterical; undoubtedly both fascist and Communist critics have made biased contributions to the *"contre-légende";* but new evidence must always result in re-evaluations of Whitman and his poetry. If his message continues to have meaning for the modern world it will lose some values and acquire others. Meanwhile, Jamati's confidence is reassuring: *"Walt Whitman, génie américain et génie universel, le plus grand du* XIX° *siècle, Walt Whitman, poète de l'avenir, est un poète d'aujourd'hui."*

Unfortunately, Jamati's biographical and critical essay contains a considerable number of petty errors. For example, Whitman did not lose every editorial position because *"il refuse toute concession dans l'expression de ses opinions";* so far as we know, this happened once. He was not *"un dandy . . . au Capitole";* that was while he was a journalist in Brooklyn. He was not editor of the New Orleans *Crescent,* only a reporter. He did not call himself "Walt" for the first time in the 1856 *Leaves* but in the first edition. And I do not agree with Jamati's description of the appearance of the 1855 *Leaves*, or with his emphasis on its failure. More important, Carlyle did not help introduce Whitman into England nor did Dante G. Rossetti assist very much; actually both disliked Whitman rather strongly. And, despite his role as the poet of athletes, Whitman did not while in Washington, or at any other time, frequent *"assidûment le gymnase"!*. M. Jamati has not been able to distinguish between fact and vicarious symbolism. Following his master, Bazalgette, he is uncritical in interpreting Whitman's own statements.

The latest French translations show continued improvement over earlier ones. Especially is this true of Roger Asselineau's *Feuilles d'herbe* (1956). He has translated the entire "Song of Myself," and generously represented the other sections of the complete (1892) *Leaves of Grass*, including, of course, all the major poems as well as excellent selections from "Inscriptions," "Children of Adam," "Calamus," and other groups. The seventeen-page introduction is accurate, as one might expect from the author of a monumental biography of Whitman. He gives a reliable account of the poet, his book, and the problems of translation. He has an accurate knowledge of English and avoids the "boners" so common in the other translations. Possibly, at times, his renderings are too literal, or slightly verbose in order to be accurate, but no French reader is likely to go far wrong on the meaning or spirit of Whitman's poems if he uses Asselineau's translation.

A more recent translation by Alain Bosquet, a young poet of considerable prestige, provides a convenient comparison. In his *Whitman* (Bibliotheque Ideale, 1959) he is direct, and sometimes more succinct than

Asselineau, but he is far less familiar with Whitman's language. At random I pick section 4 of "Song of Myself," quoting first the original for easy reference:

Trippers and askers surround me,
People I meet, the effect upon me of my early life or the
    ward and city I live in, or the nation,
The latest dates, discoveries, inventions, societies, authors
    old and new,
My dinner, dress, associates, looks, compliments, dues,
The real or fancied indifference of some man or woman I
    love,
The sickness of one of my folks or of myself, or ill-doing
    or loss or lack of money, or depressions or exaltations.
Battles, the horrors of fratricidal war, the fever of
    doubtful news, the fitful events;
These come to me days and nights and go from me again,
But they are not the Me myself.

Apart from the pulling and hauling stands what I
    am, . . .

Bosquet:

Contradicteurs et questionneurs m'entourent,
Les gens que je rencontre, l'effet sur moi des mes jeunes
    années ou du quartier et de la ville que j'habite, ou le
    pays,
Les derniers rendez-vous, découvertes, inventions, groupe-
    ments, auteurs anciens et nouveaux,
Mon dîner, mes habits, associés, apparences, compli-
    ments, obligations,
L'indifférence réelle ou imaginaire d'un homme ou d'une
    femme que j'aime,
La maladie d'un des miens ou de moi-même, le méfait, la
    perte ou le manque d'argent, les découragements ou les
    exaltations,

Les batailles, les horreurs de la guerre fratricide, la fièvre
  des nouvelles douteuses, les événements qui changent;
Toutes ces choses me viennent jour et nuit, et me quittent
  à nouveau,
Mais elles ne sont pas mon propre Moi.
En dehors de ce qui me tire et pousse, se dresse ce que je
  suis, . . .

Asselineau:

Des gens qui aiment prendre en défaut et questionner
  m'entourent,
Ceux que je rencontre, l'effet sur moi de mes premières
  années ou du quartier et de la ville que j'habite, ou de
  ma nationalité,
Les découvertes, les inventions, les associations, les événe-
  ments les plus récents, les auteurs anciens et nouveaux,
Mon dîner, mon vêtement, mes compagnons, mon air, les
  compliments que je fais, les obligations sociales,
L'indifférence réelle ou imaginaire d'un homme ou d'une
  femme que j'aime,
La maladie d'un des miens ou de moi-même, le méfait, la
  perte ou le manque d'argent, les moments de dépression
  ou d'exaltation,
Les batailles, les horreurs de la guerre fratricide, la
  fièvre des nouvelles douteuses, le cours irrégulier des
  événements,
Toutes ces choses s'approchent de moi, nuit et jour, puis
  s'éloignent de moi,
Mais elles ne sont pas mon Moi véritable.
A l'écart de tout cela qui me tire et m'entraîne se tient
  celui que je suis, . . .

Asselineau's "*les événements les plus récent*" (third
verse) is of course right, and Bosquet's colloquial interpretation of "dates" is wrong. Actually the only
real colloquialisms in the passage are "trippers," meaning those who would entrap by deceptive questions, and

"pulling and hauling," meaning trying to influence, or exerting pressure to influence. The latter phrase both translators render fairly accurately by keeping the same figure of speech. But "trippers" are more than "contradictors," and Asselineau is nearer the bull's-eye.

Aside from these technical considerations, Bosquet's book is quite different from Asselineau's. He gives a much longer and more detailed account of Whitman's life, but often with a seeming condescension, as if to expose the poet's weaknesses. Also, his judgments often seem wrong, or at least to me, as when he comments on the "*pauvrité du style*" of the 1855 Preface. It is rhetorical and a little high-flown in a nineteenth-century way, but if the style is bad, then so is Whitman's poetic style—and, in fact, whole sentences were later taken over into poems.[4] Also I believe that Bosquet is quite wrong in thinking that Whitman revised his poems and prefaces to avoid shocking, or to cater to the taste of his "*clientèle*." Perhaps many of Whitman's revisions did not improve his poems, but there can be no doubt that he revised for (intended) aesthetic reasons, and he often did improve the rhythm and sometimes the diction.

Bosquet's book contains less than fifty pages of poems, a few pages of prose fragments, a garrulous interview with Whitman in 1879 (the poet was seldom at his best in an interview), brief comments by writers from Thoreau to Allen Ginsberg, a bibliography of "Iconographie," and other curiosities. French readers should find this an entertaining introduction to Whitman, though perhaps a misleading one.

This new French admiration reminds one of Germany in the pre-Nazi days. There in three separate periods Whitman became a cult, and after World War I he was one of the most discussed authors in Germany and Austria. Hans Reisiger's complete version of *Leaves of Grass* and selected prose became a classic in German literature soon after its appearance in 1922. Reisiger prefaced his work with an eloquent introduction (reprinted in pamphlet form in 1946) that deeply impressed Thomas Mann. Reisiger admired Whitman as a democratic symbol, which Mann identified with the humanity of Goethe and Novalis.

The appearance in 1948 of a handsome book of German translations—and from the hand of Georg Goyert, the distinguished translator of James Joyce, who has also turned Henry Seidel Canby's biography into German—was a significant event. Georg Goyert's translation is prefaced by no eloquent introduction, although it does contain a brief (and accurate) factual biographical note, which mentions the strength of the poet's voice for democracy and freedom. The poems translated, however, are those of more psychological and literary than social or political interest, beginning with "There Was a Child Went Forth," ranging through selections from "Children of Adam" and "Calamus," the great poems such as "Out of the Cradle . . . ," "When Lilacs Last . . . ," "Prayer for Columbus," and on to the old-age poems, "Darest Thou Now O Soul" and "After the Supper and Talk." It is a splendid collection, impressively translated, and it has been well received by German reviewers.

Goyert's translation of Mr. Canby's biography has apparently also been widely approved by German critics; but in the reviews which I have been able to examine I find no such idealistic acclaim for Whitman as Reisiger's work produced in the decade before Hitler's rise to power. The shorter reviews are mainly factual and noncommittal. A critic in the *Tägliche Rundschau* (June 1, 1947) refers to the "*flutenden Gesänge der Demokratie, die auch in Europa auf Dichter wie Ver-*

haeren, Richard Dehmel, Gerrit Engelke und Wladi-
mir Majakowskij anspornend und wegweisend wirkte."
A long review by Herbert Pfeiffer in *Der Tages Spie-*
gel (April 21, 1948), entitled "*Die Umkehr in der*
Biographie," sees in this biographer more of an advo-
cate than a critic. ("*Es ist mehr Hingabe in ihm als*
Abstand"). Pfeffer thinks it is the custom in America
for a biographer to make a hero of his subject, and says
that perhaps Mr. Canby's American audience influenced his lack of objectivity and complete frankness.
But he seems to envy a country that can still regard
the individual as capable of being a hero in biography
or fiction, and he commends this situation as healthier
than the determinism of Taine, Emil Ludwig, and André Maurois, which makes the individual the product
of his environment.

Die erste massive Biographie, die von Amerika nach dem
Kriege zu uns kommt, zeigt, dass die Auslegung der Per-
sönlichkeit aus sich selbst drüben bereits wieder stärker
als bei uns über die rein soziologische oder geistesge-
schichtliche Beleuchtung hinausgewachsen ist. Liegt es im
Empfinden der Zeit, das Leben wieder mehr oder sogar
ganz als individueller Held zu ertragen? Es scheint ein
Widerspruch, denn die Politik ist immer kollektivisti-
scher geworden. Aber vielleicht beginnt gerade hier die
geistige Korrektur, die das seit Jahrzehnten von der Poli-
tik verkannte Individuum aus seiner Rolle als Massen-
faktor löst. Die Herrschaft der Milieutheorie hat jeden-
falls, das bestreitet heute niemand mehr, die Idee der per-
sönlichen Willensfreiheit, der persönlichen Initiative, des
Individuums als Welt für sich nicht zum besten unserer
Entwicklung, nicht zu unserem Glück verdrängt.

Although Rudolph Schmidt translated *Democratic*
Vistas into Danish in 1874, *Leaves of Grass* did not attract Scandinavian translators until the twentieth cen-

tury, and not until recently have there been transla-
tions in the three countries, Denmark, Norway, and
Sweden. Frederik Schyberg, a famous literary critic in
Copenhagen, was largely responsible for the present
Scandinavian interest in Whitman. His selected *Walt
Whitman Digte* (1933) and his biographical study,
Walt Whitman (1933), both completed while he was
still a university student, have attracted attention in
Sweden and Norway. K. A. Svensson confessed his in-
debtedness to Schyberg in the introduction to his
Strån av Gräss (Stockholm, 1935); and Per Arne-
berg in his Norwegian edition of *Sangen om Meg Selv*
(Oslo, 1947) acknowledges and plainly reveals the in-
fluence of Schyberg in his critical introduction.

Arneberg's book is the most eye-appealing translation of Whitman I have seen, beautifully printed on
fine paper, as most Scandinavian books are, and illustrated with highly symbolical drawings by Kai Kjell.
I find the drawings more Norse than Whitmanesque in
spirit, but perhaps this is a favorable sign that the
American poet is being acclimatized.

Especially to be commended is the translation of the
entire "Song of Myself" instead of fragmentary selections, a common practice, for this one poem contains
much of the substance of the entire *Leaves*. Moreover,
Whitman's style cannot be adequately indicated by little snippets, like those in the Bokanowski collection.
Arneberg's translation appears to be remarkably close
to the original in meaning and style. I do not know
whether the excellence is due to his having profited
from the examples of Schyberg and Svensson, to the
greater adaptability of the Norwegian for Whitman's
language, or simply to the translator's genius; but this
is certainly close to the original:

> *Jeg lovpriser meg selv og synger meg selv,*
> *Og hva jeg dristig gjør skal også du gjøre,*

For hvert atom i meg tilhører likegodt deg.
             (First strophe, sec. 1)

The initial reiterations (or "psychic rime") and parallelism are carefully preserved:

Smil, å vellystige, kjøligåndende jord!
Jord av de slumrende saftfulle trær!
Jord av den sluknede aftenrøde—jord av de tåkeomhyllede tinder!
Jord av fullmånens glassklare flom med det blå skjær!
Jord av marmorerende lys og mørke over flodenes tidevann!
Jord av skyers gjennomsiktige grå, lysere og klarere for min skyld!
Fjerntfavnende, svingende jord—rikt epleblomstrende jord!
Smil, ti din elsker kommer.
             (Seventh strophe, sec. 21)

And so also the elliptical sentence:

Et rop midt i mengden,
Min egen stemme, fulltonende, omslyngende, avgjørende.
A call in the midst of the crowd,
My own voice, orutund sweeping and final.
             (First strophe, sec. 42)

The similarity of modern Norwegian to English enables Arneberg to come very near to catching Whitman's "organic" rhythms:

Jeg farer bort som luft, jeg ryster mine hvite lokker mot den flyktende sol,
Jeg gyter mitt kjøtt ut i hvirvlene, og lar det drive som trasete flak.
I depart as air, I shake my white locks at the runaway sun,
I effuse my flesh in eddies, and drift it in lacy jags.
             (Fourth strophe, sec. 52)

Arneberg's translation moved Kjell Krogvig to write an article for *Samtiden,* "Til Whitman Gjennem Wergeland," pointing out the similarity between Whitman and Henrik Wergeland, the author of the great Norwegian epic, *Skabelsen, Mennesket, og Messias* ("Creation, Mankind, and Messiah") as an aid for Norwegians in understanding the American poet— or more specifically, Arneberg's translation. Others, particularly Schyberg, have noted the remarkable parallels in thought and even style between these two great poets who did not know each other. Since the Norwegians themselves are beginning to publish comparative studies, it seems likely that Walt Whitman still has a future in Norway.

Several translations have appeared in languages in which I have little competence, or none whatever, but even at second- or third-hand some pertinent facts can be assembled. I offer these notes, therefore, as part of the record of recent translations of Whitman.

The country that has produced the greatest number of Whitman translations since World War II is Japan. Whitman had attracted some attention in Japan as early as 1892, and the second World War interrupted Shigetaka Naganuma's work on a Japanese version of *Leaves of Grass.* But by 1946 he was able to publish his first volume of *Kusa no Ha* (*Leaves of Grass*), and a complete translation of the *Leaves,* in two volumes, in 1950. In *Walt Whitman Abroad* (pp. 280–81) I listed ten translations reported to me by Mr. Mitsuru Ishii, president of the Japanese Publishers Association, but by 1960 over twice that number had been published in Japan, though none complete except Naganuma's. In 1957 Haruo Shimizu, Professor of American Literature in Otaru University, in Otaru, Hokkaido, published *A Study of Whitman's Imagery,* and there have been several studies of Whitman's reception and influence in Japan, including two in English, one in 1957 by Iwao Matsuhara and another in 1959 by Ota Saburo (see the Check List).

The most comprehensive translation, aside from Reisiger's in German, is Enzo Giachino's *Foglie d'erba e Prose* (1950), including all of *Leaves of Grass* and 70 pages of prose, 958 pages in all. In a brief Preface the translator shows himself to be well acquainted with modern Whitman scholarship. Competent judges have praised the accuracy and style of the translation. Three years later (1953) Francisco Alexander, in Quito, Ecuador, published another complete translation of *Leaves of Grass*. In a letter to me Mr. Alexander said that his chief ambition was to make his translation "faithful," and Professor Fernando Alegría, author of a comprehensive book on Whitman in Spanish America, tells me that it is, both in language and style.

In 1956 Mihnea Gheorghiu, of Bucharest, Rumania, published a substantial volume called *Walt Whitman: Opera Alese*. This Rumanian translation has a long introduction by the translator, over two hundred pages of poems and as many of prose, selected letters, an essay discussing Whitman and the Russian poet Maiakovski, Lorca's "Ode to Walt Whitman" (in Rumanian), and poems to Whitman by Pablo Neruda and Geo Bogza.

Since the Communist countries are continuing to show an active interest in Whitman, it is perhaps not surprising that a Chinese translation should be published in Peking. In reviewing this book, called *Selections from Whitman's "Leaves of Grass"* (1955), in the *Walt Whitman Newsletter* (now *Walt Whitman Review*) of September, 1958, Angela Chih-ying Jung Palandri translated the "translator's Note," in which T'u-nan Ch'u reported:

I began translating Whitman's poems shortly after 1930. During that period of a fugitive existence, I sent out the rendered pieces, a few at a time, to the periodicals that would accept them. Later they were collected and published in book form. The quality of this translated work would be far from satisfactory, appraised in the light of today. For this reason I made no attempt to have it reprinted after the Liberation. However, in response to the exhortation of the World Peace Committee in commemoration [1955 was the Centennial of *Leaves of Grass*] of this most outstanding poet of America, I asked Comrade Min-yan Wang to edit it for re-publication.

Apparently a Chinese version was published some twenty years ago. And it is hardly surprising that this second edition has been edited to conform to Chinese Communist politics. But despite the presentation of Whitman "as a visionary poet of the proletarian revolution," the reviewer hopes that "the seeds of freedom and democracy of *Leaves of Grass* may be sown in the hearts of Chinese readers and bear fruit eventually."

No one who has followed the use of Whitman in revolutionary movements will be much surprised at the publication of a translation of his selected poems in Peking. The only surprise is that T'u-nan Ch'u was working on his translation as early as 1930. And this leads one to wonder whether others in China were interested in Whitman that early. It seems that the answer is "yes."

In the summer of 1954 at the Indiana University Conference on Oriental-Western Literary Relations Professor Achilles Fang, of Harvard University, read a paper with the title, "From Imagism to Whitmanism in Recent Chinese Poetry: A Search for Poetics that Failed."[5] Here we learn that in 1916 Hu Shih, then a student at Columbia University, wrote a poem in the American-British "Imagistic" tradition and started a brief but abortive "literary revolution" in China. Though this experiment failed, it was soon followed by Kuo Mo-jo's poems in imitation of Walt Whitman, and these apparently had more influence, though Professor Fang thinks that many followers of this new literary revolution did not know the part that Whitman played in it. He also says, "Whitmanism, which propelled literary malcontents toward revolutionary literature, has not succeeded in producing great poetry in China, in spite of the fact that it has been the dominant trait of the new poetry." That he is referring to Chinese poetry on the mainland is made clear by the statement that the two main aspects of "recent Chinese poetry [are] ebullient national spirit and the apotheosis of the working-man." This leaves little doubt as to who is using Whitman, and once more as a symbol of proletarianism.

It is a pleasure to turn to other parts of the world where a different use is being made of Whitman in translation. In 1952 Professor Simon Halkin, of Hebrew University in Jerusalem, published a volume of selections from *Leaves of Grass* translated into Hebrew. Dr. Sholom J. Kahn reviewed the book in *Scopus* of March, 1952: "Professor Halkin's poetical genius, critical insight, and passion for American democracy fuse in his version of *Leaves of Grass*. . . . Whitman seems to 'belong' in Hebrew. Many of his passages read like echoes of oriental 'widsom' literature—as if Ecclesiastes and the author of Proverbs were to speak with a modern accent." And earlier S. Shalom, a journalist and poet of Tel-Aviv, who has translated a number of Whitman's poems, declared:[6] "Whitman's pioneering is very close to us, and so are his Biblical rhythms. To translate him into Hebrew is like translating a writer back into his own language."

Many critics have noticed the similarities of Whitman's rhythms to those of the Bible, and some have thought that Hebrew poetry in English translation may have been the source of his versification.[7] It is doubly interesting, therefore, to find that his poetry has such affinity for modern Hebrew poets.

The most ambitious of all translations of Whitman is now under way in India, where the National Academy (Sahitya Akademi) at New Delhi is sponsoring the translation of Whitman's poems into the fourteen major languages of India. This chapter, still being written, should be one of the most important in the whole history of Whitman's expanding world reception. Advance rumors intimate that in that country which Whitman called "reason's early paradise" students are finding him more like one of their great ancient mystics than a twentieth-century poet.

THREE

The Legend

I skirt sierras, my palms
cover continents . . .

1

WHITMAN'S IMAGE
IN THE TWENTIETH CENTURY

WALT WHITMAN was already a legend when he died in 1892, but since his death *the legend* (perhaps already plural before he died) has flowered into other legends, until today it is almost impossible to read the poems without being influenced by the extraneous accumulations. In fact, one of the perennial games of both biographers and critics of Whitman is to explode the "myth," to unveil the "secret," to reveal finally— so the blurbs of the numerous books claim—*the truth* about Walt Whitman. But somehow the dragon-mystery never stays dead and the truth proves as elusive as ever.

As I have indicated in the first part, the poet himself started some of the legends, and his friends, the "hot little prophets,"[1] willingly perpetuated them. But neither the poet nor his friends can be blamed for the bewildering diversity of the many points of view of his twentieth-century critics, which has resulted from their

difficulty in coming to terms with him. The most significant fact about Whitman's critics of the present
century, especially in his own country, is that they
could not ignore him, though many would have preferred to do so. One phase of this curious fact was illustrated by Barrett Wendell in his *Literary History
of America* (New York, 1901). Wendell, a professor
of English at Harvard and personal friend of the major New England writers, devoted fourteen and a half
pages to Whitman, approximately the same space
given to Longfellow and Whittier. He did not like either Whitman or his poems, but he felt compelled to
reckon with both. His sympathies were with Lowell,
who (p. 465) "lived all his life amid the gentlest aca-
demic and social influences in America." Whittier, he
pointed out, had as humble an origin as the New York
poet, but he had grown up "and lived almost all his life
amid guileless influences. Whitman, born of the artisan
class in a region close to the most considerable and corrupt centre of population on his native continent, had
a rather vagrant youth and manhood." Whitman's re-
jection of traditional standards and values Wendell
thus blamed on "the corrupt centre of population" in
which he lived, but the professor did not think this centre was typically American: Whitman's "conception
of equality, utterly ignoring values, is not that of
American democracy, but rather that of Europe."

Wendell realized that the American nation—and indeed Western civilization—was changing, but he had
grave misgivings about the future. Whitman's individualistic style seemed to him to have "strayed dan-
gerously far from its vital origin." Like Carlyle's or
Browning's, his style, Wendell thought, was one "which
in the history of literature suggests a familiar phase
of decline," and was "as little characteristic of America
as his temper is of traditional American democracy."

This conservative literary historian recognized that Whitman had the gifts and instincts of a poet; what he really objected to—and feared—was the experience that this poet had drawn upon in writing his poems, and the influence that his thought and art might have on the future course of American literature (p. 478):

For want of other surroundings he was content to seek the meaning of life amid New York slums and dingy suburban country, in the crossing of Brooklyn Ferry, or in the hospitals which strove to alleviate the drums and tramplings of civil war. His lifelong eagerness to find in life the stuff of which poetry is made has brought him, after all, the reward he would most have cared for. In one aspect he is thoroughly American. The spirit of his work is that of world-old anarchy; its form has all the perverse oddity of world-old abortive decadence; but the substance of which his poems are made—their imagery as distinguished from their form, or their spirit—comes wholly from our native country.

And much as Wendell disapproved this uncouth, turbulent, unorthodox poet, he concluded that he might, nevertheless, throw light on the future of literature in America, for (p. 479)

he can make you feel for the moment how even the ferry-boats plying from New York to Brooklyn are fragments of God's eternities. Those of us who love the past are far from sharing his confidence in the future. Surely, however, that is no reason for denying the miracle that he has wrought by idealizing the East River. The man who has done this is the only one who points out the stuff of which perhaps the new American literature of the future may in time be made.

What Wendell seems to be saying is that Whitman
was after all a poet, maybe even a poet who presaged
the future development of American literature, but in
1900 this cultivated professor of humane letters
dreaded the prospect of a literature dominated by men
who had grown up in the slums of the great cities and
who would draw their subject matter from experience
quite unlike that of Longfellow, Lowell, and Whittier.
As a matter of fact, Stephen Crane, Frank Norris,
and Theodore Dreiser (*Sister Carrie* was first printed
though not distributed in 1900) were already doing exactly that in the novel, but Whitman was still the only
poet of consequence in America who had used such realistic experience in poetry. And he was not a Realist, as
Wendell was aware when he praised his "idealising"
the East River.

George Santayana, a poet and philosopher also
teaching at Harvard in 1900, was more intellectually
sophisticated than Barrett Wendell, but he too found
the poetry of Walt Whitman something of a shock. He
was unconcerned over Whitman's "Americanism."
What he found in *Leaves of Grass* was one of the finest examples of a return to "The Poetry of Barbar-
ism." Santayana defined the "barbarian" as a "man
who regards his passions as their own excuse for being;
who does not domesticate them either by understanding
their cause or by conceiving their ideal goal." Taking
quite literally Whitman's own poetic descriptions of
his indiscriminate joy in all things, without distinction
or gradation, Santayana saw in him a poet who
"merely feels and acts," delighting in "abundance and
vehemence," respecting only the "quantity and splendour of materials."[2]

We find the swarms of men and objects rendered as they
might strike the retina in a sort of waking dream. It is the

most sincere possible confession of the lowest—I mean the most primitive—type of perception. All ancient poets are sophisticated in comparison and give proofs of longer intellectual and moral training. Walt Whitman has gone back to the innocent style of Adam . . .

As Whitman himself indicated in his 1855 Preface, he was trying to get back to primacies, to recover and embody in his poetry the aboriginal potency of Nature. He would not, therefore, have been altogether displeased with Santayana's characterization, in which there is considerable truth and insight. Yet at the same time this is a superficial view of Whitman's poetry, which is not entirely given over to cataloging swarms of men and objects. Those were to be found mainly in "Song of Myself" and would some day be praised for their aesthetic effect. Nor was Whitman as ignorant of history (e.g., the "Long Journey" motif) or unindebted to books and libraries as Santayana and his contemporaries supposed, having accepted too literally the poet's assertion of his freedom from the literature of the past.

Santayana granted that when Whitman "afterward became aware that there was or had been a world with a history, he studied that world with curiosity and spoke of it not without a certain shrewdness." And then Santayana acutely observed, anticipating R. W. B. Lewis (*The American Adam*, 1955) by half a century, that Whitman always regarded history as "a foreign world and imagined, as not a few Americans have done, that his own world was a fresh creation, not amenable to the same laws as the old."[3] As we shall see, later critics have found a great deal more in Whitman than a prototype of "the American Adam," but this was one of the roles he played with greatest delight.

In 1901 Dr. R. M. Bucke, the Canadian alienist

who had written the second biography of Whitman
(1883), believed *Leaves of Grass* to belong "to a religious era not yet reached." In his *Cosmic Consciousness* (New York, 1901) he devoted a chapter to Whitman as "the best, most perfect example the world has
so far had of the Cosmic Sense." By this term Dr.
Bucke meant the same phenomenon that William
James the following year in *The Varieties of Religious
Experience* called the "mystical experience." It is interesting to note that James was chairman of the Department of Philosophy in which Santayana taught at
Harvard. Both James and Bucke cited as an example
of "cosmic consciousness" or "mysticism" the passage
in "Song of Myself" in which the poet records that

Swiftly arose and spread around me the peace and joy
and knowledge that pass all the art and argument of
the earth . . .

Bucke, mystically inclined himself, had no doubt that
this "cosmic sense" was of divine origin, that it pene-
trated intuitively to the bedrock of reality, and consti-
tuted the highest authority for human conduct. Consequently, to him Walt Whitman was a veritable saint,
whose every gesture and word was perfect. James, too,
admired Whitman, and an eminent philosopher in
France, Jean Wahl,[4] thinks that *Leaves of Grass* influenced the development of James's "Pluralism." But
James studied the phenomenon of the "mystical experience" as a scientist and attempted to describe each example with detached impartiality.

Even Dr. Bucke must have approved of James's discussing Whitman under the classification of "The Religion of Healthy-Mindedness"; and what James called
the poet's "mystical ontological emotion" closely resembles Bucke's "cosmic consciousness":

[Walt Whitman] owes his importance in literature to the systematic expulsion from his writings of all contractile elements. The only sentiments he allowed himself to express were of the expansive order; and he expressed these in the first person, not as your mere monstrously conceited individual might so express them, but vicariously for all men, so that a passionate and mystic ontological emotion suffuses his words, and ends by persuading the reader that men and women, life and death, and all things are divinely good.[5]

To these qualities in Whitman's poems James attributed the fact that he had become the focus of a cult of "natural religion." Societies, he pointed out, were being formed in his name (a reference to the "Walt Whitman Fellowship," which had chapters in several American cities), and Horace Traubel conducted a magazine called *The Conservator* for the propagation of this new religion: "Lines of orthodoxy and heterodoxy are already beginning to be drawn; hymns are written by others in his peculiar prosody; and he is even explicitly compared with the founder of the Christian religion, not altogether to the advantage of the latter."

Although Whitman himself had asked that societies not be formed in his name, in his old age he could not resist the adulation of Traubel, Edward Carpenter, Johannes Schlaf and, until his disillusionment, Dr. Eduard Bertz in Germany, Gabriel Sarrazin in France, and numerous others of less eminence. These cults were, in fact, to have the most profound influence on Whitman's twentieth-century fame. On the one hand, they gained him "disciples" and admirers, but these were most likely to be emotionally unstable, of uncertain sexual psychology, or subliterary minds who applied too literally Whitman's injunctions against literary conventions. Not all the adherents were "crack pots," though most were at least slightly eccentric— and already the reputation of Whitman was such that praise of him was likely to be regarded by the arbiters of literary taste as eccentric conduct. Some of the greatest writers of the age were at least sympatheti- cally interested in Whitman, such as Tolstoy, Tur- genev, Bjørnsen, Papini, Tagore, and Gide.[6] But more conventional and less independent minds were re- pelled by the cultists.

William James himself was sufficiently repelled to be on his guard and to write of Whitman with a twinge of irony. He could not, for example, agree with those critics who called Whitman (usually with admiration) a "pagan." Sometimes the term was used, he pointed out, to mean "the mere animal man without a sense of sin; sometimes it means a Greek or Roman with his own peculiar religious consciousness." But James thought that Whitman was not a pagan in either sense: "He is aware enough of sin for a swagger to be present in his indifference towards it, a conscious pride in his freedom from flexions and contractions, which your genuine pagan in the first sense of the word would never show."[7] Citing the often quoted passage, "I could turn and live with animals, they are so placid and self-contain'd," James says this could never have been written by a "natural pagan." And on the other hand, "Whitman is less than a Greek or Roman; for their consciousness, even in Homeric times, was full to the brim of the sad mortality of this sunlit world, and such a consciousness Walt Whitman resolutely refused to accept."

Although it is possible to accuse James of superficial reading of Whitman and exaggerating the poet's "swagger," it is true that both Whitman and his fol- lowers, but especially the latter, emphasized his Mes- sianic and iconoclastic role. If James did not give an

entirely reliable interpretation of Whitman and his
poems, he at least correctly epitomized the religious aspects, both positive "ontology" and negative cultism
flourishing at the time.

The precariousness of fame resting on cult worship
was brilliantly demonstrated by the disillusionment of
Dr. Eduard Bertz in Germany. After first accepting
Whitman as a saintly prophet, he became suspicious of
the poet's avidity for fame and began to examine him
more critically. Such European scholars as Dr. Albert
Moll of Berlin, E. von Krafft-Ebing of Vienna, Au-
guste Florel in France, and Havelock Ellis in England
had been writing pioneer works for several decades in
the psychology and pathology of sex. With the help of
this literature on sexual abnormality, Dr. Bertz wrote
a paper on Whitman for the *Jahrbuch für sexuelle
Zwischenstufen* (1905), and the same year published
a book with the ironical title *Der Yankee-Heiland*
(The Yankee Saint). Although he still professed to regard Whitman as one of the major lyric poets of the
world, he insisted that the traits of character which he
had encouraged his readers to interpret as those of the
prophet of a new democratic love between men were
actually manifestations of homosexuality:

The feminine and even hysterical *Grundton* of his being is
obvious to any observant reader, in the emotional, impassioned character of his world-outlook. No one familiar
with modern psychology and sex-pathology is in the
slightest doubt that the erotic friendship, which is found
in the poetry and life of our wonderful prophet, is to be
explained in any other way than by his constitutional
deviation from the masculine norm.[8]

By a curious paradox, three men in England who
warmly admired Whitman helped to corroborate Dr.
Bertz's interpretation. They were John Addinton Sy-

monds, Edward Carpenter, and Havelock Ellis. Symonds, a scholar of the Renaissance and classical Greek and Latin literature, recognized in the "Calamus" poems emotions similar to those of "Greek friendship" between men and the homosexuality of Renaissance artists (Symonds wrote a critical biography of Michelangelo). After repeatedly asking Whitman about these similarities, Symonds received from him in 1890 an indignant "disavowal" of such "morbid inferences," which he called "damnable." In this same letter he also declared that he had had six illegitimate children. Symonds was not entirely convinced, but he later refrained from the outright inferences to which the poet had objected, saying that the "adhesiveness" of comradeship in the "Calamus" poems "is meant to have no interblending with the 'amativeness' of sexual love," for "it is undeniable that Whitman possessed a specially keen sense of the fine restraint and continence, the cleanliness and chastity, that are inseparable from the perfectly virile and physically complete nature of healthy manhood."[9]

However, Symonds admitted that "those unenviable mortals who are the inheritors of sexual anomalies, will recognize their own emotions in Whitman's 'superb friendship . . . latent in all men.' " And he wondered whether the poet's "own feelings upon this delicate topic may not have altered since the time when *Calamus* was first composed."

It was Edward Carpenter who first made known Whitman's letter to Symonds. This was not until his autobiographical *Days with Walt Whitman* (London, 1906), published a decade after Symonds's death, but he has been discussing the subject with Symonds and some of Whitman's friends in America since his visit to the poet in 1877. Of all Whitman's English male friends (which excludes the marrying-minded Mrs. Gilchrist),

Carpenter was the one who felt the most intimate sympathy and identity with him.[10] He not only shared Whitman's feelings for other men, he also believed that secrecy regarding sex should be broken down and that a stronger, more socially-beneficial love between men was possible. In 1896 he published *Love's Coming of Age* to bring about better "Relations of the Sexes." At that time his purpose was to combat prudery and to show that spiritual and sexual love were not antagonistic—could, in fact, strengthen each other.

In 1902 Carpenter published *Ioläus: An Anthology of Friendship*, with examples ranging from pagan to modern times but with special attention to the Greek and Roman ages, in which a friend of the same sex was often called a "lover," as in Whitman's "Calamus" poems included in this anthology. In his *Days with Walt Whitman* (p. 78) Carpenter emphasized the poet's mysticism, finding a continuity between his universal sympathy and the writings of the mystics of all ages, from the *Vedas* to Christian Scripture. But, "He seems to *liberate* the good tidings and give it a democratic scope and world-wide application unknown in the elder prophets, even in the sayings of Buddha." So far, Carpenter's theory did not differ radically from Dr. Bucke's, but whereas the doctor believed Whitman's "cosmic consciousness" to be a forerunner of a superior mentality and spirituality, Carpenter saw in Whitman the forerunner of a superior sexual type of man, which he described in *The Intermediate Sex* (New York and London, 1912).

Carpenter was well acquainted with the German literature on homosexuality, and in his *Intermediate Sex* took over some of its terms, such as "Urning" and "homogenic." He liked K. H. Ulrich's "Uranian," derived from *Uranos*, heaven, because "the Uranian love was of a higher order than the ordinary attachment"

(p. 20). Carpenter also followed his German authorities in recognizing a considerable variety of characteristics in the "Uranian," ranging from the extremely masculine woman and effeminate man to the apparently masculine man and effeminate woman but with subjective "inversions"—a masculine body with a feminine "soul" or vice versa. Although he did not specifically say so, Carpenter evidently regarded Whitman as a "normal . . . Uranian" (pp. 31–32):

If now we come to what may be called the more normal type of Uranian man, we find a man who, while possessing thoroughly masculine powers of mind and body, combines with them the tenderer and more emotional soul-nature of the woman—and sometimes to a remarkable degree. Such men, as said, are often muscular and well-built, and not distinguishable in exterior structure and the carriage of the body from others of their own sex; but emotionally they are extremely complex, tender, sensitive, pitiful and loving, 'full of storm and stress, of ferment and fluctuation' of the heart; . . . for nursing and waiting on the needs of others they have often a peculiar gift; at the bottom lies the artist-nature, with the artist's sensibility and perception.

Although Carpenter admitted that the Uranians were a statistical minority in society (contemporary estimates ranged all the way from one in ten to one in five hundred), he thought it doubtful "whether the higher heroic and spiritual life of a nation is ever quite possible without the sanction of this attachment in its institutions, adding a new range and scope to the possibilities of love." And Whitman "could not have spoken, as he did, with a kind of authority on this subject, if he had not been fully aware that through the masses of people this attachment was already alive and working" (pp. 69–71).

Havelock Ellis did not hold a mystique of Uranian love, feeling in himself less psychological need for approving it than Carpenter evidently felt, but he was no less tolerant of deviations from the normal. In his first essay on Whitman (1880) Ellis had seen in the poet "an almost colossal largeness, a coarse healthfulness, a hearty world-embracing sympathy . . . which unites him to such men as Rabelais and Rubens."[11] Even in his more famous essay in *The New Spirit* (1890), he had, as he recalled in his autobiography, "passed over the homosexual strain in Whitman in a deprecating footnote, as negligible."[12] In fact, he had not recognized the symptoms of Lesbianism in the woman he married until forced to do so by painful experience. In *The New Spirit* he quoted Whitman's

I give you nothing as duties,
What others give as duties I give as living impulses,
(Shall I give the heart's action as a duty?)

and commented: "Morality is thus the normal activity of a healthy nature, not the product either of tradition or of rationalism."[13]

Shortly after this Ellis collaborated with John Addington Symonds on a book called *Sexual Inversion* (1896), based on case histories collected by the authors. Ellis's studies of "inversion" (i.e. persons with habitual homoerotic emotions) led him to modify his opinion of Whitman's normality and healthfulness, but he continued to admire the poet for his tolerant understanding of human nature. In 1923 in *Impressions and Comments* (Third Series) Ellis criticized the psychoanalysts for being too "materialistic," though he approved their tolerance: "So the way is open for a new vision of the soul, a new vision of the world, a new vision even of the human body, what would once have been called a new Gospel of Life. The psychoanalysts

are not themselves the people who can bring it. But
glimpses were caught of it—as by Whitman before
they even existed."[14]

By the time Ellis wrote these words Whitman's
reputation had been subjected to and survived bitter
attacks from both old and new critics. The most formi-
dable in English was Dr. W. C. Rivers in a pamphlet
called *Walt Whitman's Anomaly* (1913), published in
London with sale "restricted to Members of the Legal
and Medical Professions." With clinical precision Dr.
Rivers collected his examples from Whitman's writings
and marshaled his arguments to prove that the poet
was a homosexual of the "passive kind, as one might
expect from his pronounced feminine nature" (p. 64).
Because he diagnosed Whitman's inverted sexuality
as "passive," Dr. Rivers said "there is no need to
charge the poet with the grossest unnatural indulgence
of an active kind." He granted that "Whitman's message certainly comprised more than inversion, still,
just as certainly, inversion was at the core of it."
The poet's indignant denial of Symond's "inferences"
was probably, Dr. Rivers thought, based on a mis-
understanding of homosexuality: "Whitman may well
have shared the popular idea of *paedicatio* as the
only manifestation of real homosexuality, and have
been repudiating with horror *paedicatio* and nothing
else" (p. 54). (Many later defenders of Whitman
were to make the same assumption; some have thought
that if they could prove that he had fathered at least
one child he could be absolved from the suspicion.[15])

The Rivers monograph is still one of the most
closely-reasoned analyses ever published on Whitman's
supposed "anomaly," but the author made two major
assumptions that are at least challengeable. First,
with Moreau, Lombroso, and Nordeau he assumed that
geniuses are exceptionally prone to physical, moral,

and mental "degeneracy," and this predisposed him to finding "anomalies" in Whitman. Second, he assumed that all erotic descriptions in Whitman's poems are literally autobiographical. A modern psychologist would regard the products of the poet's fantasy as important clues to his unconscious and his innate character, but he would not interpret them as literally as Dr. Rivers did.

However, whether this interpretation is true or false, or half-true and half-false, it is doubtful that it greatly dented Walt Whitman's fame. The tone of the monograph is entirely negative, but it has never had a wide circulation. Yet it was symptomatic of a crisis in Whitman's reputation just before World War I. The very same year (1913) a controversy began in the *Mercure de France* in which many of the same charges were made, with the addition of other sensational accusations without any factual basis. It began on April 1, 1913, in a letter by Guillaume Apollinaire,[16] in which he purported to describe the funeral of Walt Whitman as related to him by an "eye-witness"—a former journalist of Philadelphia who remained anonymous throughout the ten-month quarrel.

Whitman's funeral, wrote Apollinaire, was attended by 3,500 people (not far from correct). It took place on a field used by traveling circuses, and the funeral itself resembled a circus in many respects. Three pavilions were erected, one for the corpse, one for a barbecue, and one for the tubs of whiskey, beer, and other refreshments. Three brass bands took turns in playing —later he says that they all played at the same time during the obsequies. All the poet's disreputable associates came, soldiers, fishermen, stage drivers, his former mistresses, his illegitimate children, and crowds of sex perverts. (No exclusiveness here in the implications of crimes and perversions!) Several speakers

spoke at the same time while the bands played, those
nearest the coffin pounding on the lid with their fists
for emphasis. Everyone drank enormously, ate water-
mellons and barbecue, and enjoyed the debauch.
Finally six drunken men on all fours crawled into the
narrow tomb with the coffin on their backs. "In this
manner the greatest of democratic poets entered his
last abode, and the crowd, singing, embracing and stag-
gering, returned by train to Philadelphia."

A decade later this account might have been taken
as the prank of a surrealist,[17] but Apollinaire maintained that he had believed his "eye-witness" to be
honest and reliable, though he finally apologized for
having provoked the controversy. On April 16, Stuart
Merrill, an American poet living in Paris, denounced
these "calumnies" on Whitman's character, pointing
out that the funeral had been fully reported in the
newspapers and in no way resembled Apollinaire's account. Other correspondents supported Merrill, to
which Dr. Bertz replied, summarizing his arguments
on the poet's homosexuality. Leon Bazalgette, Whitman's French biographer, replied to Bertz and this
resulted in the exchange of international insults. Finally on February 1, 1914, Harrison Morris, one of
Whitman's pall-bearers and a former resident of
Philadelphia, who was then in Rome as Commissioner
for the United States to the International Exhibition
of Fine Arts, brought the quarrel to a close by giving
a factual account of the funeral as he had witnessed
it.[18] A tent had been erected at the cemetery for the
funeral ceremonies, but they had been conducted with
solemnity, dignity, and without any interruptions.

Morris added that he did not attach much importance to the rumors "of a wild and vagabond Whitman"
which the *Mercure de France* had circulated: "Dear
old Walt's ideas and inspirations fly over the world

with a greater speed than the evil rumors . . . His place in the world of ideas is assured. No one can injure his memory from now on. The evil disposed persons who bear false witness must expect to see the consequence of their falsehoods recoil upon themselves."

Harrison Morris's affirmation of faith in the inviolability of Whitman's "place in the world of ideas" was not the judgment of an impartial critic, for he had been a member of Traubel's "Walt Whitman Club," which aided the poet with money and services during his last years. Furthermore, he was a Quaker, and the Quakers, especially of the Philadelphia region, had come to regard Walt as one of their own, though they admired him as a mystic and poet rather than as the Messiah of a new religion.[19]

But Whitman continued posthumously to play the role of a prophet. His English biographer, Henry Bryan Binns, accepted the poet's ambition "to make the American people a book which should be like the Bible in spiritual appeal and moral fervour,"[20] but rejected the Christ-role in which some of his fanatical adherents cast him, believing rather that the "peasant-born son of Manhattan, an average American artisan," incorporated America herself. And Binns made his "prophet" even more human by creating for him a sensual romance in New Orleans. The woman, Binns suggested, was of a higher social rank than the poet and for this reason never acknowledged him as the father of her child, or "perhaps, in after years, of her children." This "romance" was to become one of the most appealing of all Whitman legends.

In 1906 Horace Traubel began publishing his notes on conversations with the poet called *With Walt Whitman in Camden.* He started these notes on March 28, 1888, and continued them until Whitman's

death. Traubel himself eventually published three fat
volumes, and left enough notes for three or four more
which Charles E. Feinberg, the great Whitman bib-
liophile of the twentieth century, has undertaken to
transcribe and publish.[21] There is no reason for dis-
trusting Traubel's integrity, but he took down his
notes in longhand (with some abbreviations) and then
expanded them as a verbatim record. Under these circumstances his own ideas and attitudes could scarcely
have failed to color the version edited for publication.
Thus Whitman in his old age appears more socialistic
and "radical" than his earlier friends, such as Charles
Eldridge and John Burroughs, had remembered him
to be. Traubel's record is certainly valuable for its
factual details and copies of letters received by Whitman, but it encouraged many additions to the legend
of Whitman as a wild-eyed revolutionary.

In the same year Bliss Perry published a scholarly biography entitled *Walt Whitman, His Life and
Work* (New York, 1906), which annoyed the most in-
fatuated of the poet's American friends (Traubel,
Morris, W. S. Kennedy, etc.). Today it is difficult to
understand what they could have found objectionable
in Perry's scrupulously prepared biography. He rejected, for example, pathological interpretations of the
"Calamus" poems. He agreed with the poet that the
roots of the first *Leaves of Grass* grew "deep down in
a young man's body and soul, a clean sensuous body
and a soul untroubled as yet by the darker mysteries"
(p. 47). But of course he did not accept the super-
man or the Messiah myths. And even his defense of
the form and style of the poems was hardly that of
Dr. Bucke or Edward Carpenter: "A generation
trained to enjoyment of Monet's landscapes, Rodin
sculptures, and the music of Richard Strauss will not

be repelled from Whitman merely because he wrote in an unfamiliar form" (pp. 282–83). Though Perry's excellent book remained for many years the most reliable biography of the poet, it probably had but little direct effect either on the growth or demolition of the Whitman legends. Cults and special pleaders continued to use Whitman as Scripture, or at least as a symbol of what they advocated.

The Unanimists in France, for instance, seized upon Whitman as a forerunner and source for their literary movement, which as Frederik Schyberg[22] says, was "a sort of lyrical socialism, paralleling the outburst of young German poets of the First World War against individualism. This group tried conscientiously to achieve Whitman's theory of adhesiveness and 'comradeship.'" Jules Romains in his novel *Les Copains* (1913) glorified Whitman's "Calamus" theme of friendship between men. But the chief propagator of the Whitman-Unanimists doctrine was Leon Bazalgette who published *Walt Whitman: L'Homme et son Oeuvre* in 1908 and a complete translation of *Leaves of Grass* (*Feuilles d'herbe*) in 1909. His attitude toward Whitman's poetry is clearly illustrated in another book published in 1921 as *Le Poème Evangile de Walt Whitman*. Both for fact and interpretation Bazalgette relied almost entirely upon Whitman's American friends (Bucke, Traubel, Burroughs): "I efface myself as much as possible in the humility of a compiler behind those who were in personal contact with him and caught him on the spot."[23]

Meanwhile in England Basil De Selincourt elaborated the New Orleans romance with fresh embellishments, and interpreted Whitman's music as spontaneous, inspired, and yet composed—much of it at least—with consummate artistry. Despite the idealization, many of De Selincourt's aesthetic interpretations were valid, and his work laid the foundation for better appreciation of Whitman as an artist.

It was in Spain and Latin America that the canonized image of Whitman became most magnified. This is the way Fernando Alegría describes it:

To the Hispanic public Walt Whitman is the bard immortalized by all the portraits—with a long beard and a shepherd's staff, wearing a wide-brimmed hat and breasting the wind. His gray figure is surmounted by a halo of indisputable sainthood. His poetry is accepted as gospel, and while this gospel appears to have its own private meaning for each poet or critic, all dip into *Leaves of Grass* with pious respect, not doubting in the slightest that somewhere in the book the expected revelation will burst forth.[24]

Spanish poets and critics were interested in Whitman at the same time that the Unanimists were writing about him in France. In fact, Bazalgette's 1908 biography was the principal one read in Spain and helped to start a cult there. In 1909 Cebría Montoliu published a translation of *Leaves of Grass* in Catalan, and four years later a study called *Walt Whitman, L'Home i sa Tasca*. In Chile Armando Donosa wrote on the Old Testament characteristics of Whitman's personality, and in Argentine, Chile, and Brazil there were translations of selected poems.

Of the many Spanish and Latin American poets to whom Whitman made a strong appeal, probably the most gifted was Federico García Lorca—though earlier Ruben Darío and about the same time Miguel de Unamuno were also attracted by the American poet. Lorca, who was both a Catholic and Socialist and was to die in the Spanish Civil War while fighting for the Loyalists, visited the United States in 1929. While in

New York he felt a special identity with Walt Whitman and wrote an ode to him, later published in *Poeta
en Nueva York* (1940).

Ni un solo momento, viejo hermoso Walt Whitman,
he dejado de ver tu barba llena de mariposas,
ni tus hombors de pana gastados por la luna,
ni tus muslos de Apolo virginal,
ni tu voz como una columna de ceniza;
anciano hermoso como la niebla,
que gemías igual que un pájaro,
con el sexo atravesado por una aguja,
enemigo del sátiro,
enemigo de la vid,
y amante de los cuerpos bajo la burda tela.

Not for one moment, handsome old Walt Whitman,
have I forgotten your beard full of butterflies,
or your corduroy shoulders worn by the moon,
or your thighs of virginal Apollo,
or your voice like a column of ashes;
old man, beautiful as the mist,
trembling like a bird,
whose sex is pierced by a needle,
enemy of the satyr,
enemy of the vine,
and lover of bodies under the coarse fabric.[25]

Edwin Honig has said that "Lorca's Catholicism as
seen through his 'Oda a Walt Whitman' is supremely
a thing of the body."[26] The saintly white-haired old
man with beard full of butterflies might well stand as
the characteristic Spanish image of Whitman, an
image still unblemished in the idealized portrait in
Concha Zardoya's introduction to her translation,
Walt Whitman, Obras Escogidas (1946).

Two years later the great Brazilian sociologist,

Gilberto Freyre, held up Whitman as the archetype of democracy and compared his conception of friendship to St. Augustine's in his *Confessions*. Like Whitman, St. Augustine writes that "he does not know how he can go on living after losing the friend who in life complemented him to such a degree that the two formed 'only one soul.' " From Whitman's poems overflowed a "personalistic and fraternalistic sense of life and community, a sense so vibrant as to seem at times homosexualism gone mad, whereas it was probably only bisexualism sublimated into fraternalism."[27]

Whitman's theme of comradeship has usually appealed to foreign critics and cults more than any of his other themes, partly, no doubt, because in translation there is always a great loss of poetic values, and partly because his symbols, like the parables of the New Testament, lend themselves readily to many applications and shades of interpretation. This has been especially true in Russia, where in the late nineteenth century he was regarded as such an encourager of revolution that the Czarist Government forbad translation or discussion of him in print. Naturally this interdiction made him a hero to the young revolutionists of the late nineteenth and early twentieth centuries. Stepanchev reports that this "revolutionary generation discovered its war slogans" in Whitman.[28]

Konstantin Balmont, the first translator of more than a scattered poem or two from *Leaves of Grass*, published his translation between 1903 and 1905, "to the sound of revolutionary guns."[29] In his essays on Whitman he stressed his importance as a symbol of freedom and the "Sovereignty of the People." Kornei Chukovsky, who was soon to become Whitman's chief translator into Russian, accepted Balmont's interpretations but rejected his inaccurate translations. He continued to translate and to write about Whitman until the Revolution, after which his versions of Whitman's poems were officially approved by the Soviet Government, which published many editions of them in large quantities. However, the complete *Leaves of Grass* has never appeared in Russian, and probably the poems have been selected to some extent at least for their propaganda value, though the most blatant examples of this ulterior use of Whitman have been in other Communist countries—and by the Communists of the United States during the 1930's and '40's.[30]

Actually, to judge by Chukovsky's long introduction to the 1914 edition of his translation, which he called *Poetry of the Future,* he proclaimed Whitman only as an "apostle of Democracy" and equality who has given mankind a new word, "comrade."

Now this wonderful sense [of comradeship] which, as we know, the poet felt so strongly that it drew him to the wounded and dying in hospitals, wards for infectious diseases, fields washed by blood—this sense has not yet found full expression in contemporary poetry. The chivalrous adoration of woman, proper to the Middle Ages, the cult of the Beautiful Lady which ennobled sexual love and achieved social refinement, is now insufficient: the future of humanity needs a cult, too—the cult of the comrade, the cult of democratic union, for a new tenderness suffuses the hearts of men, a love of the fellow warrior, co-worker, fellow traveler, of him who journeys with us shoulder to shoulder and takes part in the general movement; it is this still weak feeling, this embryo or beginning of feeling, that the poet strengthened in his gigantic soul, brought to flame, to passion, to that all-encompassing, grand emotion with which, as he believed, he transfigured himself in a vision of the world triumph of democracy.

He anticipated the future even in this. And if today his odes to comrades, to those whom he called *camerado,*

seem unreal, strange, and remind one of serenades to a
lover—they are excessively pleading and flamingly affectionate—that is so because the days have not yet come
when our hearts, too, can flame with such magnificient
passion.

Chukovsky translated a whole anthology of the "Calamus" poems and said that he regretted that the word
"comradeship" was inadequate to express Whitman's
full meaning: "This is a burning, stormy, almost
alarming love of man for man, and without it, as the
poet believed, democracy is only a shadow, an illusion." Thus the emotion which Dr. Rivers called
pathological, Chukovsky regarded as a necessary
prerequisite for a new and happier society.

A 1935 edition of Chukovsky's translation was in-
troduced by a truly great critical essay on Whitman
by D. Mirsky, which recognized his limitations as well
as his achievements, but, notably, did not try to fit him
into a Marxist mould. "That reality which Whitman
affirmed was a bourgeois reality," Mirsky declared.
"But in his affirmation, the poet stressed not that which
was essentially bourgeois, but that which was creative
and progressive." Sometimes, though, "the poet loses
his realistic concreteness," and then his verse "degener-
ates into a noisy rhetoric."

It was not actually the man Walt Whitman that
Mirsky admired, contrary to Whitman's often expressed wish, but the symbolical man in the poems:
"The 'Walt Whitman' whom Whitman 'celebrated' was
not an individual endowed with a definite biography,
a definite personality differentiating him from others;
he was a metonymical type, the average man, the average American, bringing from out the American masses
the sum and substance of the contemporary scene."
Mirsky even criticized Whitman for the image of

himself the poet tried to create in his numerous prefaces and "program" poems:

In thinking out, intellectually, the subjects that he took for his verse, Whitman was led to abandon a poetic concreteness of imagery for a false and one-sided process of abstract generalization which comes as a break in the true pathos of his work. It is Whitman the prophet acting as self-interpreter for Whitman the poet. Inasmuch as it is difficult to demarcate one from the other with exactitude, we should proceed from the premise that the prophet's interpretations not only are not binding upon us, but that they actually interfere with a proper understanding of the poet.

Mirsky also criticized Whitman for his delusion that he was the poet of his people: "Whitman gave expression to the masses, but he did not speak *for* them. He spoke in their name, but not to them. This was because he failed to realize that poetry written for the masses must first of all be easy-flowing, readily memorizable, and that therefore it must possess a rhythmic transparency of form . . . But Whitman—in his own eyes —was first of all a prophet."[31]

Although Mirsky finally claimed Whitman for "socialism," he did so only because he believed him to be a great poet who envisioned the "full man." This is an abstraction if ever there was one, and the implied definition of a poet contains a good deal of the "prophetic" (in Whitman's sense). But at least Mirsky recognized Whitman's importance without falsely interpreting it.

On the whole, it would seem that Whitman was very fortunate in his two major interpreters to Communist Russia, Mirsky and Chukovsky. As a final confirmation of this conclusion, the June 13, 1960, issue of *Time* magazine contained a picture of Chukovsky

at Boris Pasternak's grave. Despite the refusal of the
Soviet Government to let Pasternak accept the Nobel
Prize or even to permit the publication in Russia of
Doctor Zhivago, Chukovsky braved official disapproval to deliver his friend's funeral oration. According to *Time,* he even defended Pasternak's criticism of
Communism, praising "his old friend as a 'splendid
fighter,' a perfect model of how an artist 'should
defend his views without fear of falling out with his
contemporaries or other disapproval, so long as he is
convinced that his word is right, so long as he is convinced that his cause is sacred!' " Thus the man who
has preached "the gospel of Whitman" (his own
phrase) in Russia since 1906 had himself not forgotten
its message of brotherhood and freedom.

Not all European critics and translators were interested in Whitman for his political and social views
or, more often, the way in which he could be used to
support their own views. A group of French poets, including André Gide, Valéry Larbaud, and Jules Laforgue were displeased with the "idealized" Whitman
presented by Bazalgette both in his translations and
his biography. Consequently, in 1913 they began
making a translation of their own. The first edition
appeared in 1914, with a long introduction by Larbaud, who attacked the nationalistic interpretation of
the American poet (including Whitman's own): "His
doctrine is German and his masters are English; as
regards his purely intellectual life he was a European
living in America. . . . Thus it was in Europe only
that he could be, and was, recognized." Larbaud also
condemned the political use of Whitman:[32]

It is . . . out of the more transient part of the work
[*Leaves of Grass*] that there have grown all the political
parasites (anarchists, sentimental socialists) who have

contributed to spread the name of Whitman and obscure the critical study of his works. A careful examination shows that in reality Whitman (who, indeed, presents himself to European revolutionaries with the red flag in his hand) is connected with anarchistic doctrines, etc., only through Hegelianism, and that he is even more conservative than most Hegelians of the left. It is certain that, to his mind, individual property is an indispensable form of liberty. So there you are.

What gave Whitman "colossal dimensions," says Larbaud, was his discovery of a new province for poetic expression: "a poetry of the self purged from egotism." His doctrine will become antiquated and the new province completely settled, but his "pure expression" will remain. "Whatever those who see works of art through political prejudices may think, it is there that the step forward has been taken, and the blow for the 'good old cause' struck; it is in the expression itself that there has been an increase in human liberty. This is the core of Whitman." This theory of Whitman as above all else a poet in the European tradition did not, of course, stabilize the image of him. In the first place, it did not halt the multiplication of other theories; furthermore, there is room for different theories of the poet, even many interpretations of Whitman's "expression."

No one has admired Whitman's expression more than Hans Reisiger, who published his first translation of selections in 1919, and a long biographical study in the 1922 complete *Leaves of Grass*. In Whitman's poems Reisiger found "a mystic force in which reality, the living dream of being, pulsates." Reduced to its simplest form, Reisiger's image of Whitman is the old romantic concept of the poet as an intuitive child of nature, such as the German critics of the eighteenth

century thought Shakespeare to have been, an un-
tutored, almost unconscious genius:[33]

Walt Whitman was one of those particularly gifted human beings who from childhood into old age remained
secure in the strength and warmth of a maternal world. In
the midst of all the visions and passions of a world free
and multiform, seizing his lonely breast, there remained
with him, at all times, the invisible smile of a child belonging to the essence out of which it had been born. Again and
again he would have only had to recall this essence in
order to return to it like a little child, in spite of the
wrinkles on his forehead and the grey hair and beard.

But this conception of Whitman as the "child-man"
did not prevent German readers from finding social
and political messages in Reisiger's translation. In
1922 Thomas Mann thanked Reisiger for his "holy
gift," and called Whitman a "profound new personification of humanity," adding that "We Germans who
are old and immature at one and the same time can
benefit from contact with this personality, symbol of
the future of humanity."[34] In the same year Mann
delivered what was to become an historic speech "Von
deutscher Republik," in which he held up Whitman
and Novalis as archtypes respectively of American
Democracy and German Humanity. Meanwhile the
socialists, the Social Democrats, the "proletarian"
poets, and the "Expressionists" took over Whitman for
their slogans and manifestoes. But of course in a short
time the "German Humanity" invisioned by Mann was
halted by the rise of National Socialism and Mann himself had to seek exile.

As early as 1905 the great Danish writer, Johannes
V. Jensen, had realized the extremes to which the cult
of Whitman could lead. In his allegorical novel called
Hjulet (The Wheel) he illustrated these extremes by

two Whitmanesque characters representing the duality
of the American poet—or at least his susceptibility to
a dualistic interpretation. A young poet named Lee
represented the positive side of Whitman, his democratic individualism, his awareness of modern reality,
his brotherly love for all mankind; but another character named Evanston was a homosexual and swindler
who preached a "new religion" out of Walt Whitman's
"Bible." Evanston based his demagogic creed on two
of Whitman's authentic doctrines, the assimilation of
the best of all religions into one composite religion and
the equality of good and evil. To Lee Whitman was a
beneficent emotional inspiration, to Evanston a perverted "program" of esoteric mysticism and eroticism.
Both characters used passages from *Leaves of Grass*
to support their doctrines, so that the novel contained a
veritable anthology of poems and extracts, translated
into Danish.

Jensen genuinely admired Whitman and in 1919 he
and Otto Gelsted published a small volume of Whitman's poetry (*Digte*), composed of Jensen's earlier
translations in *Hjulet* and additional ones by Gelsted.
In an introduction Jensen called him "a Prince of
Words and a gateway to America," but he admitted
that at the moment his influence did not seem "fruitful": "I see that some rejoice in his doctrine that the
Libido shall rule unchecked, without regard to sex, a
world of nothing but 'Camerados,' which would certainly be a snug monkey-cage. His irresponsible va-
grancy, vagabondage, the baring of his soul, which
made him akin to the Russians and Verlaine, seems to
attract many, a symptom of a decadent period."[35] But
notice that Jensen blamed the period as much as, if not
more than, Whitman. Thus one may regard his double
Whitman-theme in *Hjulet* either as an interpretation of a duality in the poet or as an illustration of the

possible perverted employment of him by an evil cult. Certainly both interpretations have often been made of Whitman in many countries.

Perhaps the most curious double image of Whitman was the one created by D. H. Lawrence in his *Studies in Classic American Literature,* a book which he worked on at intervals between 1915 and 1922. He began his chapter on Whitman with a wittily sarcastic travesty of Whitman's abstractions: "Democracy," "En Masse," "Identity," "amorous love," etc., his female universe and his being in love with death. He was especially severe with the poet's tendency to "merge" with everybody and everything, to share vicariously the suffering of anyone sick, wounded, or mistreated. This, Lawrence insisted, was not genuine sympathy but sentimental escapism, or even (Lawrence implied but did not actually say) morbid masochism. The sick man wants—or should want—to get well, not to have someone share his sickness. "Merging" leads only to death. And yet:

Whitman, the great poet, has meant so much to me. Whitman, the one man breaking a way ahead. Whitman, the one pioneer. And only Whitman. No English pioneers, no French. No European pioneer-poets. In Europe the would-be pioneers are mere innovators. The same in America. Ahead of Whitman, nothing. Ahead of all poets, pioneering into the wilderness of unopened life, Whitman. Beyond him, none. His wide, strange camp at the end of the great high-road. And lots of new little poets camping on Whitman's camping ground now. But none going really beyond. Because Whitman's camp is at the end of the road, and on the edge of a great precipice. Over the precipice, blue distances, and the blue hollow of the future. But there is no way down. It is a dead end.[36]

But Lawrence also insisted that Whitman was a "great moralist" and "a great leader," because he was "the first heroic seer to seize the soul by the scruff of her neck and plant her down among the potsherds." This was: "A doctrine of life. A new morality. A morality of actual living, not of salvation." By "salvation" Lawrence meant Christian asceticism. And the source of this "new morality" was the unconscious, which he also, like Whitman, called "the soul," the source of healthy, life-giving impulses: "It is not I who guide my soul to heaven. It is I who am guided by my own soul, along the open road, where all men tread. Therefore, I must accept her deep motions of love, or hate, or compassion, or dislike, or indifference. And I must go where she takes me. For my feet and my lips and my body are my soul. It is I who must submit to her."[37]

This Lawrence thought to be Whitman's true message of American democracy, "where soul meets soul, in the open road." Clothes, family, reputation have nothing to do with the soul. It is recognized only for itself by another soul on the same road. But the recognition will be accompanied by the "love of man and woman . . . and a communion of worship." Thus, though "Love" and "Merging" brought Whitman to the "Edge of Death" the essence, or as Lawrence said, "the exultance of his message still remains. Purified of MERGING, purified of MYSELF, the exultant message of American Democracy, of souls in the Open Road, full of glad recognitions, full of fierce readiness, full of joy of worship, when one soul sees a greater soul."[38]

Whether or not Lawrence misunderstood or perverted Whitman's doctrine of "Love" and his psychology of "merging," it is obvious that he greatly admired the American poet. In fact, some recent scholars have convincingly demonstrated the deeply permeating influence of Whitman in Lawrence's own writings, and James E. Miller, Jr., concludes that

Lawrence and Whitman were brothers of the blood, both calling for a joyous affirmation of life and a courageous confrontation of the here and now with a robust and singing soul. They both sketched remarkably similar embryos of a new kind of man and drew strikingly similar blueprints of a new social order. In short, they were Camerados of the spirit, strolling together, in their lifelong quests, down the same open road, yet neither violating the sacred separateness of the other. Poet and novelist, their art was the dance of rapture, their connection the "living organic connection with the cosmos."[39]

The period of Whitman's greatest acceptance in his own country was from about 1910 to 1930. Then— if ever—he most strongly influenced American literature, though the influence was general and pervasive rather than specific in theme, prosody, imagery, etc. Furthermore, influence is not exactly the subject of the present examination of Whitman's "image" in the twentieth century, for in real influence the work is more important than the man. In Whitman's case, however, it was the example of the man—or perhaps the man as example—that appealed to many of the writers of his own country during the second and third decades of the present century. This was a time of rebellion against the past, of search for new standards, and, above all, of experimentation. And, naturally, the most famous rebel against convention and most original experimenter in the history of American poetry became a figure around whom the iconoclasts could rally. In strict accuracy, no new image of Whitman appeared; it was simply a case of rendering long-overdue homage to a "pioneer."

In *America's Coming of Age* (1915) Van Wyck Brooks declared that in the past nearly all major American authors had been too delicate, too refined, and too British. Only Whitman "gave us the sense of something organic in American life." The others and especially in New York during Whitman's lifetime, "had the temperament of collectors and connoiseurs; and Whitman came in upon them thundering and with his coat off, like an inconvenient country uncle, puddling their artistic expectations." Though Brooks thought Whitman's "social ideal" only "a collection of raw materials," and that he "was lost on the plane of ideas,"[40] he felt a strong affection for the "country uncle," and so did many of Brooks's contemporaries.

In observance of the first centennial of Whitman's birth, May 31, 1919, poets, critics, and journalists paid special tributes to him. Percy Boynton called him the "animating force" in contemporary poetry. Louis Untermeyer thought he had influenced Carl Sandburg, Sherwood Anderson, Vachel Lindsay, Edgar Lee Masters, Robert Frost, Theodore Dreiser, and James Oppenheim.[41] He was almost certainly wrong in naming Frost, but the others admired Whitman and may have been influenced to some extent. But about all that any of these poets got specifically from Whitman was an example of metrical freedom, and possibly of nationalism. Amy Lowell claimed Whitman in her camp because he had written "free verse." Sandburg later wrote an introduction to an edition of *Leaves of Grass*, and in *The Litany of Washington Street* (1929) Lindsay whimsically insisted that Whitman was a "statesman" like Jefferson.

The only poet of this period who is generally thought to have been profoundly influenced by Whitman was Hart Crane, and his case is worth mentioning here because the critics who have most emphasized this supposed influence contributed thereby a strong negative image of Whitman, counteracting the affectionate approval of men like Brooks. It was Crane's avowed intention[42] in *The Bridge* to carry on the binding and "incarnating" themes of Whitman, making the poem into a cultural bridge between past and present, reconciling sectional differences, and bringing the whole nation together by adhesive love. The intention was certainly Whitmanian, but Crane had also been studying the French Symbolists, especially Rimbaud and Laforgue (though mainly in translations) and he was likewise acquainted with Eliot's poems and opinions. Thus, even if, as Yvor Winters flatly asserted, "Crane's thought . . . was derived from Whitman," his imagery, discontinuity of structure, and prosody owed a large debt to the Symbolists and Eliot.

Winters, however, did not stop at condemning Crane for borrowing his "thought" from Whitman; he accused Whitman (and Emerson as Whitman's mentor) of being responsible for Crane's suicide. This is Winters's logic:[43]

The doctrine of Emerson and Whitman, if really put into practice, should naturally lead to suicide: in the first place, if the impulses are indulged systematically and passionately, they can lead only to madness; in the second place, death, according to the doctrine, is not only a release from suffering but is also and inevitably the way to beatitude. There is no question, according to the doctrine, of moral preparation for salvation; death leads automatically to salvation.

Whitman has been accused of many crimes, but this is the first time, to my knowledge, that anyone has denounced him as an encourager of suicide. More often the "caresser of life" has been condemned for enjoying life too much, of being a hedonist. But, at any rate, he was once more condemned on moral grounds.

Allen Tate[44] also thought that Whitman's influence on Crane was unfortunate, but he more plausibly attributed the suicide to neuroses produced in Crane during his youth by his quarreling parents. Tate points out too that Rimbaud, whose "spiritual heir" he sought to be, taught Crane to use the fused metaphor, and both Eliot and Laforgue "heavily influenced" the style of *The Bridge*. That Crane admired Whitman is beyond question, and he longed to see a nation cemented by the fraternal love that Whitman expressed in his socialized "Calamus" poems. (It is very surprising that Winters did not blame Crane's homosexuality on Whitman!) Yet Whitman's influence on Crane has undoubtedly been exaggerated.

But Winters's charges were symptomatic of a new period of opposition to Whitman in his own country. As a critic Winters represented almost a school-of-one, but his rational-moralistic aesthetic was similar to that of the New Humanists, led by Irving Babbitt and Paul Elmer More. They opposed all forms of Rousseauism and "obscurantism" (Winters's *bête noire*), of which Emerson and Whitman were prime examples. Ernest Boyd, bitter enemy of H. L. Mencken and other foes of "Puritanism," also called Whitman "the first of the literary exhibitionists whose cacophonous incongruities and general echolalia are the distinguishing marks of what is regarded as poetry in aesthetic circles today."[45] And Harvey O'Higgins, of the psychoanalytic-school (though then more a fad than a school), said that Whitman's mother fixation and narcissism made him completely unfit for the role of "poet of Democracy."[46]

More important was the growing prestige of Ezra Pound and T. S. Eliot. Pound's attitude toward Whit-

man vacillated for several decades. In 1916 in a poem
called "A Pact" he made "a truce" with Whitman, because "We have one sap and one root," but he continued to criticize him sarcastically. The actual influence of Whitman on Pound has been much debated,
but Babette Deutsch has reasonably declared that
in certain of his poems Pound has written "not in
Walt's accents but surely with his animus," and concluded: "The great difference between Pound and
Whitman is not between the democrat looking hope-
fully toward the future and the fascist madly in love
with the past. It is that between the woodsman and
woodcarver. It is that between the mystic harking back
to his vision and the artist whose first allegiance is to
his craft, and so to the reality it presents." By 1940
the woodcarvers were in the ascendant and the woods-
men out of favor in American poetic circles. Only William Carlos Williams of the major poets in favor
(Sandburg was out) remained loyal to Whitman.[47]

The great influence of T. S. Eliot on American poets
during the 1940's and early '50's was, however, the
most decisive deterrent to any influence Whitman
might have had on this generation of poets. A New
Zealand scholar, S. Musgrove,[48] has discovered what
he thinks are unmistakable internal evidences of
Whitman's influence on Eliot himself, but his examples
are not entirely convincing. Eliot says that he "had to
conquer an aversion to his form, as well as much of his
matter" before he could read Whitman at all. And
Eliot's religious, social, and political views are almost
the exact antithesis of Whitman's. Thus both by his
ideas and his literary practices Eliot, to say the
least, severely discouraged young poets from reading
Whitman, and in the early years of the "New Criticism" Whitman was simply ignored.

Scholarship has, at best, an indirect and usually

delayed effect on a poet's reputation in any given period. Critics, other poets, and even journalists usually produce more immediate results. But eventually the discoveries and theories of the scholars modify the popular image of a renowned writer.

Until Emory Holloway came on the scene, Whitman had had only one real scholar, Bliss Perry, who published only one book, a biography in 1906. Although on the whole he gave a favorable picture of the poet, his book should have destroyed the saintly-carpenter image of O'Connor, but it did not. And the sentimental biographies of Binns (1905) and Bazalgette (1908) had more popular appeal. For one thing, by presenting a hypothetical "romance" in New Orleans they provided love interest, and both regarded the poet as heterosexual. Actually, little was known about Whitman's life before 1855 except what he had published himself in his autobiographical writings or given to Burroughs and Bucke for their biographies.

Professor Holloway published his first important book on Whitman in 1921, entitled *Uncollected Poetry and Prose of Walt Whitman* (two volumes), in which he printed valuable extracts from Whitman's notebooks, reprinted poems and sketches published by Whitman in magazines and newspapers before 1855, and traced in a long introduction the poet's early life as a printer, school teacher, conventional poet, and author of sentimental short stories and a prohibition novel. From this material and Holloway's researches an image emerged of a young man so mediocre that some critics said the professor should not have raided the junk heap. And indeed Whitman was an undistinguished editor and third-rate poet before he startled the world with the first edition of *Leaves of Grass.*

Five years later Holloway published his *Whitman,*

An Interpretation in Narrative (New York, 1926),
which won a Pulitzer prize. Here he emphasized the
"miracle" that took place in the writing of the 1855
Leaves of Grass. And he also tried to dispose of the
problem which would continue to trouble him and
Whitman scholarship and criticism for many years to
come. Although in a previous article he had ridiculed
the "New Orleans romance" of Binns and Bazalgette,
he was now convinced that Whitman had experienced
heterosexual love and sex in the exotic South. But he
also recognized in some of the "Calamus" poems an
"unhealthy mood" (p. 173) ; however, he believed that
the poet's work among the soldiers in the hospitals during the Civil War cured him. After 1870 he was
a changed man, sure of his destiny, stable of character, a poet of the Ideal—with religious overtones—
and heroic in old-age sickness, neglect, and poverty.
Holloway's Whitman after 1870 is not unlike the saint
of O'Connor, Burroughs, and Bucke. Subsequent editions of "uncollected" writings[49] filled in more details
of Whitman's life as man and poet, but did not essentially change Holloway's portrait of 1926.

The next important scholar to appear was Jean
Catel in France, who had visited Holloway while doing
research in this country. Catel called his first book
Walt Whitman: La Naissance du Poète (Paris, 1929).
To trace the "birth" of his poet, Catel examined
everything he could find written by Whitman before
1855, and used this knowledge to interpret the '55
poems. His book was a psychological and critical study,
making some use of Freud's then-popular theories.
Catel's thesis was that an inner conflict in Whitman's
life, partly subconscious, had given him a compulsion
to write the first edition. There he revealed the secret
which he "consecrated his life to disguise." And "for
what he hid Whitman substituted the soul of a poet

ready to receive the habiliments of glory. To his real self, he preferred a legend" (p. 11). But he forgot one thing: that first edition. "After that edition is pruned, recast, and diluted into the later editions of *Leaves of Grass* it lacks the air of reality of that first long, revealing cry."

What did Whitman try to conceal? First his ancestry, which was not the healthy, sane, peasant stock that Whitman and his collaborating biographers claimed. It was, on the contrary, mediocre, harassed by poverty, and probably tainted by disease (the implication is that venereal disease was responsible for the congenital crippling of Walt's youngest brother, Edward, and possibly affected other brothers and sisters). Then, too, young Whitman never had a proper home; this is why at fifteen he roamed the streets of Brooklyn and New York and learned to love crowds, ferries, and omnibuses. As a young man, working successively as printer, country school teacher, and journalist, he was a failure. He probably also indulged in promiscuous sexual pleasures, but he was naturally autoerotic and this caused him to feel maladjusted and lonely. He sought compensations in dreams and poetic phantasies, from which grew the themes and images of the 1855 poems.

No one before Catel had attempted systematically to account for the origins and nature of Whitman's imagery. He also quoted passages, showed how images grew into symbols, and drew conclusions that made all previous criticism of Whitman tame and pedestrian in comparison. Of course this new image of the dreamer compensating for his inner weaknesses owed a great deal to the intellectual climate of the 1920's, and it need not be accepted as the final truth, but Catel all but demolished the image created by the three B's.

The next important attempt at a new portrait of
Whitman was the work of a young man in Denmark,
who was soon to become the most influential literary
critic in Scandinavia since Georg Brandes. Frederik
Schyberg wrote his *Walt Whitman* (1933) with the
most extensive knowledge of comparative literature of
anyone who had published a book on the American
poet. He was interested, however, not in sources or
influence (old-style philological studies), but in literary types, psychology, and the light that one author
can throw on another. He also demonstrated how much
could be learned about Whitman from the study of his
textual changes, his rearrangements of his poems, and
his suppression or expansion of themes.

Of course any interpretation of this kind is likely
to be influenced by the critic's own personality and
character, and it is probable that Schyberg found
much of himself in the lonely, frustrated man who
sought all his life for "equals" and "lovers" and never
found them in reality. Schyberg also thought that a
tragic flaw in Whitman's psyche caused him to think of
love and death together, to find satisfaction only in the
thought of love through or after death. Once again,
this is a very subjective interpretation. But some of
Schyberg's deductions based almost entirely on the
study of the text of *Leaves of Grass* were brilliant.
He decided, for instance, that Whitman experienced a
spiritual and perhaps moral crisis about 1858–59, and
later research corroborated this deduction.[50] He was
also one of the first to point out the importance of the
1860 edition in Whitman's spiritual biography, an
opinion held by many critics today.

But Schyberg did not think Whitman an immoral or
perverted person. He saw great similarities between
him and D. H. Lawrence, both of whom "released their
erotic impulses in their work, not in their lives."[51]

Also, "the puberal and effeminate character of Whitman's eroticism" is paralleled in the writings of other great mystics in world literature, such as the medieval Heinrich Suso, the Persian Rumi, or Swedenborg who saw "heated visions of Paradise."[52] Like the great mystics, too, Whitman sublimated his erotic impulses in a "city of friends," a truly sublime vision of a society ruled by love.

In 1937 Edgar Lee Masters published a biography titled simply *Whitman* in which he called the poet a "Uranian" but begged his readers to be tolerant and understanding because this literary pioneer inaugurated a better respect for the body and "stood for sanity in matters of sex." However, all Masters accomplished was to shock most of his readers by his admission of Whitman's anomalous sexuality and failed to gain the respect for the poet which he had intended.

The following year Esther Shephard in *Walt Whitman's Pose*, advanced the thesis that Whitman had surreptitiously borrowed his poetic program from George Sand's *Journeyman Joiner* and *Countess of Rudolstadt*. She may not have intended to accuse Whitman of dishonesty, but most reviewers thought that "Pose" implied deception, perhaps even fraud. The fact that the book received a very bad press gives some indication of the esteem in which Whitman was generally held by reviewers, journalists, and scholars in the 1930's.

Also in 1938 Newton Arvin, at that time an ardent Marxist, published a study, *Whitman*, aimed ostensibly at proving the poet a socialist. But even in his Marxist phase Arvin was too honest to claim more than the facts warranted, and he ended by lamenting Whitman's indifference to socialism and trade unionism, though he stood for "democratic and fraternal humanism."

At this time Mrs. Katherine Molinoff was making

extensive investigations on Long Island into the Whitman family, which she published in a 1941 monograph. Here for the first time the sordidness of the poet's family was fully revealed, the whining, dejected mother (in contrast to the genial old Quaker lady of the early Whitman hagiography), her headstrong oldest daughter, and her imbecile youngest son. Her oldest son, Jesse who died in a lunatic asylum, and a younger, Andrew, married a street-walker, became a drunkard, and died of "tuberculosis" (cancer?) of the throat. After Andrew's death his wife returned to her old profession and set her children to begging in the street. Another daughter, Hannah, was a neurasthenic. These depressing revelations gave a better understanding, Mrs. Molinoff said, of "that baffling reluctance of the poet to mention any member of his family which is so puzzling to biographers."[53]

But oddly enough, they did not cause a reaction against Whitman. The first biographer to use these facts (aside from Clifton Furness, who got so involved in his materials that he was never able to write a publishable book),[54] was Henry Seidel Canby, in *Walt Whitman, an American* (1943). He called his book frankly "an interpretation." He suppressed no pertinent fact and gave a vivid account of the national scene, but he agreed with Catel that "a satisfactory biography of Whitman must be essentially a biography of an inner life and of the mysterious creative process of poetry." To him Whitman was "the American poet," who articulated the American dream "of a continent where the people should escape from injustices of the past and establish a new and better life in which everyone would share." His Whitman, therefore, had as much social and political as aesthetic importance.

Canby distinguised between the actual man Walt

Whitman and the symbolical self of his poems. The "I" of his poems was neither his own ego nor the editorial "we," but "my soul," by which Whitman meant "an identification of himself with the power to greatness which he felt intuitively to be entering his own spirit." But the "soul" that Whitman dramatized had for years been passionately absorbing the life of his country, so that the symbolic "Walt Whitman" did actually represent his America; hence, Canby's title.[55]

The next major contribution to twentieth-century interpretation of Whitman was Roger Asselineau's *L'Evolution de Walt Whitman après la Première Edition des Feuilles d'Herbe* (1954). The title suggested that this was a continuation of Catel's study, and in a sense it was, but it was also much more: in fact, a full-scale biography, meticulously researched, and presented with rich details skilfully handled. Agreeing in part with Catel and Schyberg, Asselineau demonstrated that Whitman's art developed out of his double ambition to create a perfect life and a literary masterpiece, and he succeeded only in the second ambition. His youth was a time of vain search for self-understanding, and for understanding of other people, and for finding a place for himself in the social and professional world. His early manhood was a time of painful frustration in his attempt to find friends and lovers to satisfy his deep sexual cravings. He was by nature homosexual and did not know how to adjust himself to a normal world. He longed to be a symbol of robust health, joyousness, and strong masculinity, but he knew where he was "most weak,"[56] and in "Starting from Paumanok" acknowledged himself to be "Solitary, singing in the West." The pathos of his life was this awareness of being different, yet longing to be typical and average, and this created a duality in his poetry, as the reader can see in the solitude of the "Calamus" poems and the vision of himself as a great leader in his manifestoes.

Asselineau, therefore, saw Whitman not so much as a pioneer, but as a poet who found therapy in his poems. His whole aesthetic grew out of this therapy, but it also happens to have therapeutic values for readers as well as the author. One of his greatest achievements was the creation and experiencing of a mysticism tied to his senses, resulting in an imagery of strong physicality, vividness, and intensity. He never entirely stilled his inner turmoils, but in his last years he almost became the wise, serene, heroic personality he dreamed of and strove for in his early editions of *Leaves of Grass*.

In general Asselineau's image of Whitman anticipated my own, presented the following year in *The Solitary Singer: A Critical Biography of Walt Whitman* (Asselineau had even emphasized the quotation which I used as title). Of course, the two books were organized differently, mine strictly chronological and his by topics, which enabled him to write neat, graceful essays.

We differed primarily on the subject of homosexuality, and perhaps more semantically than actually. I avoided, so far as possible, the term "homosexual" and called Whitman "homoerotic," a perfectly legitimate psychological term meaning that he habitually felt stronger affection for men than for women and often expressed it in erotic imagery. In English (or at least in American English) "homosexual" suggest pederasty or perverted sexual practices. I found no evidence for such perversion in Whitman's life, though it could have been kept a secret. It seemed, instead, that in some of his poems Whitman unleashed the floodgates of damned-up sexuality, finding relief not in physical but vicarious, imaginative satisfaction. Although the condition that produced the eroticism in Whitman's poems could be called pathological, the release was beneficial, healthful, both to the poet and potentially to the reader.

Back of this interpretation was a theory of poetry, derived in part from J. Middleton Murry,[57] which seemed to me demonstrated by Whitman. This theory is that a poem originates, perhaps in the subconscious, in a turmoil in the poet's psyche. If he tries to write the poem while the turmoil is still intense, he will likely botch it, but "recollected in tranquility," he can or may create a work of art. Some of Whitman's poems show the turmoil, and this accounts for his contradictions, vacillations of purpose (e.g., in "Starting from Paumanok" he cannot make up his mind whether he wants to be a national poet-leader or a resigned, retired lover of one person, a man), and the uneven style and structure of his early poems.

My biography was widely praised for its massive details, but some critics thought it neglected criticism. Whether right or wrong, the whole biographical narrative rested on major critical interpretations—in which I had been powerfully aided by, though I did not always accept, the interpretations of Catel, Schyberg, and Canby. Above all, I agreed with Canby that it was Whitman's spiritual and creative life that mattered, and for this reason tried to correlate his physical life, external circumstances (local and national), and the record of his psychic life in his letters, diaries, notebooks, poem manuscripts, published poems, and revisions in his editions. Before publishing the biography I greatly feared that I had given too much space to literary criticism, but if so the critics did not notice it.

In his 1855 Preface Whitman called Faith the

"antiseptic of the soul," and, both by theory and practice, he wrote his poems to acquire and disseminate
faith. As a physician of the soul he sought first of all
to cure himself. He did not entirely succeed, but in
Leaves of Grass he has left us one of the great spiritual
autobiographies of world literature.

An indication of how unfashionable Whitman had
become, and at the same time an omen of a change
in his American reputation, was an article in the
Kenyon Review in 1952 by Randall Jarrell, called
"Walt Whitman: He Had His Nerve." Jarrell said
"something odd has happened to the living changing
part of Whitman's reputation; now always it is people
who are not particularly interested in poetry . . .
who admire Whitman most." He referred sarcastically to "a war in which Walt Whitman and Henry
James chose up sides," meaning Philip Rahv's "Paleface and Redskin" in the *Kenyon Review* (Summer
1939).

Jarrell was right: In literary circles Whitman had
come to be thought of as an antithesis of James, Eliot,
and Pound—in short, as not an artist. Jarrell's
strategy was simply to quote Whitman in order to show
how good he was, at least in his best passages. Perhaps
most significant, however, was the fact that John
Crowe Ransom printed this article in the *Kenyon
Review*, which had never before contained an article on
Whitman or scarcely mentioned him.

Although a respected poet and critic, Jarrell could
hardly by himself bring about a revival in Whitman's
sliding reputation, but the tide was about to turn. Perhaps the arrival of 1955, the centennial of the first
Leaves of Grass, was partly responsible in directing
attention once more to Whitman, for the year produced an avalanche of books on the poet, some good,
some bad, but most discussion-provoking. The first was

a symposium edited by Milton Hindus, with essays by
William Carlos Williams, Richard Chase, Leslie
Fiedler, Kenneth Burke, David Daiches, and J. Middleton Murry (*Leaves of Grass One Hundred Years
After*, Stanford, Calif.). These might be classified
(perhaps too conveniently) as the young men, Chase
and Fiedler, who found themselves a bit embarrassed to
be writing on Whitman; Burke and Daiches, who approached the poet without much previous knowledge
and were astonished by the originality of the language
and ideas, which they found still challenging; Murry
and Hindus (introduction), who revived the old-
fashioned view of Whitman as "the poet of democracy,"
whose nationalism was anything but shoddy; and Williams, whose one idea, apparently, was to use Whitman
to beat Eliot over the head.

This symposium settled nothing, but a number of
interesting and pertinent observations were made.
Both Chase and Fiedler insisted on the comic element
in *Leaves of Grass*, certainly a neglected observation,
though Chase, to my mind, made too much of it in his
book, *Walt Whitman Reconsidered* (1955). But perhaps Fiedler's most valuable contribution was his insistence that, "He is a poet whom we must begin now
to rescue from parody as well as apotheosis." This was
indeed a problem.

Of course Fiedler was not the first to recognize this
fact, but his witty treatment of it was badly
needed. Recently (1951) in Italy Cesare Pavese had
rejected the image of Whitman as "a bearded cen-
tenarian intent on contemplating a butterfly and gathering into his mild eyes the final serenity of all the
joys and miseries of the universe . . . the legend of
Walt Whitman as a seer, an illuminee, the founder of
new religions." Whitman, he insisted, was an artist, but
his early work was his best. "He did not write the

primitive poem of which he dreamed, but the poem of that dream."[58] A nice distinction. Few students of Whitman have realized how much he thought about the nature of poetry and the poet. Not only his many prefaces and "program" poems but also most of his major poems are about how the American poet is to live, be, and write the great poem.

Whether my own biography had any influence in creating a truer image of Whitman, I cannot say. But I do think that the introduction which Charles Davis and I wrote for a selected edition of *Walt Whitman's Poems*[59] has had some effect in getting college students to read Whitman's poems as poems, and to realize that the author was at times a great poet, the master of his artistic medium, which he had largely created for his special purpose. Fortunately, others have helped to encourage this point of view. James E. Miller, Jr., wrote *A Critical Guide to Leaves of Grass* (University of Chicago Press, 1957) with the conviction that "Whitman's poetry was not formless but sensitively ordered and that the nature of the form originated not from fraudulent pose but from genuine drama." The same intention guided Miller in his Riverside Edition of *Complete Poetry and Selected Prose* (1959) and Leslie Fiedler in his shorter but brilliant Laurel Edition (Dell Books, 1959).

One of the latest contributions has a more equivocal value: *Start with the Sun: Studies in Cosmic Poetry*, by James E. Miller, Jr., Karl Shapiro, and Bernice Slote. The chapters on Whitman's "Cosmic Consciousness" and "Cosmic Poetics" have many fresh and useful observations, despite the fact that others, from Dr. Bucke to myself have emphasized Whitman's cosmic aspects. Also the demonstration of the deep influence of Whitman on D. H. Lawrence and the slighter but still not insignificant influence on Dylan

Thomas are very important additions both to criticism
and knowledge of Whitman's importance. But these
positive and considerable values are somewhat un-
dermined by Shapiro's using Whitman as William
Carlos Williams had done, to denigrate Eliot and
berate the present generation of poets for not following the "Whitman tradition" instead of an alien, syn-
thetic, and meretricious cult. Berating Eliot—who is a
major poet, like him or not—to elevate Whitman will
never do anyone any good, least of all Walt.

Perhaps it is too soon to vote with or against
Shapiro in his championing of Henry Miller as the
Walt Whitman and the greatest writer of this century
—or in the cute phrase which Shapiro uses from
Miller, "The greatest living Patagonian." Shapiro admires Miller for the same reasons that prompt him to
urge the Whitmanian tradition: "Miller leads us away
from the charnel house of nineteenth-century poetry;
he does not even recognize the existence of twentieth-
century poetry. For poetry has lost its significance, its
relevance, and even its meaning in our time. To begin
again it must repair to the wilderness, outside society,
outside the city gates, a million miles from books and
their keepers. Almost alone of the writers of our time
Henry Miller has done this" (p. 205).

In other words, Miller, like Whitman, is a new symbol
of revolt against everything that Shapiro dislikes
in the present age. The "beatniks," too, have embraced
Whitman for much the same reason. His defiance of
custom in poetry, dress, and earning a living, for
which he was slighted, denounced, and at times
ostracized, endear him to them, though a "square"
would guess that the man and his gestures mean more
to them than his poems. With Allen Ginsberg, however,
the identification has probably gone deeper. In his
poem to Whitman called "A Supermarket in Cali-

fornia" he sees the poet, a "childless, lonely old grubber, poking among the meats in the refrigerator and eyeing the grocery boys." The young poet wonders what he and Walt will do after the supermarket closes:

> Will we stroll dreaming of the lost America of love past blue automobiles in driveways, home to our silent cottage?
> Ah, dear father, graybeard, lonely old courage-teacher, what America did you have when Charon quit poling his ferry and you got out on a smoking bank and stood watching the boat disappear on the black waters of Lethe?[60]

In an article in the *Evergreen Review* Ginsberg said that in writing "Howl" he realized "that Whitman's form had rarely been further explored (improved on even) in the U. S.—Whitman always a mountain too vast to be seen. Everybody assumes (with Pound?) (except Jeffers) that his line is a big freakish uncontrollable necessary prosaic goof. No attempt's been made to use it in the light of early XX Century organization of new speech-rhythm prosedy [*sic*] to *build up* large organic structures."[61] Ginsberg has made this experiment in "Howl" and other poems, and already other young poets have begun to study Whitman's line. This could have vital consequences.

But it has remained for Malcolm Cowley, who has been trying to size up Whitman for years, to make the most interesting and perhaps fruitful re-evaluation of the present century. In 1955 he decided that the 1855 edition of *Leaves of Grass* contained some of the finest poetry written in America, and published in the *New Republic* a selection of twelve extracts to demonstrate his claim. Then in 1959 he republished the entire first edition with a long introduction of his own.[62] Here, he said, is Whitman at his best, but he has often been mis-

understood because these poems have been compared
with the wrong works of other authors:

I might suggest that the real nature of the poem ["Song
of Myself"] becomes clearer when it is considered in relation to quite another list of works, even though Whitman had probably read none of them in 1855. Most of
them he could not have read, because they were not yet
written, or not published, or not translated into English.
That other list might include the *Bhagavad-Gita*, the
Upanishads, Christopher Smart's long crazy inspired
poem *Jubilate Agno*, Blake's prophetic books (not for-
getting *The Marriage of Heaven and Hell*), Rimbaud's
Illuminations, *The Chants of Maldoror*, and Nietzsche's
Thus Spake Zarathustra, as well as *The Gospel of Sri
Ramakrishna* and a compendious handbook, *The Philosophy of India* by Heinrich Zimmer (New York, 1951). I
am offering what might seem to be a curious list of titles,
but its double purpose is easy to explain. "Song of Myself" should be judged, I think, as one of the great inspired (and sometimes insane) prophetic works that have
appeared at intervals in the Western World, like *Jubilate Agno* (which is written in a biblical style sometimes
suggesting Whitman's), like the *Illuminations*, like *Thus
Spake Zarathustra*. But the system of doctrine suggested
by the poem is more Eastern than Western, it includes
notions like metempsychosis and karma, and it might almost be one of those *Philosophies of India* that Zimmer
expounds at length.

"Song of Myself," continues Cowley, "is hardly at
all concerned with American nationalism, political
democracy, contemporary progress, or other social
themes that are commonly associated with Whitman's
works." The subject is mystical "illumination," and
the poem describes three separate moments of ecstasy.
Recently James E. Miller, Jr., analyzed "Song of My-

self" as "inverted mysticism,"[63] which was the right
approach, according to Cowley, but Miller arrived at
the wrong conclusions.

Many years ago a few poets and scholars in India, or
of India, began to recognize in *Leaves of Grass* close
parallels to the writings of the great Indian mystics,
and at present two young scholars, Dr. V. K. Chari,
and Dr. O. K. Nambiar, are systematically re-examin-
ing this whole question. The publication of their
studies could not only corroborate Malcolm Cowley but
also have a most useful and salutary influence toward
reorienting Whitman (no pun intended). This need
not be a return to the image the "hot little prophets"
held of Whitman as a "prophet" and might help prevent his being used as a propaganda symbol or slo-
gan for every sort of "ism." Furthermore, it would
emphasize Whitman's importance as a poet, and center
attention on and encourage scholars to search for the
meaning of his poems instead of his mysterious and
elusive illegitimate children.

The Sahitya Akedemi (National Academy of Letters) of India has undertaken the translation and publication of Whitman's poems in the fourteen major
languages of India and recently invited me to con-
tribute an introduction for use in these editions. In it[64]
I expressed the hope that Indian studies of Whitman
would not only bring about a better understanding
of Whitman and America in India, but might also do
the same for India in America. If Walt Whitman's
passage to India can become a two-way cultural journey, our poet will have achieved the transcendent
stature which he invisioned for "the poet" in his 1855
Preface.

While this survey was being written the *Walt Whitman Review* completed publication of its symposium,
"Whitman: 1960." In the June, 1960, issue the out-

standing critic and recent Whitman scholar, David Daiches, describes so well the change that has taken place in the modern image of this poet that I cannot do better than end my essay by quoting him:

It was not so long ago that it was generally maintained that if you liked Whitman you couldn't like Eliot, and admirers of Whitman were regarded by the most fashionable critics as simple-minded readers who mistook the flamboyant affirmations of democratic or patriotic sentiment for great poetry. The richness, complexity, and variety of Whitman's work have recently been excitingly explored with the result that, in the minds at least of those who have followed Whitman criticism of the last ten years or so, the idea of him as the over-excited Voice of America has been replaced by that of a haunting and challenging poet whose counterpoint of elegy and hope, of affirmation and doubt, of American expansiveness and American self-criticism, is far removed indeed from mere rhetorical gush.

What all this amounts to is that modern Whitman criticism has at last come to concern itself with Whitman's poetry rather than with the idea of Whitman as it came down in diluted form from the nineteenth century. . . .

Whitman therefore stands today not as a poet disposed of and "taped," but as a mystery and a challenge whose poems demand the same kind of sympathetic critical attention as those of Eliot or Yeats. . . . Recent Whitman criticism has shown us how much there is to be said about both the man and his work, and in revealing a Whitman more sympathetic to modern taste has also suggested how much more there is still left to reveal.

". . . how much more there is still left to reveal!" As I said in the preface to this book, each study that I have completed of Whitman or his poetry has called for another, and then another and another. The most important fact about Whitman today, in the sixth decade of the twentieth century, is that an increasing number of people all over the world are also finding Whitman unexhausted. *Leaves of Grass* is indeed a hardy perennial, adaptable to various climates and seasons, and at the present time it is sprouting in many parts of the world.

2

SOME LETTERS CONCERNING WHITMAN

THE OHIO WESLEYAN UNIVERSITY LIBRARY has a number of letters written by and to Edward Carpenter which throw considerable light on the "image of Whitman" held by several of his intimate friends and early biographers between 1877 and 1910, though they are mainly concerned with controversies that affected the poet's reputation in the early twentieth century. One of these letters (no. 4) has been quoted in part many times from the text printed by Carpenter in *Days with Walt Whitman,* p. 142 ff. And the core of no. 6 was printed by H. B. Binns in his *Life of Walt Whitman,* p. 349. Several of the others I have quoted in part myself in *The Solitary Singer.* These letters, therefore, are known in Whitman biography only in fragments and indirect sources. The custodians of the Ohio Wesleyan University Library permit scholars to use them, but I believe a complete text should be made available to the public, and Dr. J. H. Lancaster, Director of Slocum Library at Ohio Wesleyan, has generously permitted me to publish them.

I first read this inside exchange of views by Whitman's friends about ten years ago. At that time the letters were owned by Mr. Edward Naumburg, Jr., of New York City, who graciously permitted me to make copies. The late William Bayley bought them before I completed my biography, but he also kindly granted me the right to quote from them as freely as I wished.

Letter no. 3, from John Addington Symonds to J. W. Wallace, was in Mr. Naumburg's collection of Edward Carpenter correspondence when I used it, and I have a photostat which he had made for me. This letter was in the batch sold to Mr. Bayley, but Dr. Lancaster cannot find it in the Slocum Library. Apparently it was misplaced or lost before Mr. Bayley turned over his collection to Ohio Wesleyan.

Two letters in the Bayley collection I have not included because they contain no pertinent information or opinion. One is a friendly but inconsequential letter of Mrs. Anne Gilchrist to Edward Carpenter, dated November 24, 1879, after she had returned to England. She gossips about her family and her impressions of America, but says nothing of importance about Whitman, whom she had tried unsuccessfully to marry. The other is a letter to Carpenter from Leonard Abbott, written on editorial stationery of the *Literary Digest*, in which he merely states his surprise over having heard Traubel read the correspondence between Whitman and Symonds on "homogenic love."

1. *CARPENTER TO "BENJAMIN"*

Montgomery Hotel / Philadelphia. / 4. May 1877. My dear Benjamin,[1] I must write to tell you [illegible] —you know. And as I have just written a letter to my sister on the same subject I shall give you extracts from it.

I need not say that I think him the most profound & wonderful thing that I have met, but I was surprised to

find (although I *had* expected it in part) *how* genial,
accessible, considerate & courteous (if you can use
such a word of a Colossus) he is. 431. Stevens Street
Camden[2] is a very well to do brick house in a long quiet
street planted with trees. Going there on Sunday afternoon last (it is only across the Delaware River from
Philadelphia.) they told me in the most nonchalant way
that he had gone away for a week or so, they didn't
know where—or when he would be back! Fancy my
disgust. However I managed to see the Sister in law,
Mrs. Whitman, a common comfortable little body
who gave me hope: and sure enough when I called
again on Tuesday morning he was there. A cry of
'Walt!' went through the house on my arrival—and in
a few moments the cleanest whitest old man (for he
looks more than 58)—long snow white hair & beard—
came slowly down stairs. We met at the bottom of the
staircase. He held my hand for a long time, looking
with clear blue eyes into mine—and then said in an unmistakably American voice 'I was afraid we would miss
each other after all.' Then he sat down & asked me
about myself, and chatted about the European war in
a way which put me at my ease at once. The thing
which strikes one about his face is the great interval between his eyes and eyebrows. That 'space in which
the soul seems to move' is very large. The eyebrows
very much arched so as to make the bridge of the nose
very long—the nose itself straight & well-propor-
tioned. The mouth & chin are covered with a fall of
white hair, but the forehead is clear & high. As to his
eyes of course it is impossible to put them into words—
the impression they produce on me is of an immense,
immense, background: Yet it is very characteristic of
them that the pupils are small & distinct, the likeness
to Christ is quite marked. I suppose it comes in the
high eyebrows. I send you a sketch[3] (!) which will give

you an idea of the proportions of the face. Put into it the extravagant prophetic look of genius, intense perceptive power, and as much sentiment as you like, and you have something like.

He was kindness itself—as he is to everybody—went out with me and fixed me up in the present hotel, wh. is cheaper & pleasanter than the other I was at, put my name down at a reading room, & gave me an introduction to the Gilchrists,[4] some excellent English people of whom more anon. Walking through the streets with him—he leaning on my arm, for one foot is still semiparalysed—it was a sight (a sight for which I know you will bless him) to see the working people come around. The 'bus drivers, the ferryboat men, jacks of all trades, *stopped* his way with greetings. One man jumped down off a dray cart. He had been a driver on Broadway, New York, 'hadn't seen 'Walt' for 3 or 4 years': tears stood in his the driver's eyes as he stood & held his hand & gazed hard in his face. One can see how it is that he has this wonderful personal influence. If he hears 'George' is ill, he must go 'right away' & see him, if anyone is in trouble he lends a patient ear for any time: he is full of kindness, yet he unites this tenderness with the most wonderful strength & persistency & self[less]ness of character that I ever saw in any one. That union of the two is what I can't get over—it alternately fascinates and awes one.

I haven't had any long conversation with him yet, for though I met him again the next day at the Gilchrists, and went a long way home with him afterwards, yet there was no opportunity for sustained & continued talk. But indeed I have felt content just to be with him without *bothering* about conversation. However I do want to tell him about friends in England, and hope I shall have an opportunity for that.

Well, I must tell you more & about myself another
time. I am *charmed* with the American people (I mean
the working folk, for the commercials are sordid) &
with their customs (except the spitting), and with the
build & plan of their towns, and with the climate. The
whole thing is a magnificent sketch, a sketch on the
grandest scale of what is to come, and I do not
doubt that in course of time it will be filled in.

If you write, it had better be shortly after receipt of
this to Post Office, New York, but do not *trouble* to. I
shall enjoy telling you about it all some time—and of
course you will have to go yourself and see.

Many greetings to Job and the genius.[5]

Ever yours, E. C.

2. *CARPENTER TO "BENJAMIN"*

1929 North 22nd St. / Philadelphia, /
20 June 1877.

Dear Benjamin, I write from the abode of the gods. I
wrote you at the beginning of my tour from this place,
but Olympus seemed too high to scale then, and I went
away sad (though happy *inside* as a Ford would say!)
I went to Niagara and sat by it, gaining strength
from its splendour, for four days, then I went down
the Hudson and on to Boston, and visited Emerson,
Holmes and the rest, and now at the last I have come
back here. And he seems to tower higher & more
splendid than ever. And he has taken me to himself.

This is the house of Mrs. Gilchrist an English lady,
widow, with two daughters and a son. She, do you
remember the name? wrote an article in the Radical
Review[6] a long time ago on Whitman. She is *first rate*.
And he has a room in the house, permanently his own,
and where he spends a good part of his days. He is stay-

ing here now, and so am I. Domestic life with him is fulfilment. He seems to bring with him an atmosphere of perfect rest and union: and to fill out the moments as they should be filled out into something great. Full of fun & laughter, his conversation half the time is on the simplest things in the world. Yesterday we all sat round the table looking at my photographs. He specially admired you three, and looked at them long. I think he remembered the name, at any rate when I told him what admirers you were he *was* pleased. I told him how much interested you were in American politics and in the future of the country; and he said warmly that hardly anything pleased him more than to find that his writings drew people to America. I picked out all the photographs in my collection of people that read his books—about 10 altogether and he looked at them carefully. He seemed much struck with my youngest sister's face among them. Then we played a game of which he is fond—called the game of 20 questions. But the best time is in the evening when we set a chair for him in the porch, and the rest of us sit round and on the steps—he generally holding some one by the hand and looking like a great god in the twilight or moonlight—with his full white hair & beard & florid face & lionlike head.—Whatever the conversation is, it is all the same. There is no effort, no constraint. Listening to others or talking himself he makes each moment *sane* and healthy. His reading is vast & varied. Though I expected that to some extent I did not realize the extent. Yet you might live with him for days and never discover that he knew anything but what Nature had taught him.

Conventionality is dead & buried in this house. He generally appears in this sultry weather with just a perfectly clean white shirt on—open at the front and showing his chest beneath his beard—that and grey trousers complete his costume: and we others dress & behave with a like ease.

Though he has such a range of interests & subjects, and seems to look out like a mountain over the world, yet I almost think his greatest delight is in doing the smallest little acts of kindness.

He never seems to go out without giving an orange or something to some child, or getting to talk to some working man & cheering him up with his strong ringing voice: and almost every afternoon since I have been here he has gone on quite a long journey to the other end of the town to see a rather common & vulgar sister in law who is unwell.

You must know these Gilchrists when they return to England—which may be in a year or two.[7] The son is an artist and the eldest daughter (she is about twenty two) is studying medicine for a profession.

Well, I won't write more now. I leave for England in 4 days. Perhaps I may add a portrait before I go. Love to your sisters.

Ever yrs Caleb.[8]

W. W. has *bagged* the photos of you three! He has written his name on one of his own in return—which I send. You will have to send *me* another set to replace these. Do so with a letter to Brighton, as soon as you get this.

3. *SYMONDS TO WALLACE*

Am Hof / Davos Platz / Switzerland / Dec. 19, 1892.

I returned a short time since from my long absence in England & Italy. Here I found the note-books of your American journey,[9] which are full of a deep and pathetic interest. I am reading them with care, & will return them duly registered.

I had nearly finished writing a "Study of Walt

Whitman,"[10] the thinker & poet, not the man. It is an attempt to show the relations of Religion, Science, Personality, Sex, Comradeship, Democracy, Literature in his writings. I think I sh[a]ll have to publish it separately as a little book.

I am still perplexed about the real drift of "Calamus." Whitman wrote me a very emphatic letter, repudiating the idea that under any circumstances the passionate attachment between friend & friend could fall into physical relations. Yet there are certainly a large number of men born with "homosexual" tendencies, who could not fail, while reading "Calamus," to think their own emotions justified by Whitman.

The subject is one of considerable interest & importance for students of W. W. I have lately been obliged to study the most recent French, German & Italian research into the phenomenon, in course of writing my new life of Michelangelo,[11] who was certainly born with innate sexual inversion. I had not any idea what a large part this anomaly plays in modern life.

By the way, I noticed in some newspaper that a prosecution was going on at Bolton under what is called "[illegible][12] Clause." Do you think that you or Dr. Johnston[13] could give me any exact information regarding it? Whatever view the physiologists may take of homosexual passion, every citizen of a free country must feel that [illegible] Clause is a disgrace to legislation, because of its vague terminology & plain incitement to false accusations.

This of course is not a matter of great moment. Still, if you can send me a report, you would oblige me.

Pray give my kindest regards to Dr. Johnston, & believe me very sincerely yours,

                              John Addington Symonds

If you have any advice to give me regarding the publication of my "Study of W. Whitman," or any suggestions to make about "Calamus," I should be grateful for them.

P. S. Since writing the enclosed, I spent the whole morning reading through your notes, & now I want to tell you what a profound & genial impression they have made on me. I seem to feel the whole of the Camden Circle quite as old friends, & to have gained a vivid presentment of them to the inner eye. But what is even more, I am immersed in a definite atmosphere of friendliness, essential kindness, fine brotherly benevolence. Of course some of Whitman's own spoken words are very frequent, & throw to a certain extent fresh light upon his works. I have been so free as to jot down a few phrases; & these, if you give permission, might, I think, be used with profit to authorize the views I have taken in my "Study of W. W." on certain points. But I will most assuredly not do so without sanction from yourself.

It seems to me that you & other friends, to whom I feel linked in bonds of sympathy through W. W., must regard me as cold, inexpressive, apathetic, about him to some extent—& also about the kindness you have shown me.

But you must remember in what a huge mass of study and literature this matter of Whitman is for me of necessity embedded. Also I am alone, quite alone here, in all that concerns him. I have as yet nowhere found men of my own pursuits & condition who sympathize with me upon this point—I mean found them through personal society & contact.

So make excuses for me, & believe that my belief in Whitman is very permanent & real, if possibly less enthusiastic & exclusive than some of his younger disciples might desire.

4. *SYMONDS TO CARPENTER*

Am Hof / Davos Platz / Dec. 29, 1892.

[Only the last part of this long letter concerns Whitman, and consequently the main body is omitted here. In it Symonds discusses his plans to collaborate with Havelock Ellis on a book devoted to homosexuality. He is particularly interested in homosexual love in ancient Greece, which he thinks might be revived as "a new chivalry," advantageous to society.]

Whitman, in Calamus, seemed to strike the key note. And though he repudiated (in a very notable letter to myself) the deductions which are logically to be drawn from Calamus, his work will remain as infinitely helpful.

South Sea Idyls, C. W. Stoddard, Boston, James N. Osgood, 1873. I got mine from Sampson Low, I think, through Nutt 270 Strand. If you cannot get a copy, let me hear, & I will send you mine. It was suppressed once in America.

Now, dear friend, farewell. I put "Private" on this letter, quie habent sua fata epistlae.

Yours in affection J. A. S.

5. *SYMONDS TO CARPENTER*

Am Hof / Davos Platz / Switzerland / Jan. 21, 1893.

My dear Carpenter

Thank you for yours of the 17th. What you say about H. Ellis in conversation is just what R. Noel[14] told me.

In correspondence I find him frank, eager, open-minded, scientifically conscientious; the sort of man, I think, to lead our joint enquiry.

When you make notes on that matter for me, will you send them to me? Of course H. E. will see the

bulk of them. But you might feel it more appropriate
to let me have things etc. you would not care to submit
to him. This is only a suggestion, arising from my desire to lose nothing you may have to say. I will copy
out for you Whitman's very singular letter to me about
Calamus, when I have time. I feel sure he would not
have written it, when he first published Calamus. I
think he was afraid of being used to lend his influence
to "sods." Did not quite trust me perhaps. In his
Symposium Speeches[15] he called me "terribly suspicious," you may remember.

I will send my Greek Study to Holmesfield.

The blending of social strata in masculine love seems
to me one of its most pronounced, & socially hopeful,
features. Where it appears, it abolishes class distinc-
tions, & opens by a single operation the cataract-
blinded eye to their futilities. In removing the film of
prejudice & education, it acts like the occulist's knife.
If it could be acknowledged & extended, it would do
very much to further the advent of the right sort of
Socialism.

I find a great deal of the emotion, in a wholly manly
& admirable form, abroad among the people here. It
does not interfere with marriage, when that is sought as
a domestic institution, as it always is among men who
want children for helpers in their work & women to
keep their households.

We have a most awful snow-storm raging here, after
2 months of cold sunny weather. I think pensively with
a troubled heart of many friends, carters, postillions,
conductors of diligences, abroad upon our passes—the
highest in Europe, averaging (five of them) 7000 feet
above the sea.

Goodnight. I respond to your greetings of affection,
& return them with my heart

                                        J A Symonds

6. *SYMONDS TO CARPENTER*

Davos, Feb: 13 1893

Dear Carpenter

I wrote in the Summer of 1890 to Whitman, asking him what his real feeling about masculine love was, & saying that I knew people in England who had a strong sexual bias in such passions, felt themselves supported & encouraged by Calamus. Unluckily I have not got a copy of my letter.

He replied (Aug: 19. / 90)

"About the questions on Calamus, etc: they quite daze me. LofG is only to be rightly construed by & within its own atmosphere & essential character—all of its pages & pieces so coming strictly under—: that the Calamus part has even allowed the possibility of such construction as mentioned is terrible—I am fain to hope the pp themselves are not to be even mentioned for such gratuitous & quite at the time undreamed & unintended possibility of morbid inferences—wh. are disavowed by me & seem damnable."

That is all that is to the point. He rambles on about his being less "restrained" by temperament & theory than I (J. A. S.) am.—"I at certain moments let the spirit impulse (female) rage its utmost wildest damnedest (I feel to do so some times in L. of G. & I do so)."

That last passage seems meant to qualify the first. But if it does so, it implies that these inferences are not so gratuitous morbid & damnable as supposed.

At the end of the letter (wh. is a long one) he resumes:

"My life, young manhood, mid-age, times South, etc. have been jolly bodily, and doubtless open to criticism. Though unmarried I have had six children—two

are dead—one living Southern grandchild—fine boy
writes to me occasionally—circumstances (connected
with their benefit & fortune) have separated me from
intimate relations."

It struck me when I first read this p. s. that W. W.
wanted to obviate "damnable inferences" about himself
by asserting his paternity.

Section X of my Modern Problems[16] treats of Calamus you will find.

My "Study of W. W." is now in the hands of J. C.
Neins. I am sure he will make a pretty book out of it,
but I doubt a cheap one. I fear the blind idolaters of
W. W. will not wholly like it.

Yours affectionately
J. A. S.

"Civilization"[17] came last night. Have not had time to
do more yet than look at p. 105—which is finely and
delicately touched.

7. TRAUBEL TO CARPENTER

Phila / Dec. 27, 1901.

Dear Carpenter—

Your paper was forwarded me after some delay.

Walt frequently in his later years made allusions to
the fact of his fatherhood, that is, to me. One night,
just previous to his death, I went with Harned to
Walt's room, at Walt's request, to get a sort of deposi-
tion in the matter—its details &c, &c. Walt always regarded Harned[18] as in a sense his attorney. He wished
to set down this affair in an unquestionable record &
proposed signing the paper we drew up. But he was
taken sick in our presence & was unable to proceed.
There the thing rested. For from that day on he grew
proportionately weaker & could never resume the sub-

ject. He wanted to have this recital "put away in Harned's safe," as he said, "in order that some one should authoritatively have all the facts at command if by some misfortune a public discussion of the incident were ever provoked." He cautioned me at the time —as he had always cautioned me on prior occasions— on no account whatever to be a party to the revelations. "Better to be forever hushed," he averred: "It involves bad feeling, passion, families, even a fortune," & so on: "and it would in at least one place create great unhappiness."

These things have come back to me as I read your paper. What do they suggest to you, dear Carpenter?

I will write you again.

Beautiful man, I love you!

Traubel.

8. *TRAUBEL TO CARPENTER*

Phila / Feb. 28, 1903.

Dear Carpenter—

I cannot discuss Bucke's[19] death. It comes too near. And yet I wish in the March number of the Conservator[20] to pay my respects to him. I am writing a few of his friends to send me such spontaneous tributes as the event may seem to suggest. Do you not feel like adding your own word to these printed pages? Words do nothing—and yet the word may live.

I send you back the Whitman Ms, dear Carpenter, because I could not print it without being involved with the interviewer. I remember my promise to Walt & must adhere to it. He did not wish the matter broached. He felt that it would indisputably do a great injury to some one—God knows who (I do not).—During Walt's last sickness his grandson came to the house.[21] I was not there at the time. When Walt mentioned the occurrence to me I expressed my regrets that I had missed him. "I wish I might see him." "God forbid." I think, dear Carpenter, that you thoroughly understand my position.

I go round the streets and to my work & try to write always with Bucke's dear face before me.

Lovingly—
Traubel.

9. *ELDRIDGE TO CARPENTER*

Washington D. C. June 24, 1902.

Dear Sir:

I have noted the article by you copied from the London (Eng) Reformer about Walt Whitman's *six* children.—I was Walt Whitman's publisher in Boston in 1860,[22] and in *Washington* from 1863 to 1873 was probably more intimate with him than any person now living.—You refer to Walt's letter to Symonds, (dated Aug 10, 1890) as your authority. I have no doubt of the authenticity of your reference, but I want to say that no such thing can possibly be *true*.—Walt was a serious invalid for over twenty years of his life, and for the last two or three years must have been subject to *delusions*. Harned and Traubel say that he never gave them any satisfaction as to when, where, or by whom he had these *six children*, or whether any of them survived.—For the last two or three years he was a *very sick man* and this was only one of the evidences that his mind had weakened.—You say in your letter that of Walt's life previous to arriving in Washington "only the barest outline is known."[23] This is a mistake.— Walt was a well known citizen of New York and Brooklyn for more than 20 years before. He edited newspapers in both cities—was a printer & reporter in New York and a builder in Brooklyn. The material for a

minute biography of his whole life at this period is ample. He was known to thousands, many of them now living.—At one time he was a Tammany orator, or stump-
speaker during a campaign.[24]—I have talked with
many persons who knew him well at that time.—I
wished to give you this view of an old and intimate
friend so you may know how the story is regarded by
some of us.

Very truly yours, Charles W. Eldridge
Address Treasury Department / Washington, D. C.

To Mr. Edward Carpenter / Holmesfield / Near Shef-
field / England.

10. *BINNS TO CARPENTER*

3 Cavendish Musus / 28 Sept. 1904.
My dear Carpenter,

Many thanks for your Snowden card. I found some
curious entries in a diary of Walt's (which Traubel
has not even read!! though it is in his possession) for
1876–1886.[25]

Nov. 25–28, 1876.   At White Horse
(Timber Creek) "Memorable talk with H. S. settles
the matter [?] for life." This I think was partly
erased, but legible. H. S. might or might *not* be Harry
Stafford.
Dec. 19 Evening sitting in room [?Camden] had serious inward revelation and conviction about H's course
in the matter. Saw clearly what it really meant. Very
profound meditation on all—more happy and satisfied
at last about it—singularly so. . . .
Apl 29, 1877—Scene with H. in the front room.
July 20, 1877—Scene "in the room at White Horse
'Goodbye.' "

Now these, it seems to me, *may* refer to the closing up of some relationship which had previously existed with some woman.

H alone might refer to the troublesome brother-in-law—Heyde—but that he is generally referred to by his initials. Do you know anything which would lead you to suppose that Harry Stafford could be referred to in these entries?—He could only have been a lad, I suppose, at the time.[26] I hoped to meet him—but was pressed for time—would have spent a whole day doing it—& was vigorously dissuaded by Traubel.

I have a mind to write and ask him for reminiscences. The Staffords were eager for news of Gilchrist—if you think of it next time you are sending me a word will you tell me how he is going on.

There is a note in the Diary of your being at Timber Creek & Mrs. Gilchrist's in May 1877—& June and a note in Sept. "Meetings with Ed. C by the pond moonlight nights." Were you still there? or is this a reference to someone else. It doesn't matter much to me: but I was interested.

Harned has a brief illiterate note written at Washington by someone who had called & missed W. W. It is dated Apl 1 1864 & is by W. E. Vandermack "to his father Walt Whitman." (sic)—I presume it is a "manner of speech."[27]

Traubel (& Harned, I think) told me Walt had five children [one may have died][28] by two Southern ladies both of high family. E. H. Griggs[29] reminded me that a Southern woman's unblemished character was the boast & most sacred asset of the South.

Walt used to feel the separation from his children as most tragic—according to Traubel, & built his huge tomb to accommodate them—but found it impossible to have them.

Traubel showed me a love letter from Ellen Eyre[30]

(? of New York) in 1862—& J. H. Johnston a photo of a young N. Y. actress who had been "one of Walt's sweethearts." Maynard[31] says that Doyle admitted he knew of a woman in Washington with whom W. had sex relations.[32] This is all I could gather on our subject.

I found great hostility to J. A. Symonds' Calamus suggestions: Maynard says that American school life is quite different in this respect from English. Evidently the Whitman set were *astonished* at the suggestions! And I gather that old Walt was, too.

I am very deep in the book.[33] My greetings to your George.

Affectionately H. B. B.

I am to have photo-illustrations of Walt's friends: may I have one of you, please: I have a delightful one of Anne Gilchrist who (they tell me) was very much in love with Walt—& Harned (?) adds offered to marry him. Harned doesn't want the family to know, though! Bother these discreet silences—I know one must tread warily.

11. *CALDER TO CARPENTER*

306 Hope Street / Providence, R. I. /
[Nov. 15, 1909]

To Edward Carpenter
Author of "Days with Walt Whitman":
Ever since I first read your "Days with Walt Whitman" in 1906, it has been in my mind to write you and say that of all the many books and papers concerning Walt Whitman not one has touched me as yours has done. Not one has seemed to me to comprehend the man as you have comprehended him.

In those short visits, it is marvelous to me that you have taken in the sweetness and sadness and lovableness and beauty of his character, as well as what you rightly call, on page 47, his "cussedness."

It was my great privilege to know him intimately from the time he came to Washington in the latter part of 1862, for many months, and for some time he was the guest of Mr. O'Connor and myself, as I have told in my Atlantic Monthly article of June, 1907.

As he himself has implied, which you quote on page 37, he had a personal love for O'Connor, but for all that, they disagreed violently in regard to giving the ballot to the Negro, Whitman opposing the idea.[34]

As you will conclude,—at the time above referred to I was the wife of the late William D. O'Connor.

Sincerely yours,

Ellen M. Calder

12. *CALDER TO CARPENTER*

306 Hope Street / Providence, R. I. /
Jan. 11, 1910.

Dear Mr. Carpenter,

Your letter of Dec. 29 has just come, and I will write you at once. It is because there were so many sides to the character of our dear Walt that I was so much impressed by your penetration. I was indeed very fond of Walt, and both myself and Mr. O'Connor knew him well. Mr. Horace Traubel was almost incredulous when he asked me if I knew of the children, and I assured him that I knew nothing of the matter, —then he said that he was sure that Walt told William,—and I was equally sure that Walt never did,— he was not that kind of a man, and we were not the sort of people that would have helped him to unburden his heart, if he had had the disposition to do so.

You ask if I have any views about the question of Whitman's children. Yes, views, theories, but no *knowledge*. You remember what he says of his trip to New Orleans, and his stop there, and all of it. My belief is that some probably light colored woman loved him, and perhaps followed him north, and no doubt there was a child born, but with you, I doubt if there was more than *one*. To me the idea that Mr. Binns[35] has elaborated is all *bosh*, if you will excuse the word. He never seduced a woman and he never was a guest in any such family as is pictured.

Horace Traubel says that Walt loved William O'Connor more than he loved any living man,—I think so, too, and Mr. O'Connor was all that you say of him, —and a most lovable and gifted man.

Will you tell me where I can get any of your books, the one on "Evolution" I want, and no doubt others.

Ever most cordially, with best wishes,

Yours truly
Ellen H. Calder

13. *CALDER TO CARPENTER*

306 Hope Street / Providence, R. I. / June 3rd, 1910.

Dear Mr. Carpenter:

I have no excuse to make for not answering your most kind letter of last February. I think it was sheer procrastination, perhaps induced by not being quite well.

I am sending you in this an article from the "Boston Globe" of last Sunday, and I see that the printer has called you out of your name, Edmund, and not Edward. Shall we forgive him!

As for any information that Traubel has about Walt's children, it is *nil*. I know all that he knows, for he has told me all, but some time the facts may be known, and then shall all wonder that we ever wondered!

Thanks for the copy of your list of books. It is "The Art of Creation" that I meant, and I shall be very glad to have it.

Yours cordially,

Ellen H. Calder

14. *CALDER TO CARPENTER*

306 Hope Street / Providence, R. I. / July 5, 1910. Dear Mr. Carpenter,

The book, "The Art of Creation" reached me safely, and I am reading it. It will take more than one careful reading to make it mine, surely.

Thank you very much for it, and for the pamphlet that you sent with it. I should like two more copies of that, for friends, who will be very glad of it. I also want a copy of "Edward Carpenter: The Man and His Message."

I will send the money for all later. I am not at home just now, but shall be, and will send soon, I trust.

I enclose a thought about Walt Whitman in regard to the children question. It may be worth nothing.

Yours cordially,

Ellen M. Calder

It has occurred to me that though my opinion is no better than that of anyone in regard to Walt Whitman, who loved him very much and knew him,—I feel that it may be in some measure correct. You remember in your "Days with Walt Whitman" on page 56 you quote a poem from the 1860 edition of Leaves of Grass, omitted later. That to me is a key to much, very much of his life. Change the pronoun for the feminine, and remember what he tells of his early life in New Or-

leans, and what he told *us*,—William and me,—and
it gives a clue to much. The love for him of the girl
who clung to him, his leaving—the long sorrow,—he
could not marry her,—he could not for many reasons,
and the long regret, all go with *his* nature to make up
the story. To me it seems almost plain.

I do not think that Traubel has any information "up
his sleeve" or anywhere. He has some notes out of which
he is trying to make something, but to me things are
plain.

II

A CHECK LIST OF WHITMAN PUBLICATIONS 1945-1960

The Check List is unselective and comprehensive, but it cannot be called exhaustive. Some items in newspapers and ephemeral publications were too trivial to include. Probably others have been overlooked or were not listed in bibliographical guides available in this country. Most of the books listed have been examined, and many of the articles in periodicals, but a few—mainly foreign titles—had to be taken from other bibliographies. If the number of pages has not been given for a book, or the inclusive pages in a periodical, the information was obtained in this way.

Alegría, Fernando. *Walt Whitman en Hispanoamerica.* Mexico City: Collecion Studium, 1954, pp. 411–19.

Allen, Gay Wilson (ed.). *Walt Whitman Abroad.* Syracuse, N. Y.: Syracuse University Press, 1955, pp. 266–81.

————. *Walt Whitman Handbook.* Chicago: Packard and Co., 1946; New York: Hendricks House, 1957; pp. 95–103, 227–35, 316–24, 372–74, 437–41, 538–45.

American Library, London. *Walt Whitman Catalogue of an Exhibition of Manuscripts, Letters and Books* . . . London: U. S. Information Service, 1954, 32 pp.

Asselineau, Roger. *L'Évolution de Walt Whitman après la Première Edition des Feuilles d'Herbe.* Paris: Didier, 1954, pp. 529–44.

Blodgett, Harold W. "Bibliographical Description as a Key to Whitman," *Walt Whitman Newsletter,* II (March–June, 1956), 8–9.

Bolton Reference Library. *A Catalogue of Works by and Relating to Walt Whitman* . . . Compiled by Harold Hamer. Bolton, England: Libraries Committee, 1955. 52 pp.

Bowen, Dorothy, and Durham, Phillip. "Walt Whitman Materials in the Huntington Library," *Huntington Library Quarterly,* XIX (1955), 81–96.

Boyce, George K. "Modern Literary Manuscripts in the Morgan Library," *PMLA,* CXVIII (1952), 31.

Brown, Glenora W., and Brown, Deming B. *A Guide to Soviet Russian Translations of American Literature.*

New York: King's Crown Press (Columbia University). 1954, p. 243.

Detroit Public Library. *An Exhibition of the Works of Walt Whitman* . . . Detroit, 1945. 48 pp.

———. *Walt Whitman, a Selection of the Manuscripts, Books and Association Items Gathered by Charles E. Feinberg* . . . Detroit, 1955. 128 pp.

Duke University Library. *Walt Whitman, a Checklist of an Exhibition of Manuscripts and Books from the Trent Collection* . . . Durham, 1955. 8 pp.

Eby, Edwin Harold. *A Concordance of Walt Whitman's "Leaves of Grass" and Selected Prose Writings*. Seattle: University of Washington Press, 1949–55. 964 pp.

Englekirk, John E. *A Literatura Norteamericana no Brasil*. Mexico City, 1950, pp. 132–35.

Frey, Ellen Frances. *Catalogue of the Whitman Collection in the Duke University Library* . . . *Trent Collection* . . . Durham: Duke University Library, 1945. 148 pp.

Leary, Lewis. *Articles on American Literature Appearing in Current Periodicals, 1920–1945*. Durham: Duke University Press, 1947, pp. 169–80.

———. *Articles on American Literature, 1900–1950*. Durham: Duke University Press, 1954. pp. 303–16.

Library of Congress. *Ten Notebooks and a Cardboard Butterfly Missing from the Walt Whitman Manuscripts in The Library of Congress*. Washington, D. C.: Government Printing Office, 1954. 38 pp.

———. *Walt Whitman, a Catalog Based Upon the Collections of The Library of Congress With Notes*. Washington, D. C.: Government Printing Office, 1955. 147 pp.

Miller, Edwin H. and Rosalind S. *Walt Whitman's Correspondence, a Checklist*. New York: New York Public Library, 1957. 161 pp.

New York Public Library. *Walt Whitman: The Oscar*

Lion Collection. New York: New York Public Library, 1953. 78 pp. (See also *New York Public Library Bulletin,* LVIII—1954—213–29, 305–8, 348–54, 397–410, 455–61, 497–514.)

Parke-Bernet Galleries. *Sporting Books in Color . . . Whitman and Other Manuscripts and Autographs . . . Public Auction Sale . . .* New York: Parke-Bernet Galleries, 1953. 93 pp.

Rumanian Institute for Cultural Relations with Foreign Countries. *Expozitia Walt Whitman, Bucresti, Noiembrie 1956.* Bucharest, 1956, 55 pp.

Spiller, R. E., Thorp, Willard, Johnson, T. H., and Canby, H. S. *Literary History of the United States.* New York: Macmillan, 1948, III, 759–68; Supplement, ed. Richard M. Ludwig, 1959, pp. 203–7.

Stark, Lewis M., and Gordan, John D. *Walt Whitman's Leaves of Grass: A Centenary Exhibition from the Lion Whitman Collection and the Berg Collection of the New York Public Library.* New York: New York Public Library, 1955. 46 pp.

Thorp, Willard. "Whitman" in *Eight American Authors: A Review of Research and Criticism,* ed. Floyd Stovall. New York: The Modern Language Association of America, 1956, pp. 271–318.

Tulsa Bibliophiles. *List of Whitman Items . . .* Tulsa, Oklahoma, 1949. 46 pp.

Walt Whitman Exhibition in Tokyo [title in Japanese], *July 21–30, 1953* [date in English and Japanese]. Tokyo: Whitman Exhibition Committee. 1953. 56 pp. (Lists 147 translations and biographies in Japanese.)

White, William. "Walt Whitman's Short Stories: Some Comments and a Bibliography," *Papers of the Bibliographical Society of America,* LII (1958), 300–306.

————. "Whitman: A Current Bibliography," *Walt Whitman Newsletter,* II (1956), 14, 29, 54; III (1957), 13–14, 33, 51, 66; IV (1958), 81–82, 97–98,

98–99 [113–114]; *Walt Whitman Review*, V (1959), 18, 37–38, 57–58, 77–78; VI (1960), 17–18, 37–38, 56–58.

"The Whitman Collection," *University of Pennsylvania Library Chronicle*, XIV (1947), 24–31.

EDITIONS AND SELECTIONS

BY YEAR OF PUBLICATION

Leaves of Grass. With a Preface by Bernard Smith. New York: Knopf, 1945. 549 pp.

A Wartime Whitman. Selections arranged with a foreword by William A. Aiken. New York: Editions for the Armed Services [1945]. 96 pp.

I Hear the People Singing: Selected Poems. Introduction by Langston Hughes; illustrated by Alexander Dobkin. New York: International Publishers [1946]. 96 pp.

Leaves of Grass. With an Introduction and Notes by Emory Holloway. London: Dent (Everyman's Library), 1947. 468 pp.

Complete Poetry and Prose of Walt Whitman. With an Introduction, "Walt Whitman, the Poet and the Mask," by Malcolm Cowley. New York: Pellegrini & Cudahy, 1948. 2 vols.

Democratic Vistas. Introduction and notes by K. Ishbash. Osaka: Kyoiku Tosho, 1948. 142 pp. (Text in English).

Walt Whitman [Poetry and Prose]. Selected and with notes and Introduction by Mark Van Doren. New York: Viking (Viking Portable Library), 1948. 698 pp.

Democratic Vistas. Introduction by John Valente. New York: Liberal Arts Press, 1949. 69 pp.

A Gathering [poetry of Whitman]. Mount Vernon, N. Y.: Peter Pauper Press, 1949. 173 pp.

Leaves of Grass and Selected Prose. Edited with an Intro-

duction by Sculley Bradley. New York: Rinehart
(Rinehart Editions), 1949. 568 pp.

Poetry and Prose. With a biographical introduction and
a basic selection of early and recent critical commentary, edited by Louis Untermeyer. New York: Simon &
Schuster, 1949. 1224 pp.

*Wound Dresser: Letters Written to His Mother from
the Hospitals in Washington during the Civil War.*
Edited by Richard M. Bucke, with an Introduction by
Oscar Cargill. New York: Bodley Press, 1949. 200 pp.

Leaves of Grass. With fifteen two-color wood-engravings
by Boyd Hanna. Mount Vernon, N. Y.: Peter Pauper
Press, 1950. 400 pp.

Leaves of Grass. With an Introduction by Oscar Cargill.
New York: Harper, 1950. 537 pp.

Leaves of Grass. Edited with an Introduction by John
Kouwenhoven. New York: Random House (Modern
Library), 1950. 769 pp.

Selected Poems. Edited by Stephen Spender. London:
Grey Walls Press, 1950. 64 pp.

Walt Whitman: His Prose & Poems. Selected and edited,
with notes, by Arata Mitsuoka. Tokyo: Ono Shobo
[1950]. 88 pp. (Text in English, notes in Japanese.)

The Best of Walt Whitman. Edited with an Introduction
by Harold Blodgett. New York: Ronald Press, 1953.
478 pp.

Leaves of Grass. With an Introduction by Sculley Bradley. New York: New American Library (Mentor
Books), 1954. 430 pp.

Leaves of Grass. Edited by Emory Holloway. Garden
City: Doubleday, 1954. 682 pp. (Reprint.)

"One Wicked Impulse" [short story], *Ellery Queen's
Mystery Magazine*, XXIII (January 1954), 92–100.

*Poet of American Democracy, Selections from Poetry and
Prose.* Edited with an Introduction by Samuel Sillen.
New York: International Publishers, 1955. 174 pp.

To a Foil'd European Revolutionnaire. Berkeley Heights, N. J.: Oriole Press, 1955. 10 pp.

Walt Whitman's Poems, Selections with Critical Aids. Edited by Gay Wilson Allen and Charles T. Davis. New York: New York University Press, 1955. 280 pp. Grove Press (Evergreen Book), 1959.

The Whitman Reader. Edited with an Introduction by Maxwell Geismar. New York: Pocket Books, 1955. 507 pp.

Eighteenth Presidency: A Critical Text. Edited by Edward F. Grier. Lawrence: University of Kansas Press, 1956. 47 pp.

Fragments from Walt Whitman; Being a Rearrangement of the Great Passages of Leaves of Grass . . . Edited by John L. Davenport. New York: Privately printed by Kurt H. Volk, 1956. 91 pp.

Poems [of Walt Whitman]. Selected with Introduction and notes by T. Funahashi. Tokyo: Kenkyusha (Kenkyusha Pocket English Series). [1956?] (Text in English, notes in Japanese.)

Poems: Song of Myself, By Blue Ontario's Shore. Introduction and annotations by William L. Moore. Tokyo: Kenkyusha, 1957. 115 pp.

Over the Carnage Rose Prophetic a Voice: The American Civil War in Prose and Verse. Edited with an Introduction by Oakleigh Ross Bush. Bussum, Netherlands: Paul Brand Ltd., 1957. 164 pp.

Leaves of Grass. With an Introduction by Gay Wilson Allen. New York: New American Library (Mentor Books), 1958. 430 pp. (Reprinted, Signet Books, 1960.)

Poetry and Prose. With an Introduction and notes by Abe Capek. Berlin: Seven Seas Books [1958]. 552 pp.

Leaves of Grass: The First (1855) Edition. Edited with an Introduction by Malcolm Cowley. New York: Viking, 1959. 145 pp.

Complete Poetry and Selected Prose. Edited with an Introduction and Glossary by James E. Miller, Jr. Boston: Houghton Mifflin (Riverside Editions), 1959. 516 pp.

Selections from Leaves of Grass. With an Introduction and notes by Leslie A. Fiedler. New York: Dell (Laurel Poetry Series), 1959. 192 pp.

Walt Whitman's Drum-Taps (1865) and Sequel to Drum-Taps (1865–66). Edited with an Introduction by F. DeWolfe Miller. Gainesville, Florida: Scholars Facsimiles and Reprints, 1959. 158 pp.

Walt Whitman's Civil War. Edited by Walter Lowenfels, assisted by Nan Braymer. New York: Knopf, 1960. 362 pp.

Leaves of Grass [reprint of 1855 edition]. Garden City: Doubleday (Dolphin Ser.) [1960]. 153 pp.

UNCOLLECTED WRITINGS

Asselineau, Roger M. "Three Uncollected 'Leaves of Grass,'" *Huntington Library Quarterly*, XXII (1959), 255–59.

———. "Un inédit de Walt Whitman: 'Taine's History of English Literature,'" *Études Anglaises*, X (1957), 128–38.

———. "Walt Whitman, Child of Adam: Three Unpublished Letters," *Modern Language Quarterly*, X (1949), 91–95.

———. "Walt Whitman to Gabriel Sarrazin: Four Unpublished Pieces," *Walt Whitman Review*, V (1959), 8–11.

Bergman, Herbert, " 'Chicago,' an Uncollected Poem Possibly by Whitman," *Modern Language Notes*, XV (November 1950), 478–81.

———. "Walt Whitman on New Jersey: an Uncollected

Essay," *Proceedings of the New Jersey Historical Society*, LXVI (October 1948), 139–54.

———. "Whitman in June 1885: Three Uncollected Interviews," *American Notes and Queries*, VIII (July 1948), 51–56.

———. "Whitman on His Poetry and Some Poets: Two Uncollected Interviews," *American Notes and Queries*, VIII (February 1950). 103–5.

Blodgett, Harold W. "An Early Whitman Manuscript," *Walt Whitman Newsletter*, IV (1958), 73–74.

———. *1855–56 Whitman Notebook: Toward the Second Edition of Leaves of Grass*. Introduction by Harold W. Blodgett, notes by William White, and a foreword by Charles E. Feinberg. Carbondale: Southern Illinois University Press. 1959, 56 pp.

———. "Toward the Second Edition of *Leaves of Grass:* An Unpublished Whitman Notebook 1855–56." *Walt Whitman Newsletter*, II (1956), 35–53.

Bowers, Fredson. "The Earliest Manuscripts of 'Passage to India' and Its Notebooks," *Bulletin of New York Public Library*, LXI (1957), 319–52.

———. "The Manuscript of Walt Whitman's 'A Carol of Harvest for 1867,'" *Modern Philology*, LII (1954), 29–51.

———. "The Manuscripts of Whitman's 'Song of the Redwood Tree,'" *Publications of the Bibliographical Society of America*, L (1956), 53–85.

———. "Whitman's Manuscripts for the Original 'Calamus' Poems," *Studies in Bibliography* (University of Virginia), VI (1953–54), 257–65.

———. *Whitman's Manuscripts: Leaves of Grass (1860)*. A Parallel Text edited with notes and Introduction. Chicago: University of Chicago Press, 1955. 264 pp.

Bradley, Sculley, and Stevenson, John A. (eds.). *Walt*

Whitman's Backward Glances: A Backward Glance O'er Traveled Roads and Two Contributory Essays Hitherto Uncollected. Edited with an Introduction. Philadelphia: University of Pennsylvania Press, 1947. 51 pp.

Brasher, Thomas L. "Sketches of the Sidewalks and Levee: With Glimpses into the New Orleans Bar (Rooms). Mrs. Giddy Gay Butterfly," *Walt Whitman Newsletter*, IV (1958), 87–90, 103–6.

Cameron, Kenneth W. "Rough Draft of Whitman's 'By Emerson's Grave,'" *Emerson Society Quarterly*, No. 13 (1958), pp. 32–34.

———. "Three Ungathered Whitman Manuscripts," *Emerson Society Quarterly*, No. 1, 4th Quarter (1955), pp. 8–9.

Freedman, Florence. *Walt Whitman Looks at the Schools* [newspaper articles and editorials]. New York: King's Crown Press, 1950. 278 pp.

Frenz, Horst (ed.). *Whitman and Rolleston: A Correspondence.* Bloomington: Indiana University Publications, Humanities Series, No. 26, 1951. 137 pp.

Gohdes, Clarence, and Silver, Rollo G. *Faint Clews and Indirections: Manuscripts of Walt Whitman and His Family.* Durham, N. C.: Duke University Press, 1949. 250 pp.

Golden, Arthur. "An Uncollected Whitman Article," *Bulletin of the New York Public Library*, LXIV (July 1960), 353–60.

Grant, Rena V. "Wood Odors" [uncollected poem], *Harper's Magazine*, CCXXI (December 1960), 43.

Harding, Walter. "A Sheaf of Whitman Letters," *Studies in Bibliography*, V (1952–53), 203–9.

Holloway, Emory. "More Temperance Tales by Whitman," *American Literature*, XXVII (January 1956), 577–78.

————. "Whitman and Band Music" [Washington, D. C., *Sunday Herald*, October 20, 1872], *Walt Whitman Review*, VI (1960), 51–52.

Hubach, Robert R. "An Uncollected Walt Whitman Letter" [November 30, 1890], *Duke University Library Notes*, No. 23 (1950), p. 13.

Miller, Edwin H. "New Letters of Walt Whitman," *Missouri Historical Society Bulletin*, XVI (1960), 99–113.

————. "Walt Whitman's Correspondence with Whitelaw Reid, Editor of the New York *Tribune*," *Studies in Bibliography*, VIII (1956), 242–49.

————. "Whitman Correspondence with Edwin Booth," *Walt Whitman Review*, VI (1960), 48–59.

Roos, Carl. "Walt Whitman's Letters to a Danish Friend" [Rudolf Schmidt]," *Orbis Literarum*, VII (1949), 31–60.

Rubin, J. J., and Brown, C. H. (eds.). *Walt Whitman of the New York Aurora*. State College, Pa.: The Bald Eagle Press, 1950. 148 pp.

Silver, Rollo G. "Whitman in 1850: Three Uncollected Articles," *American Literature*, XIX (January 1948), 301–17.

White, William. "I am a Born Democrat: An Unpublished Whitman Fragment," *Notes and Queries*, VI (1959), 454–44.

————. "Walt Whitman to U. S. Grant: An Unknown Exchange [of letters]," *Prairie Schooner*, XXXIV (Summer 1960), 120–22.

Whitman, Walt. "Tear Down and Build Over Again" [reprinted from *American Review*, XI (November 1845), 234–38)], *Walt Whitman Birthplace Bulletin*, III (July 1960), 16–19.

————. " 'Kentucky': Unpublished Poetic Fragment by Walt Whitman, Edited, with a Commentary, by William White," *Prairie Schooner*, XXXII (fall 1958), 170–78.

————. "Logan Pearsall Smith on Walt Whitman: A Correction and Some Unpublished [Whitman] Letters," *Walt Whitman Newsletter*, IV (1958), 87–90.

————. "Three Unpublished Whitman Fragments," *Walt Whitman Review*, V (1959), 75–76.

————. "Walt Whitman and Osler: Three Unpublished Letters," *Journal of the History of Medicine and Allied Sciences*, XI (1956), 348–49.

Anonymous. "Two Civil War Letters" [one by Mark Twain and one by Whitman], *American Heritage*, VIII (1957), 62–64.

————. "Unpublished Notes," *Wake*, VII (1948), 6–22.

TRANSLATIONS

CHINESE

Selections from Whitman's "Leaves of Grass" [title in Chinese]. Translated and Selected by T'u-nan Ch'u. Peking: People's Literary Publishing Society, 1955. 324 pp.

Song of the Open Road and Other Poems [title in Chinese]. Translated by Kao Han. Shangai: Tu-shu cheu-pan she, 1947. 273 pp.

Whitman: Selections [title in Chinese]. Translated by Chow Tao-Naa. Peking: People's Literary Publishing Society, 1957. 324 pp.

CZECH

Walt Whitman: Demokracie, Zeno Ma! [Democracy, Ma Femme!]. Translated and edited by Pavel Eisner. Prague: Jarvslav Podrouzek, 1945. 181 pp.

Walt Whitman: Pozdrav Svety [Selected Poetry—poetry, prose, and letters]. Translated by Jan Boor. Bratislava: SVKL, 1956. 224 pp.

DANISH

Walt Whitman: Digte [Poetry—selected]. Translated
by Frederik Schyberg. København: Gyldendal, 1949
(2nd rev. ed.). 133 pp.
Walt Whitman: Fuldkommedage [Specimen Days—se-
lections]. Translated by P. E. Seeberg. København:
Steen Hasselbachs Forlag (Hasselbachs Kultur-Biblio-
tek, Bind XCV), 1950. 55 pp.

DUTCH

Grashalmen [Leaves of Grass]. Translated by Maurits
Wagenvoort. Antwerp: Wereld-Biblioteek, 1956 (3rd
ed.).

FINNISH

Walt Whitman: Ruobonlehtiä [Selections]. Translated
by Viljo Laitinet. Turku: Suomentjan Kustantama,
1954. 114 pp.

FRENCH

Walt Whitman: Choix de Poèmes. Traduction et préface
de Pierre Messiaen. Paris: Aubier [1951]. 354 pp.
Walt Whitman: Choix des Textes. Traduction par Hélène Bokanowski. Paris: Guy Levis Mano, 1947. 69 pp.
Walt Whitman: Feuilles d'herbe (Choix). Introduction et
traduction de Roger Asselineau. Paris: Société D'Edition "Les Belles Lettres," 1956. 358 pp.
"Walt Whitman: Fragments politiques inédits en fran-
çais" [extracts from "The Eighteenth Presidency!",
Democratic Vistas, and a letter to a would-be Russian
translator], *La Nouvelle Critique,* VII (juil.-août
1955), 239–56.

"Walt Whitman, Perspectives Democratiques" [selections from *Democratic Vistas*] in *L'Énigme du Nouveau-Monde*. [Introductory note and translation by] Ch. Neveu. Paris: Flammarion [1946], pp. 41–72.

Walt Whitman: Une Etude, un Choix de Poèmes. Par Paul Jamati. Paris: Pierre Seghers, 1948. 238 pp.

Whitman [biographical-critical study with translation of selected poetry and prose]. Par Alain Bosquet. Paris: Gallimard (La Bibliotheque Ideale), 1959. 270 pp.

GERMAN

Gesang von Mir Selbst [Song of Myself]. Deutsch von Hans Reisiger. Berlin: Suhrkamp Verlag, 1946. 52 pp.

Salut au Monde. Deutsch von Hans Reisiger. Berlin: Suhrkamp Verlag, 1946. 60 pp.

Tagebuch: 1862–1864, 1876–1882 [selections from *Specimen Days*]. Deutsch von Hans Reisiger. Berlin: Suhrkamp Verlag, 1946. 84 pp.

Grashalme [Leaves of Grass]. Auswahl von Georg Goyert ins Deutsche übertragen. Berlin: Lothar Blansvalet Verlag, 1948. 106 pp.

Grashalme. In Auswahl neu übertragen von Elisabeth Serelman-Küchler und Walther Küchler. Erlangen: Dipax Verlag, 1947. 331 pp.

Walt Whitmans Werk [complete *Leaves of Grass*]. Übertragen und eingeleitet von Hans Reisiger. Hamburg: Rowohlt Verlag, 1956. 502 pp.

HEBREW

"Crossing Brooklyn Ferry" [translated into Hebrew by Simon Halkin], *The Hebrew Monthly*, XX (1949), 163–69.

Aleyesev . . . [*Leaves of Grass*, being a selection and translation into Hebrew with notes and an essay on the poet's life and work]. By Simon Halkin. Jerusalem: Workers Book Guild, 1952. 550 pp.

HUNGARIAN

Költeményei. Keszthelyi Zoltán, fordításában. Budapest: Magyar-Amerikai Társaság, 1947. 91 pp.

INDIAN (Oriya)

Walt Whitman: Durbadala. Translated by Inanindra Barma. Cuttack, India: Prophulla Chandra Dasa. n.d. 74 pp.

ITALIAN

Walt Whitman: Foglie d'erba e Prose [*Leaves of Grass* and (selected) Prose]. Traduzione di Enzo Giachino. Torino: Giulio Einaudi, 1950. 958 pp.

JAPANESE

Kusa no Ha [*Leaves of Grass*]. Translation and introduction by Shigetaka Naganuma. Tokyo: (vol. I) Nippon Dakusho Kumiai, 1946; (vol. II) Mikasa Shobo, 1950. 354 and 345 pp. (Complete *Leaves of Grass* in 2 vols., based on 1892 text.)

Kusa no Ha. Translated by Saika Tomita. Tokyo: Asahi Shimbun-sha, 1950. 502 pp.

Minshu-shugi Tenbo [*Democratic Vistas*]. Translated with Preface by Sota Kimura. Tokyo: Nippon Dokusho, 1947. 251 pp.

Minshu-shugi Tenbo. Translated by Masaru Shiga. Tokyo: Sogen-sha, 1949; Iwanami Bunko (Library) Series, 1953. 123 pp.

Wago Kuso yo Saraba [*Good Bye My Fancy*]. Translated by Izumi Yanagida. Tokyo: Nippon Dokusho Kumiai, 1947. 295 pp.

[*Whitman's Letters to His Mother and to Jeff*]. Translated by Shigetaka Naganuma. Tokyo: Arechi Shuppan-sha, 1958. 270 pp.

Whitman Shisen [Selected Poems of Whitman]. Translated by Koju Kiguchi and Masao Yaku. Tokyo: Azuma Shobo, 1949. 279 pp.

Whitman Shishū [Poems—selected]. Translated by Makoto Asano. Tokyo: Sojinusha. 1953. 294 pp.

Whitman Shishū. Translated by Akira Asano. Tokyo: Kanto-sha (229 pp.) and Sojin-sha (294 pp.), 1950.

Whitman Shishū. Translated by Shogo Shiratori. Nara: Yotoku-sha, Tambashi-machi, 1947, 128 pp.; Tokyo: Oizumi Shoten, 1949, 285 pp.; Tokyo: Shincho-sha (Bunko Series), 1954, 171 pp.

JUGOSLAVIAN (Serbo-Croatian)

Vlati Trave [*Leaves of Grass*—selections]. Translated by Tin Ujević; Preface by Gustave Krklec. Zagreb: Zora, 1951. 140 pp.

NORWEGIAN

Walt Whitman: Sangen om Meg Selv [Song of Myself] *av Leaves of Grass*. Oversettelse og Innledning ved Per Arneberg. Tegninger [illustrations] av Kai Fjell. Oslo: Forlagt av H. Aschehoug & Co., 1947. 123 pp.

POLISH

"Tobie O Demokracjo" [To You O Democracy], translated by Sydor Rey, in *Pieśni Mowione*. New York: St. Marks Printing Corp., 1945, pp. 39–40.

PORTUGUESE

Canção da Estrada Larga. Traducão de Luis Cardim. Lisbon: Cadernos da "Seara Nova" Secção de Textos Literários, 1947. 26 pp.

Cantos de Walt Whitman. Traducão de Oswaldino Margues; introducão de Anibal Machado. Rio de Janeiro: Editora José Olympio, 1946. 88 pp.

Videntes e Sonambulos: Coletaneo de Poemas Norte-Americanos [Collection of North American Poems]. [Edited and translated by] Oswaldino Margues. Rio de Janeiro: Ministerio do Educacio e Cultura, 1955, Whitman, pp. 36–79.

RUMANIAN

Poeme, Talmaciri. Commenta si Vignete de Margarcta Sterian. Bucuresti: Pro Pace, 1945. 38 pp.

Walt Whitman: Opere Alese [Selections]. Traducere si presentare de Mihnea Gheorghiu. Bucuresti: Editura de Stat Pentru Literature si Arta, 1956. 592 pp.

RUSSIAN

Uolt Uitmen: List'ya Travy [Walt Whitman: *Leaves of Grass*—selected]. (Introductions by Kornei Chukovsky and M. Mendelssohn; several translators, including Chukovsky.) Mosco: OGIZ [Government Publishing Office for Belles Lettres], 1955. 355 pp.

SPANISH

Cantando a la Primavera. Tradución y prólogo de Concha Zardaya. Madrid: Editorial Hispánica, 1945. 83 pp.

Hojas de Hierba [*Leaves of Grass*]. Version directa e integra conforme al texto de la edicion definitive de 1891–2. Por Francisco Alexander. Quito [Ecuador]: Casa la Cultura Ecuatoriana, 1953. 653 pp. (Complete *Leaves of Grass.*)

La ultima vez que florecieron las lilas en el patio ["When Lilacs Last in the Dooryard Bloom'd"]. Traducción de Arturo Torres-Rioseco. Mexico City: Coleccion Literaria de la Revista Iberioamericana, 1946. 13 pp.

Saludo al Mundo ["Salut au Monde!"]. Traducción de Gregorio Gasman. Santiago, Chile: Libreria Negra, 1949. 44 pp.

Walt Whitman, Cantor de la Democracia: Ensayo biográfico y breve antologia [Walt Whitman, Poet of Democracy: Biographical Essay and brief Anthology]. Por Miguel R. Mendoza. Mexico City: Secretaría de Educación Pública, 1946. 76 pp.

Walt Whitman: Obros Escogidas: Ensayo Biográfico-crítico [selections with a biographical-critical essay]. Versión, notas, y bibliografía de Concha Zardoya; prólogo de John Van Horne. Madrid: M. Aguilar, 1946. 851 pp.

Whitman y Otras Cronicas [Whitman and Other Chronicles]. Selección prólogo y notas de Emilio Abreu Gomez. Washington, D. C.: Unión Panamericana, 1950. "Yo Canto al cuerpo eléctrico de Walt Whitman" ["I Sing the Body Electric"], introducción, traducción y notas por Fernando Alegría, *ARS*, No. 1 (October–December 1951), pp. 47–54.

BOOKS ABOUT WHITMAN

Alegría, Fernando. *Walt Whitman en Hispanoamerica.* Mexico City: Ediciones Studium, 1954. (Collecion Studium 5.) 419 pp.

Allen, Gay Wilson. See *Invitation to Learning.*

———. *The Solitary Singer: A Critical Biography of Walt Whitman.* New York: Macmillan (1955), Grove Press—Evergreen Editions (1959); London: John Calder, 1959. 616 pp.

———. "Walt Whitman" in *Cyclopedia of World Authors.* New York: Harper, 1958, III, 1155–57.

———. "Walt Whitman" in *Encyclopaedia Britannica.*

——— (ed.). *Walt Whitman Abroad.* Syracuse: Syracuse University Press, 1955. 281 pp.

———. *Walt Whitman Handbook.* Chicago: Packard, 1946; New York: Hendricks House, 1957. 560 pp.

———. "Walt Whitman the Man" in *Walt Whitman: Man, Poet, and Philosopher—Three Lectures,* Washington, D. C.: Library of Congress, 1955. pp. 1–14.

Arnavon, Cyrille. *Les Lettres américaines devant la Critique française 1887–1917.* Paris: Les Belles Lettres, 1951, pp. 51–70. (Reception of *Leaves of Grass* in France 1887–1917.)

Asselineau, Roger. *L'Evolution de Walt Whitman après la première Édition des Feuilles d'herbe.* Paris: Didier. 1954. 567 pp.

———(author and translator). *The Evolution of Walt Whitman: The Development of a Personality* [first half of *L'Evolution de . . .*]. Cambridge: Harvard University Press, 1960. 376 pp.

Bab, Julius. *Amerikas Dichter.* Berlin: Im Christian, 1949. Whitman, pp. 54–58.

Baldini, Gabrielle. *Poeti americani.* Torino: De Silva, 1949.

Beaver, Joseph. *Walt Whitman, Poet of Science.* New York: King's Crown Press, 1951. 178 pp.

Berrill, N. J. *You and the Universe . . . with Support from Walt Whitman.* New York: Dodd, Mead, 1958. 215 pp.

Bertri, Luigi. *Storia della letteratura americano.* Milano, 1950. Vol. II.

Bowers, Fredson. *Textual and Literary Criticism.* The Sandors Lectures in Bibliography, 1957–58. Cambridge, England: Cambridge University Press, 1959, pp. 35–65.

Bowra, C. M. "Walt Whitman" in *The Saturday Book.* Sixth Year. London: Hutchinson, 1946, pp. 280–84.

Briggs, Arthur E. *Walt Whitman, Thinker and Artist.* New York: Philosophical Library, 1952. 489 pp.

Brooks, Van Wyck. *The Times of Melville and Whitman.* New York: E. P. Dutton, 1947. 489 pp.

Brown, C. S. "Musical Development of Symbols: Whitman" in *Music and Literature.* Athens: University of Georgia Press, 1948, pp. 178–94.

Burroughs, John. "Boston Criticism of Whitman" in Langer, S. K. K. (ed.). *Reflections on Art.* Baltimore: Johns Hopkins University Press, 1958, pp. 229–33.

Canby, Henry Seidel. *Walt Whitman, Ein Amerikaner.* Uebersetzt von Georg Goyert. Berlin: Lothar Blansvalet Verlag, 1947. 454 pp.

Carpenter, F. I. "Walt Whitman's Eidolon" in *American Literature and the American Dream.* New York: Philosophical Library, 1955, pp. 40–50.

Cestre, Charles. "Walt Whitman, 1819–1892" in *Les Poètes américains*. Paris: Presses Universitaires de France, 1948, pp. 61–85.

Chapman, John J. "Walt Whitman" in *Selected Writings* . . . New York: Farrar, Straus and Cudahy, 1957, pp. 141–49.

Chase, Richard. *Walt Whitman Reconsidered*. New York: Sloane, 1955. 191 pp.

Chesterton, G. K. "Conventions and the Hero" in *Lunacy and Letters*. New York: Sheed, 1958, pp. 62–65.

Chiarini, Giuseppe. *Pasculi nel centenario della nascita*. Milano: Mondadori, 1955.

Clark, Leadie Mae. *Walt Whitman's Conception of the American Common Man*. New York: Philosophical Library, 1955. 178 pp.

Cohen, Jacques-Fernand. *La Literature Americaine*. Paris: Presses Universitaires de France, 1950. Whitman, pp. 39 ff., *passim*.

Conner, Frederick William. *Cosmic Optimism: A Study of the Interpretation by American Poets from Emerson to Robinson*. Gainesville: University of Florida Press, 1949. Whitman, pp. 92–127.

Cory, Donald Webster. *The Homosexual in America*. New York: Greenberg, 1951, pp. 162–66.

Cowie, Alexander. "Walt Whitman" in *Rise of the American Novel*. New York: American Book Co., 1948, pp. 306–9.

Daiches, David. See *Invitation to Learning*.

———. "Walt Whitman as Innovator" in Carl Bode (ed.). *The Young Rebel in American Literature*. London: Heineman, 1959, pp. 25–48.

———. "Walt Whitman, The Philosopher" in *Walt Whitman: Man, Poet, Philosopher—Three Lectures* . . . Washington, D. C.: Library of Congress, 1955, pp. 35–53.

———. "Walt Whitman's Philosophy" in *Literary Es-*

says. New York: Philosophical Library, 1957, pp. 62–87.

De Moshinsky, Aizén Elena. *Walt Whitman y La América Latina.* Mexico City: Universidad Nacional Autonomade Mexico, 1950. 100 pp.

De Selincourt, Ernest. *Wordsworthian and Other Studies.* Oxford: Clarendon Press, 1947. Whitman, pp. 129–53.

Dickason, David Howard. "Whitman" in *The Daring Young Men.* Bloomington: Indiana University Press, 1953, pp. 228–31 *passim.*

Dyson, Verne. *Whitmanland: West Hills Memories of the Poet and His Ancestors.* Brentwood, Long Island: Published by the author, 1960. 72 pp.

Faner, Robert D. *Walt Whitman and Opera.* Philadelphia: University of Pennsylvania Press, 1951. 249 pp.

Fang, Achilles. "From Imagism to Whitmanism in Recent Chinese Poetry: A Search for Poetics that Failed" in *University of North Carolina Studies in Comparative Literature* (1955), pp. 177–89.

Fausset, Hugh I'Anson. "Whitman's Mysticism" in *Poets and Pundits: Essays and Addresses.* London: Jonathan Cape, 1947, pp. 31–51.

Floan, Howard R. "Whitman" in *The South in Northern Eyes, 1831–1861.* Austin: University of Texas Press, 1958, pp. 164–83 *passim.*

Franco, Luis L. *Walt Whitman.* Buenos Aires: Ed. Americalee [1945]. 240 pp.

Frank, Waldo. *The Rediscovery of Man: A Memoir and a Methodology of Modern Life.* New York: Braziller, 1958. Whitman, pp. 363–68 *passim.*

Freyre, Gilberto. *O Camarada Whitman:* Conferencia lida na Sociedade dos Amigos da América, do Rio de Janeiro, em 22 de Maio de 1947. Rio de Janeiro: Olympio, 1948. 63 pp.

Funnell, Walter S. *A Short History of the Long Islander*

[founded by Walt Whitman]. Huntington: Long Islander Press, 1947. 13 pp.

Gohdes, Clarence L. "Democracy in Free Verse" in A. H. Quinn (ed.). *Literature of the American People*. New York: Appleton-Century-Crofts, 1951, pp. 598–621.

Hamlin, F. "Walt Whitman" in *Land of Liberty*. New York: Crowell, 1947, pp. 226–51.

Hindus, Milton (ed.). *Leaves of Grass One Hundred Years After*. Essays by William Carlos Williams, Richard Chase, Leslie A. Fiedler, Kenneth Burke, David Daiches, and J. Middleton Murry . . . with an Introduction by Milton Hindus. Stanford: Stanford University Press, 1955. 149 pp.

Hoffman, F. J. "Emerson, Whitman, and the Silhouette of Sweeney" in *The Twenties*. New York: Viking, 1955, pp. 123–31.

Holloway, Emory. *Free and Lonesome Heart: The Secret of Walt Whitman*. New York: Vantage Press, 1960. 232 pp.

Holmes, O. W. "On Whitman" in Brown, C. A. (ed.). *Achievements of American Criticism*. New York: Ronald, 1954, pp. 367–68.

Holyroyd, Stuart. "Walt Whitman's Healthy-Mindedness" in *Emergence from Chaos*. Boston: Houghton Mifflin, 1957, pp. 95–112.

Ibarra, Luis F. *El genio de une vaza y la riqueza de un continente*. Paris, 1948.

Invitation to Learning. "Walt Whitman: *Leaves of Grass*. (As broadcast February 13, 1955.) Gay Wilson Allen. David Daiches. Lyman Bryson." In *The Invitation to Learning Reader*, vol. 5, no. 1 (1955), pp. 46–54.

Jackson, Holbrook. "Whitman" in *Dreamers of Dreams: The Rise and Fall of Nineteenth Century Idealism*. London: Faber, 1948, pp. 253–80.

James, Henry. "Mr. Walt Whitman" in *The Portable*

Henry James. New York: Viking, 1951, pp. 426–33.

Jarrell, Randall. "Some Lines from Whitman" in *Poetry and the Age.* New York: Knopf, 1953, pp. 112–32.

Jones, P. M. "Whitman and the Symbolists" in *The Background of Modern French Poetry.* Cambridge: Cambridge University Press, 1951, pp. 69–88.

Kazin, Alfred. *The Open Street.* New York: Reynal and Hitchcock, 1948. 22 pp.

Kenner, Hugh. "Whitman's Multitudes" in *Gnomon: Essays on Contemporary Literature.* New York: McDowell, Obelensky, 1959, pp. 67–69.

Kindilien, Carlin T. "Whitman and the Vagabondians" in *American Poetry in the Eighteen Nineties.* Brown University Studies, vol. 20 (1952), pp. 169–90.

Koht, Halvdan. *The American Spirit in Europe: A Survey of Transatlantic Influences.* Philadelphia: University of Pennsylvania Press, 1949. Whitman, pp. 195–201.

Kumei, Tsukasa. *Children of Leaves of Grass.* Tokyo: Tokyo Publishing Co., 1952. 214 pp.

Lawrence, David Herbert. "Whitman" in *Studies in Classic American Literature.* New York: Doubleday (Anchor Books), 1953, pp. 174–91. Also in *D. H. Lawrence: Selected Literary Criticism.* New York: Viking, 1956, pp. 392–407. And Edmund Wilson (ed.). *The Shock of Recognition.* New York: Farrar, Straus and Cudahy, 1955, pp. 1061–77.

Lenhart, Charmenz S. "Walt Whitman and Music in Leaves of Grass" in *Musical Influences on American Poetry.* Athens: University of Georgia Press, 1956, pp. 161–209.

Lewis, R. W. B. *American Adam: Innocence, Tragedy and Tradition in the Nineteenth Century.* Chicago: University of Chicago Press, 1955. See index—numerous references.

Lewis, W. "Walt Whitman: American Baby" in *L. A.*

Fiedler (ed.). *Art of the Essay.* New York: Crowell, 1958, pp. 584–87.

Lieberman, Elias. "Walt Whitman" in G. R. Mason (ed.). *Great American Liberals.* Boston: Starr King Press, 1956, pp. 83–95.

Lynd, R. "Whitman, Man and Poet" in *Books and Writers.* London: Dent [1952], pp. 1–7.

McCarthy, Sir Desmond. "Walt Whitman, 1945" in *Memories.* London: MacGibbon & Kee, 1953, pp. 132–36.

McCormick, Edward Alley. *Die Sprachliche Eigenart von Walt Whitmans Leaves of Grass in deutsche Uebertragung: Ein beitrag zur Übersetzungs Kunst.* Berne: Paul Haupt, 1953. 118 pp.

Martí, José. "The Poet Walt Whitman" in *Selected Writings: The America of José Martí.* Translated by Juande Onis. New York: Noonday, 1953, pp. 239–58.

Massis, Mahfud. *Walt Whitman el Visionario de Long Island.* Chile, 1953.

Matejka, Ladislav. *K Ceskym pre Kladum Walta Whitmana.* New York: Moravian Library, 1957. 16 pp. (Czech interest in Whitman; 1 p. summary in English.)

Matthiessen, F. O. "Whitman" in *The Responsibilities of the Critic; Essays and Reviews.* Selected by John Rackliffe. New York: Oxford University Press, 1952, pp. 215–23.

Mencken, H. L. "Whitman" in *Mencken Chrestomathy.* New York: Knopf, 1949, pp. 482–83.

Mendoza, Miguel R. *Walt Whitman (Cantor democracia).* Ensayo biográfico y breve antologia. Mexico: Secretaría de Educación Publica (Biblioteca Enciclopedia Popula, No. 111), 1946. 76 pp.

Miller, F. DeWolfe. "Melville, Whitman and Forty Immortals" in *English Studies in Honor of James Southall Freeman.* Charlottesville, Va., 1951, pp. 23–24.

Miller, James E. *A Critical Guide to Leaves of Grass.*

Chicago: University of Chicago Press, 1957. 268 pp.

Morgan, Manie (Kendley). "Memories of Walt Whitman" in *The New Stars: Life and Labor in Old Missouri*. Arranged by Jennie L. Morgan. Yellow Springs, Ohio: Antioch Press, 1949; pp. 283–88, 294–97, 298–300.

Morley, Christopher D. "Atom Splitter" in *Ironing Board*. New York: Doubleday, 1949, pp. 179–86.

Murry, J. Middleton. *Unprofessional Essays*. London: Cape, 1956. (Fielding, Clare, Whitman, and T. S. Eliot.)

Musgrove, S. *T. S. Eliot and Walt Whitman*. Wellington: New Zealand University Press, 1952. 93 pp.

Myers, Henry A. "Walt Whitman" in *Tragedy: A View of Life*. Ithaca: Cornell University Press, 1956, pp. 78–97.

Ota, Saburo, and Rikutaro, Fukuda. *Footprints of Foreign Literature in Japan*. Tokyo: Japan P. E. N. Club, 1957.

Pavese, Cesare. "Whitman—Poesie del far poesia" in *La Letteratura Americana e Altri Saggi*. Turin: Einaudi, 1951. Translation by Roger Asselineau: "Whitman—Poetry of Poetry Writing" in G. W. Allen (ed.). *Walt Whitman Abroad*. Syracuse: Syracuse University Press, 1955, pp. 189–97.

Peltola, Niilo. *The Compound Epithet and Its Use in American Poetry: Bradstreet through Whitman*. Helsinki: Suomalainen Tiedakatemia, 1956, pp. 140–60.

Phillips, James E. *Walt Whitman, Philosopher, Psychologist and Prophet*. A lecture delivered at the New York Theosophical Society on August 12, 1953, Privately printed. 24 pp.

Pochmann, Henry A. "Walt Whitman" in *German Culture in America: 1600–1900*. Madison: University of Wisconsin Press, 1957, pp. 416–70.

Pritchard, John Paul. "Walt Whitman" in *Criticism in America*. Norman: University of Oklahoma Press, 1956, pp. 112–20.

Ramsey, Warren. *Jules Laforgue and the Ironic Inheritance*. New York: Oxford University Press, 1953, pp. 152–54 *passim*.

Read, Herbert E. "Figure of Grammar: Whitman and Lawrence" in *True Voice of Feeling*. New York: Pantheon Books, 1953, pp. 432–44.

Redmond, Louis. *What's a Poet For? Let's Take Walt Whitman*. Illustration by William A. Smith. Winter Park, Florida: Angel Alley Press, 1955. 4 pp.

Reisiger, Hans. *Walt Whitman* [biography-criticism]. Berlin: Suhrkamp Verlag, 1946. 104 pp.

Resnick, Nathan. *Walt Whitman and the Authorship of the Good Gray Poet*. Brooklyn: Long Island University Press, 1948. 38 pp.

Romig, Edna D. "More Roots for Leaves of Grass" in *Elizabethan Studies and Other Essays in Honor of George F. Reynolds*. University of Colorado Studies in the Humanities, vol. 2, no. 4, pp. 322–27.

Rukeyser, Muriel. *The Life of Poetry*. New York: Wynn, 1949, pp. 72–87.

Rusev, Rusi. *Literaturnite S'zhdeniya na Uot Uitman* [The Literary Judgment of Walt Whitman]. Annual of the Faculty of History and Philology at the University of Sofia, vol. 42, 1946.

Salvatore, Rosati. *Storia della Letteratura Americana*. Torino: R.A.I., 1956.

Sandburg, Carl. *Abraham Lincoln: The Prairie Years and the War Years*. New York: Harcourt, Brace, 1954. See index.

Sandeen, Ernest Emanuel. "Ego in New Eden" in *American Classics Reconsidered*. New York: Scribner, 1958, pp. 229–63.

Schyberg, Frederik. *Walt Whitman*. Translated from the

Danish by Evie Allison Allen. Introduction by Gay
Wilson Allen. New York: Columbia University Press,
1951. 387 pp.

Shimizu, Haruo. [A Study of Whitman's Imagery—title
in Japanese.] Tokyo: Shinozaki-Shorin. 1957. 233 pp.

Sitwell, Edith. *The American Genius*. London: Lehman,
1951, pp. x–xiii, 40–70 (anthology).

Spencer, Benjamin T. "Half-Century of Whitman (1842–
1892)" in *The Quest of Nationality: An American
Literary Campaign*. Syracuse: Syracuse University
Press, 1957, pp. 219–51.

Spiller, Robert E. "Romantic Crisis: Melville, Whitman"
in *Cycle of American Literature*. New York: Macmillan, 1955, pp. 89–110.

Thorp, Willard. "Walt Whitman" in Floyd Stovall
(ed.). *Eight American Authors*. New York: Modern
Language Association, 1956, pp. 271–318.

Traubel, Horace. *With Walt Whitman in Camden: January 21—April 17, 1889*. Carbondale: Southern Illinois University Press, 1959. 528 pp.

Untermeyer, Louis. "Glory of the Commonplace: Walt
Whitman" in *Lives of the Poets* . . . New York: Simon and Schuster, 1959, pp. 558–77.

———. "Walt Whitman" in *Makers of the Modern
Word*. New York: Simon and Schuster, 1955, pp. 34–
46.

Usinger, Fritz. *Walt Whitman*. Wiesbaden: Steiner,
1957.

Van Doren, Mark. "[Walt Whitman] The Poet" in *Walt
Whitman: Man, Poet, and Philosopher—Three Lectures*. Washington, D. C.: Library of Congress, 1955,
pp. 15–33.

Vasseur, Armando. *Los discos poéticos de Walt Whitman*.
Leido por radio en Montevideo. Buenos Aires: Ed.
Shapire, 1950.

Warfel, Harry (Ed.). *Studies in Walt Whitman's Leaves*

of Grass. Written by students at Philipps-Universität
. . . Gainesville, Florida: Scholars' Facsimiles and
Reprints, 1954. 116 pp.

Watson, Georgia M. *So We Bought a Poet's Shrine.* New
York: Pageant, 1955. 116 pp.

Wescott, Ralph W. *Walt Whitman in Camden.* Trenton:
Walt Whitman Foundation and State of New Jersey
Dept. of Conservation & Economic Development, 1952.
24 pp.

Willard, Charles B. *Whitman's American Fame.* Providence: Brown University Press, 1950. 269 pp.

Williams, Stanley T. *Tres escritores clásicos de la literatura, de los Estados Unidos: Whitman, Mark Twain,
Poe.* Traducción de Filberto Gomez González. Prefacio
de Juli Torri. Mexico: Instituto Mexicano-Norteameri-
cano de Relaciones Culturales, IX, S. A. (Conferncias
dadas en la Universidad de Mexico, 1947.)

Winn, R. B. "Walt Whitman" in *American Philosophy.*
New York: Philosophical Library. 1955, pp. 262–64.

Woolf, Virginia S. "Visits to Walt Whitman" in *Granite
and Rainbow.* New York: Harcourt, Brace, 1958, pp.
229–31.

Ackerman, Catherine A. "The Mystique of Walt Whitman." *Lockhaven Bulletin* (State Teachers College, Lockhaven, Pa.), no. 1 (1959), pp. 66–67.

Acquaoni, José Luis. "Walt Whitman: Mensaje en cuerpo y alma," *Revista Shell* (Caracas, Venezuela), VII (March 1958), 21–27.

Adams, Charles M. "Whitman's Use of 'Grass,' " *American Notes and Queries*, VI (February 1947), 167–68.

Adams, Richard P. "Architecture and the Romantic Tradition: Coleridge to Wright," *American Quarterly*, IX (1957), 46–62.

———. "Romanticism and the American Renaissance." *American Literature*, XXIII (January 1952), 419–32.

———. "Whitman: A Brief Revaluation," *Tulane Studies in English*, V (1955), 111–49.

———. "Whitman's 'Lilacs' and the Traditional Pastoral Elegy," *PMLA*, LXXII (1957), 479–87.

Åhnebrink, Lars. "Whitman and Sweden," *Walt Whitman Review*, VI (1960), 43–44.

Alegría, Fernando. "El Whitman de José Martí," *Humanismo* (Mexico), III (1954), 239–49.

———. "The Whitman Myth," *Américas*, VI (1954), 9–11, 41–42.

Alexander, Francisco. "Los Primeros cien axos de Hojas de Hierba," *Letras del Ecuador*, no. 102 (1955), pp. 4, 36.

Alexander, S. "Permanence of Walt Whitman," *Reporter*, XII (May 19, 1955), 43–45.

Alicata, Mario. "Note su Whitman." *Rinascita*, VIII (May 1951), 249–54.

Allen, Charles A. "The Whitman Centenary: A Publisher's View." *New Mexico Quarterly*, XXV (1955–56), 387–92.

Allen, Gay Wilson. "On the Trochaic Meter of 'Pioneers! O Pioneers!,'" *American Literature*, XX (January 1949), 449–51.

———. "Regarding the Publication of the First 'Leaves of Grass,'" *American Literature*, XXVIII (1956), 78–79.

———. "The Young Whitman," *The Youth's Companion* (Tokyo), December 1955, pp. 6–9.

———. "Walt Whitman: 'Cosmos-Inspired,'" *New World Writing*, Eighth Mentor Selection (1955), pp. 266–80.

———. "Walt Whitman: Passage to India," *Indian Literature* (New Delhi), II (1959), 38–44.

———. "Walt Whitman the Man, an Introduction," *American Literary Review* (Tokyo), September 1955, pp. 1–2.

———. "Walt Whitman's Reception in Scandinavia," *Papers of the Bibliographical Society of America*, XL (1946), 259–75.

———. "Whitman Abroad [translations]," *Comparative Literature*, I (Summer, 1949), 272–77.

———. "Whitman Edition: Progress Report," *Walt Whitman Newsletter*, IV (1958), 71–72.

———. "Whitman in Japan, China, and Finland," *Walt Whitman Newsletter*, III (1957), 25–27.

———. "Whitman's 'When Lilacs Last in the Dooryard Bloom'd,'" *Explicator*, X (January 1952), 55.

Allen, Walter. "Kosmos, of Manhattan the Son," *New Statesman* (London), LVIII (September 12, 1959), 327.

Amacher, Richard E. "Whitman's 'Passage to India,'" *Explicator*, IX (December 1950), 2.

Andrews, Elizabeth Robert. "Walt Whitman: American Poet (1819–1892)," *Canadian Poetry Magazine*, XIX (1955), 27–30.

Armand, E. "Resurrexit Walt Whitman," *L'Unique* (France), CXVII (Jan.–Feb. 1955), 16–18.

Asselineau, Roger. "A Footnote to Whitman's Essay on Taine," *Walt Whitman Newsletter*, IV (1958), 93–94.

———. "A propos de Walt Whitman," *Langues Modernes*, XLII (Aug.–Oct. 1948), 62–65.

———. "État Présent des Études Whitmanienes," *Étude Anglaises*, XI (1958), 31–40.

———. "La Théme de la Mort dans L'Oeuvre de Walt Whitman," *La Revue des Lettres Modernes*, November 1954, pp. 33–48.

———. "Un poéte cosmique américain: Walt Whitman," *Mystére solaire* (France), no. 13–14 (January 1954).

———. "Walt Whitman—or Nature Imitates Art," translated by Edward F. Grier. *Walt Whitman Newsletter*, III (1957), 22–24.

———. "Whitman Agonistes," translated by Edward F. Grier. *Walt Whitman Newsletter*, III (1957), 3–5.

———. "Whitman et Wordsworth—étude d'une influence indirecte," *Revue de Littérature Comparée*, XXIX (1955), 505–12.

———. "Whitman in France in 1960," *Walt Whitman Review*, VI (1960), 4–5.

Baker, Carlos. "The Road to Concord: Another Milestone in the Whitman-Emerson Friendship," *Princeton University Library Chronicle*, VII (April 1946), 100–117.

Balseiro, José A. "Emerson y Whitman," *Atlántico* (Madrid), no. 2 (1956), pp. 49–71.

Barahona, Melvin Rene. "Escuha Walt Whitman," *Suplemento Mensual de Revista de Guatemala*, nos. 2 and 3 (February 1952).

Basler, Roy P. "Out of the Cradle Endlessly Rocking," *Explicator*, V [59] (June 1947).

Beatty, R. C. "Whitman's Political Thought," *South Atlantic Quarterly*. XLVI (1947), 72–83. Reprinted in *Fifteen Years of the South Atlantic Quarterly* (1952).

Beaver, Joseph. "Walt Whitman, Star-Gazer," *Journal of English and Germanic Philology*, XLVIII (July 1949), 307–19.

Begg, Edleen. "Larks, Purple Cows and Whitmania," *University of Texas Library Chronicle*, II (Spring 1947), 190–92.

Bergman, Herbert. "A Poet's Western Visit," *Missouri Historical Review*, VIII (1949), 74.

———. "Ezra Pound and Walt Whitman," *American Literature*, XXVII (1955), 56–61.

———. "Sir Edwin Arnold and Walt Whitman," *Notes and Queries*, CXCIII (August 21, 1948), 366.

———. "The Whitman-Twain Enigma Again," *Mark Twain Journal*, X (1956), 12–23.

———. "Walt Whitman Parodies," *American Notes and Queries*, VIII (August 1948), 74.

———. "Whitman and Tennyson," *Studies in Philology*, LI (1954), 492–504.

———. "Whitman on Beethoven and Music," *Modern Language Notes*, LXVI (December 1952), 556–57.

———. "Whitman on Politics, Presidents and Hopefuls," *American Notes and Queries*, VIII (May 1948), 19–26.

Bermann, Gregorio. "Sarmiento y los Estados Unidos," *Cuadernos Americanos*, no. 5 (Sept.–Oct. 1945).

Bernbrock, John, S. J. "Whitman's Language Study: Work in Progress," *Walt Whitman Review*, VI (December 1960), 69–72.

Billy, A. "Le plus grand Genie du XIX siècle [Walt Whitman]," *Figaro Litteraire*, May 8, 1948, p. 2.

Blanck, Jacob. "News from Rare Book Sellers," *Publishers' Weekly*, CLIII (September 27, 1947), B201–B202.

Blanco, Manuel García. "Walt Whitman y Unamuno," Notas para la Historia de la Difusion de la Obra del

Poeta Norteamericano en Espana, *Cultura Universitaria* [Universidad Central de Venezuela], no. 52 (Nov.–Dec. 1955), pp. 76–102.

———. "Walt Whitman y Unamuno," *Atlántico* (Madrid), no. 2 (1956), 5–47.

Blodgett, Harold W. "A Note on Whitman's Poetic Fragments," *Walt Whitman Newsletter*, II (1956), 26–27.

———. "Take My Leaves America," *Virginia Quarterly Review*, XXXII (1956), 147–50.

———. "Whitman and the Linton Portrait," *Walt Whitman Newsletter*, IV (1958), 90–92.

———. "Whitman in Iran," *Walt Whitman Review*, V (1959), 11–12.

Bo, Carlo. "Riflessioni critiche—Whitman," *Paragone*, II (October 1951), 37–52.

Bode, Carl. "Whitman at Oxbridge," *Walt Whitman Review*, VI (1960), 5–6.

Boroff, David. "Walt Whitman's Brooklyn and Mine," *Nocturne* (Brooklyn College), VII (Spring 1955), 29–32.

Bowers, Fredson. "The Manuscripts of Walt Whitman's 'A Carol of Harvest, for 1867,' " *Modern Philology*, LII (August 1954), 29–51.

———. "The Manuscript of Whitman's 'Passage to India,' " *Modern Philology*, LI (November 1953), 102–17.

———. "Whitman's Manuscripts for the Original 'Calamus' Poems," *Studies in Bibliography* (Papers of the Bibliographical Society of the University of Virginia), VI (1953–1954), 257–65.

Bradley, Sculley. "Growth of the Leaves," *Walt Whitman Foundation Bulletin*, III (March 1950), 11–12.

———. "Introduction to With Walt Whitman in Camden Volume 4," *Walt Whitman Foundation Bulletin*, VI (April 1953), 11–14.

————. "Whitman and the Charcoal Burner," *Walt Whitman Newsletter*, II (1956), 21–23.

————. "Walt Whitman y el Mundo de Post Guerra," *Temas*, 81 (August 1945).

Brasher, Thomas Lowber. "Organized Labor Versus Whitman's 'Immutable Truth,'" *Walt Whitman Review*, VI (December 1960), 63–66.

————. "Whitman and Emma Willard's 'Rocked in the Cradle of the Deep,'" *Walt Whitman Newsletter*, IV (1958), 78.

————. "Whitman and the Crescent: A Conjecture," *Walt Whitman Newsletter*, III (1957), 24–25.

————. "Whitman and Universalism," *Walt Whitman Newsletter*, III (1957), 40–42.

————. "Whitman on the 'Atrocious Practice of Publishing Letters,'" *Walt Whitman Newsletter*, III (1957), 63.

————. "Whitman, Robert Owen and Radical Reform," *Walt Whitman Review*, V (1959), 72–73.

————. "Whitman's Conversion to Opera," *Walt Whitman Newsletter*, IV (1958), 109–10.

————. "Whitman's Conversion to Phrenology," *Walt Whitman Newsletter*, IV (1958), 95–97.

Brown, Charles H. "Young Editor Whitman: An Individualist in Journalism," *Journalism Quarterly*, XXVII (spring 1950), 141–48.

Brown, Clarence A. "Walt Whitman and Lincoln," *Journal of Illinois Historical Society*, XLVII (1954), 176–84.

Bychowsky, Gustav. "Walt Whitman—A Study in Sublimation," *Psychoanalysis and the Social Sciences*, III (1950), 223–61.

Cakurov, K. D. "Uolt Uitman," *Liteaturen Front* (Sofia), XI (1955), 4.

Cambon, Glauco. "Ancora su Whitman," *aut, aut*, no. 42 (1957), pp. 469–85.

――――. "Whitman e ul Mito di Adamo," *aut, aut*, no. 40 (1957), pp. 315–30.

――――. "Walt Whitman in Italia," *aut, aut*, no. 39 (1957), pp. 244–63.

Cameron, Kenneth W. "Emerson's Recommendation of Whitman in 1863: The Remainder of the Evidence," *Emerson Society Quarterly*, no. 3 (2nd quarter, 1956), pp. 14–20.

Camillucci, Mareella. "Walt Whitman," *Idea*, VIII (February 12, 1956) 1.

Cantoni, Louis T. "Walt Whitman, Secular Mystic," *Personalist*, XXXVI (1955), 379–84.

Capek, Abe. "Walt Whitman: A Centennial Re-Evaluation," *Philologico* (Prague), VII (no. 2–3, 1955), 30–45.

Cardona Pena, Alfredo. "La India Rusia y Walt Whitman," *Repertorio Americano*, no. 17 (March 13, 1948), p. 269.

Cestre, Charles. "L'Evolution de Walt Whitman," *Les Langues Modernes*, LI (1957), 158–60.

Chace, F. F. "Notes on Whitman's Mocking Bird in 'Out of the Cradle Endlessly Rocking,' " *Modern Language Notes*, LXI (February 1946), 93–94.

Chadbourn, Charles C., Jr. "A Note on the Publication of The Good Gray Poet," *Books at Brown* [University], XV (June 1953), 1–4.

Chaplin, G., and Mazo, E. "Poet of Democracy: New Jersey to Honor Memory of Whitman with a Shrine," *Christian Science Monitor Magazine*, August 23, 1947, p. 4.

Chari, V. K. "A Critical Approach to Whitman," *Walt Whitman Review*, VI (1960), 54–56.

――――. "Whitman and Indian Thought," *Western Humanities Review*, XIII (1959), 291–302.

――――. "Whitman and the Christian Sensibility," *Walt Whitman Review*, VI (1960), 6–7.

Chase, Richard. "Walt Whitman as American Spokesman," *Commentary*, XIX (March 1955), 260–65.

Chitlick, V. L. O. "A Footnote to *Tales of the Sea* [Mac-Mechan]," *Dalhousie Review*, XXXVI (1956), 275–78.

Chupak, Henry. "Walt Whitman and the Camden Circle," *Proceedings of the New Jersey Historical Society*, LXXII (1955), 274–99.

Ciardi, John. "Whitman's Principle of Selection," *Walt Whitman Newsletter*, II (1956), 10–11.

Clark, George Peirce. " 'Saerasmid,' an Early Promoter of Walt Whitman," *American Literature*, XXVII (May 1955), 259–62.

————. "Solitude: An Early Whitman Imitation," *Harvard Library Bulletin*, VIII (spring 1954), 213–23.

Coffman, S. K., Jr. " 'Crossing Brooklyn Ferry,' a Note on the Catalog Technique in Whitman's Poetry," *Modern Philology*, LI (May 1954), 225–32.

————. "Form and Meaning in Whitman's 'Passage to India,' " *PMLA*, LXX (June 1955), 337–49.

————. "Whitman's 'Song of the Broad-Axe,' Stanza 1, Section 1," *Explicator*, XII, no. 6 (April 1954), item 39.

Coleman, Rufus A. "Further Reminiscences of Walt Whitman," *Modern Language Notes*, LXIII (April 1948), 266–68.

————. "Trowbridge and Burroughs," *Modern Language Quarterly*, XIV (June 1953), 154–62.

————. "Trowbridge and O'Connor: An Unpublished Correspondence with Special Reference to Walt Whitman," *American Literature*, XXIII (November 1951), 323–31.

————. "Trowbridge and Whitman," *PMLA*, LXIII (May 1948), 262–73.

Cooke, Alice Lovelace. "American First Editions of Texas

University: IV Walt Whitman (1819–1892)," *University of Texas Library Chronicle*, II (1946), 95–105.

———. "The Centennial of Walt Whitman's Leaves of Grass," *University of Texas Library Chronicle*, V (spring 1955), 13–17.

———. "A Note on Whitman's Symbolism in 'A Song of Myself,'" *Modern Language Notes*, LXV (April 1950), 228–32.

———. "Notes on Whitman's Musical Background," *New England Quarterly*, XIX (June 1946), 224–35.

———. "Whitman as a Critic: *Democratic Vistas* with Special Reference to Carlyle," *Walt Whitman Newsletter*, IV (1958), 91–95.

Cormac, Philip. "Walt Whitman's Diagnosis of Democracy," *America*, XCIV (November 5, 1955), 157–59.

Cowley, Malcolm. "Guru, the Beatnik and the Good Gray Poet," *New Republic*, CXLI (October 26, 1959), 17–19.

———. "Walt Whitman—The Miracle," *New Republic*, CXIV (March 18, 1946), 385–88.

———. "Walt Whitman—The Philosopher," *New Republic*, CXVII (September 29, 1947), 29–31.

———. "Walt Whitman—The Secret," *New Republic*, CXIV (April 8, 1946), 481–84.

———. "Whitman—The Poet," *New Republic*, CXVII (October 20, 1947), 27–30.

———. "Whitman: A Little Anthology: Lyrical Passages from Leaves of Grass, Selected and with Commentary," *New Republic*, CXXXIII (July 25, 1955), 16–21.

———. "Walt Whitman's Buried Masterpiece," *Saturday Review*, XLII (October 31, 1959), 11–13, 32–34.

Cox, Leo. "A Whitman Pilgrimage," *Canadian Poetry Magazine*, XIX (1955), 27.

D'Agnostino, Nemi. "La letteratura americana e altri saggi Cesare Pavese," *Belfagor*, VII (November 1952), 710–17.

———. "Poe, Whitman, Dickinson," *Belfagor*, VIII (September 30, 1953), 517–38.

Da Ponte, Durant. "Whitman's 'Young Fellow Named Da Ponte,'" *Walt Whitman Review*, V (1959), 16–17.

Davis, David B. "The Movement to Abolish Capital Punishment in America, 1787–1861," *American Historical Review*, LXIII (1957), 23–46.

De Graaf, Daniel A. "Arthur Rimbaud et Walt Whitman," *Levende Talen* (November 1953), pp. 363–72.

———. "Walt Whitman et les Pays-Bas," *Walt Whitman Newsletter*, III (1957), 48–50.

De Jouvenel, Renaud. "Walt Whitman," *Europe*, XXXIII (Nov.–Dec. 1955), 91–107.

———. "Walt Whitman." *Lettres Françaises*, no. 586 (September 22–28, 1955), pp. 1, 9.

De Maria, Federíco. "Walt Whitman, poeta di Ieri e di Sempre," *Cittá di Vita*, XIII (1958), 462–74.

Doyle, John R., Jr. "The Poetry of Walt Whitman," *English Studies in Africa*, III (March 1960), 33–47.

DuBois, Arthur E. "Keeping Whitman's Tally," *Modern Language Notes*, LXVII (June 1952), 414–17.

Eby, E. H. "Did Whitman Write 'The Good Gray Poet?'" *Modern Language Quarterly*, XI (December 1950), 445–49.

———. "The Future Looks at Walt Whitman," *Walt Whitman Review*, VI (1960), 8–9.

Eleanor, Sister Mary. "Hedge's 'Prose Writers of Germany' as Source of Whitman's Knowledge of German Philosophy," *Modern Language Notes*, LXI (June 1946), 381–88.

Elliott, Jorge. "Walt Whitman y nuestra poesía," *Annales de la Universidad de Chile*, XIV, no. 101 (1956), 121–25.

Emerson, R. W. "But Would He be a Security Risk? Letter Dated 10 January 1863 [recommendation of Whitman]," *Harper's Magazine*, CCXII (February 1956), 71.

Englekirk, John E. "Walt Whitman 'indomable e intraducible,' " [Proceedings] *Sexto Congreso del Instituto Internacional de Literatura Ibero-americana* (Mexico, 1954), pp. 65–79.

―――. "Whitman en costellano," *Atlántico* (Madrid), no. 2 (1956), pp. 73–87.

―――. "Whitman y el anti-moderismo," *Revisto Ibero-americana*, October, 1947.

Ernest, Joseph M., Jr. "Holmes to Whittier re Whitman," *Walt Whitman Newsletter*, IV (1958), 76–77.

―――. "Whittier and Whitman: Uncongenial Personalities," *Bulletin of Friends of History Association*, XLII (Autumn 1953), 21.

Faner, Robert D. "Whitman and Alboni," *Walt Whitman Newsletter*, III (1957), 6.

Feidelson, C., Jr. "Centenary of Leaves of Grass," *Yale Review*, XLV (September 1955), 135–40.

Feinberg, Charles E. "A Whitman Collector Destroys a Whitman Myth," *Papers of the Bibliographical Society of America*, LII (1958), 73–92.

―――. "Percy Ives, Detroit and Walt Whitman," *Bulletin of Detroit Historical Society*, XVI (1960), 4–11.

Feldman, E. "Posthumous Additions," *Saturday Review*, XXXVII (August 7, 1954), 21.

Feo, José Rodriguez. "Walt Whitman y la Literatura," *Sur*, no. 239, pp. 13–24.

Fiedler, Leslie A. "Revaluaciones: Walt Whitman," *Ciclon*, I (1955), 46–54.

―――. "Walt Whitman Reconsidered," *New Leader*, XLII (March 2 and 9, 1959), 20–22, 19–21.

Figueira, Gastón. "Poetas y Prosistas de América: Walt

Whitman," *Revista Iberoamericana,* XI (June 1946), 113–16.

Finkel, William L. "Sources of Walt Whitman's Manuscript Notes on Physique," *American Literature,* XXII (November 1950), 308–31.

————. "Walt Whitman's Manuscript Notes on Oratory," *American Literature,* XXII (March 1950), 29–52.

————. "Whitman and the Calendar," *Word Study,* XXV (February 1950), 3–4.

————. "Robert Ingersoll's Oratory and Walt Whitman's Poetry," *Speech Monographs,* XVI (1949?), 41–56.

Fleisher, Frederic. "Walt Whitman's Swedish Reception," *Walt Whitman Newsletter,* III (1957), 19–22, 44–47, 58–62.

Fletcher, E. G. "Pioneers! O Pioneers!" *American Literature,* XIX (November 1947), 259–61.

Flint, R. W. "The Living Whitman," *Partisan Review,* XXII (1955), 391–94.

Flood, M. M. "To You, Endless Announcements, an Imaginary Conversation with Whitman and Saroyan," *Saturday Review of Literature,* XXVIII (September 8, 1945), 14–15.

Fogg, John M., Jr. "Walt Whitman—Poet of Science," *Walt Whitman Foundation Bulletin,* IV (April 1951), 13.

Ford, Nich Aaron. "Walt Whitman's Conception of Democracy," *Phylon,* XI (1950), 201–6.

Ford, Thomas W. "Significance of Whitman's Revisions in 'Excelsior,'" *Walt Whitman Review,* V (1959), 69–72.

Francis, K. H. "Walt Whitman's French," *Modern Language Review,* LI (October 1956), 493–506.

Frank, Waldo. "With a Voice as Big as America," *New York Times Book Review,* July 3, 1955, pp. 1, 13.

Frenz, Horst. "Karl Knortz, Interpreter of American Literature and Culture," *American Germanic Review*, XIII (December 1946), 27–30.

──────. "Walt Whitman's Letters to Karl Knortz," *American Literature*, XX (May 1948), 155–63.

Fussell, Edwin. "Leaves of Grass and Browning," *American Literature*, XXXI (1959), 77–78.

Gamby, Erik. "Whitman i Europa," *Perspectiv* (Sweden), VI (1955), 264–70.

Garcés, Jacome Alfredo. "Walt Whitman, el poeta y su época," *Lettras del Ecuador*, no. 102 (1955), pp. 5–6.

Gary, L. M. "Imagery: Walt Whitman's," *Poet Lore*, LII (1946), 360–61.

Geismar, Maxwell. "The World of Walt Whitman," *Nation*, CLXXX (1955), 265–67.

Gertzog, Alice. "Public Employees' Hall of Fame: Walt Whitman, Poet of America," *The Public Employee* (AFL-CIO), XXII (1957), 6–7.

Getto, Giovanno. "Pascoli e l'America," *Nuova Antologia*, XCI (October 1956), 159–78.

Gogoberidze, L. L. "Uitmen-pevec Prostogo Naroda Ameriki," *Izvestija Akademi Nauk* (Moscow), XIV (1955), 225–66.

Gohdes, Clarence. "A Comment on Section 5 of Whitman's 'Song of Myself,'" *Modern Language Notes*, LXIX (1954), 583–86.

──────. "Nationalism and Cosmopolitanism in Whitman's *Leaves of Grass*," *Walt Whitman Review*, V (1959), 3–7.

──────. "Section 50 of Whitman's 'Song of Myself,'" *Modern Language Notes*, LXXV (December 1960), 654–56.

Golden, Harry L. "We Need Whitman Today Even More than Shakespeare," *Carolina Israelite*, XVII (1959), 5–6.

Gordan, John D. "Berg Collection's 1867 *Leaves of*

Grass," *Walt Whitman Newsletter,* II (1956), 30.

Grant, Rena V. See under "anonymous" at end of this section.

Green, David Bonnell. "Charles Ollier: An Early English Admirer of Walt Whitman," *Walt Whitman Newsletter,* IV (1958), 106–8.

Grier, Edwin F. "Walt Whitman, the *Galaxy* and *Democratic Vistas,*" *American Literature,* XXIII (November 1951), 332–50.

―――. "Whitman's Attack on the Temperance Movement," *Walt Whitman Newsletter,* IV (1958), 78.

Griffith, C. "Sex and Death: The Significance of Whitman's Calamus Themes," *Philological Quarterly,* XXXIX (January 1960), 18–38.

Grover, Edwin Osgood. "The First Words of Warm Approval," *Walt Whitman Review,* V (1959), 30–33.

Guéhenno, Jean. "Rousseau et Whitman," *Figaro,* November 22, 1955, p. 1.

Gummere, Richard M. "Whitman and His Reaction to the Classics," *Harvard Studies in Classical Philology,* LX (1951), 263–89.

Hackman, Martha. "Whitman, Jeffers, and Freedom," *Prairie Schooner,* XX (1946), 182–84.

Hall, Martha K. "Joseph Whitman of Long Island," *Walt Whitman Birthplace Bulletin,* I (1957), 3–4.

―――. "Old Salt Kossabone," *Walt Whitman Birthplace Bulletin,* I (1958), 13–14.

―――. "Whitman Acres in Huntington," *Walt Whitman Birthplace Bulletin,* I (1958), 7–10.

Harding, Walter. "A Glimpse of Walt Whitman," *Walt Whitman Newsletter,* III (1957), 7.

Hardy, John Edward. "Stephen Crane, Whitman, Auden and a Poetry Handbook," *Poetry* (Chicago), XCII (1958), 116–20.

Harrison, Joseph M., Jr. "John Burroughs' Review of

the 1867 Leaves of Grass," *Walt Whitman Review*, VI (1960), 45–48.

Hastings, William. "Jean Catel's Interpretation of Walt Whitman," *The Annotator* (Purdue), no. 3 (May 1954), pp. 5–9.

Hendrick, George. "Mrs. Davis' Claim Against the Whitman Estate," *Walt Whitman Birthplace Bulletin*, IV (October 1960), 6–8.

———. "Walt Whitman and Sadakichi Hartman," *Emerson Society Quarterly*, no. 11 (1958), pp. 50–52.

———. "Whitman and Sir Edwin Arnold," *Western Humanities Review*, XIV (Winter 1960), 83–89.

———. "Whitman's Copy of the *Bhagavad-Gita*," *Walt Whitman Review*, V (1959), 12–14.

Hentges, Phyl, and Hentges, Pierre. "Walt Whitman, Poète d'une Nouveau Monde," *Nouvelle Critique*, VII (Sept.–Oct. 1955), 84–104.

Herra, Maurice. "Feuilles d'Herbe en Europe et en Amèrique Latine," *Europe*, XXXIII (Nov.–Dec. 1955), 137–45.

Hertel, Lev. "Walt Whitman Kenntnis Deutscher Literatur," *German Quarterly*, XXI (January 1948), 16–24.

Hindus, Milton. "Whitman and Poe: A Note," *Walt Whitman Newsletter*, III (1957), 5–6.

———. "Dostoyevsky's Religion and Whitman's," *Walt Whitman Review*, VI (December 1960), 66–69.

Hogan, Robert. "The Amorous Whale: A Study in the Symbolism of D. H. Lawrence [and Whitman]," *Modern Fiction Studies*, V (1959), 39–46.

Hollis, C. Carroll. "Names in 'Leaves of Grass,'" *Names*, V (1957), 129–56.

———. "Whitman and the American Idiom," *Quarterly Journal of Speech*, XLIII (1957), 408–20.

———. "Whitman and William Swinton: A Cooperative Friendship," *American Literature*, XXX (1959), 425–49.

———. "Whitman in 1960," *Walt Whitman Review*, VI (1960), 9–11.

———. "Whitman on 'Periphrastic' Literature . . . Speculations on an Unpublished MS. Fragment," *Fresco*, X (1960), 5–13.

———. "Whitman's 'Ellen Eyre,'" *Walt Whitman Newsletter*, II (1956), 24–26.

———. "Whitman's Language Study: Work in Progress," *Walt Whitman Review*, VI (December 1960), 69–72.

———. "Whitman's Word-Game," *Walt Whitman Newsletter*, IV (1958), 74–76.

Holloway, Emory. "A Whitman Source," *Walt Whitman Newsletter*, II (1956), 23–24.

———. "Whitman Pursued [with text of Lion copy of Ellen Eyre letter]," *American Literature*, XXVII (March 1955), 1–11.

———. "Whitman's Last Words," *American Literature*, XXIV (November 1952), 367–69.

———. "Whitman's Message for To-Day," *American Mercury*, LXII (February 1946), 202–6.

———. "Why Whitman Lives," *Walt Whitman Review*, VI (1960), 11–12.

Housser, F. B. "The Creative Man, from an Unpublished Manuscript 'Whitman to America: The Study of an Attitude,'" *The Canadian Theosophist*, May 15, 1947, pp. 87–91; June 15, 1947, pp. 100–103.

Howarth, Herbert. "Whitman Among the Irish," *The London Magazine*, VII (January 1960), 48–55.

Howell, A. C. "Walt Whitman, Singer of the American Spirit," *English Language and Literature* (English Literary Society of Korea), no. 4 (1957), pp. 265–78.

Hubach, Robert R. "Walt Whitman and Taliessin," *American Literature*, XVIII (January 1947), 329–31.

Hubbell, Jay B. "The Centenary of a Book," *Virginia Quarterly Review*, XXXI (1955), 486–90.

Huggard, W. A. "Whitman's Poem of Personalism," *Personalist*, XXVIII (July 1947), 273–78.

Hume, Robert A. "Walt Whitman and the Peace," *College English*, VI (March 1945), 313–19.

Idzerda, Stanley. "Walt Whitman Politician," *New York History*, XXXVII (1956), 171–84.

Iglesias, A. "Classic Blend in Literature," *Saturday Review of Literature*, XXXIII (January 14, 1950), 31–32.

Jamati, Paul. "Leon Bazalgette Introducteur de Whitman," *Europe*, XXXIII (Nov.–Dec. 1955), 135–37.

Jarrell, Randall. "Walt Whitman: He Had His Nerve," *Kenyon Review*, XIV (Winter 1952), 63–71. Reprinted as "Some Lines from Whitman" in *Perspectives*, no. 2 (Winter 1953), pp. 61–77. As "Walt Whitman, il avait du cran" in *Profils*, no. 2 (January 1953), pp. 98–119.

Johnson, C. W. M. "Whitman's 'Out of the Cradle Endlessly Rocking,' " *Explicator*, V (May 1947), note 52.

Johnson, Jane. "Whitman's Changing Attitude toward Emerson," *PMLA*, LXXIII (September 1958), 452.

Jones, Joseph. "Carlyle, Whitman, and the Democratic Dilemma." *English Studies in Africa*, III (September 1960), 179–97.

———. "New Acquisitions: Rare Book Collections: Walt Whitman," *University of Texas Library Chronicle*, VI (1958), 44–46.

———. "Whitman's 'When Lilacs Last in the Dooryard Bloom'd,' " *Explicator*, IX (April 1951), note 42.

Jones, P. M. "Whitman and the Origins of 'Vers Libre,' " *French Studies* (Oxford, England), II (April 1948), 129–39.

Kahn, Sholom. "American Backgrounds of Whitman's Sense of Evil," *Scripta Hierosolyminata* (Jerusalem), II (1955), 82–118.

———. "Eliot's 'Polyphiloprogenitive': Another Whitman Link?" *Walt Whitman Review*, V (1959), 52–54.

————. "Towards a Popular Edition of Whitman's 'Complete Poems,' " *Walt Whitman Review*, V (1959), 23–26.

————. "Walt Whitman in Hebrew," *Scopus* (Jerusalem), VI (March 1952), 6–7.

————. "Whitman's Black Lucifer: Some Possible Sources," *PMLA*, LXXI (December 1956), 932–44.

————. "Whitman's Vision and Art," *Walt Whitman Review*, VI (1960), 12–14.

Kallsen, T. J. " 'Song of Myself': Logical Unity through Analogy," *West Virginia University Bulletin*, IX (1953), 33–40.

————. "The World of 'When Lilacs Last in the Dooryard Bloom'd,' " *University of Virginia Philological Papers*, VIII (1951), 59–65.

Kamei, Shunsuka. "Walt Whitman and Takeo Arishima," *Walt Whitman Birthplace Bulletin*, IV (October 1960), 8–12; (January 1961), 3–7.

Kenner, Hugh. "Whitman's Multitudes," *Poetry*, LXXXVII (December 1955), 183–89.

Kinnaird, John. "The Paradox of an American Identity," *Partisan Review*, V (1958), 380–405.

Kouwenhoven, John A. "What's American about America," *Harper's Magazine*, CCXIII (July 1956), 25–33.

Krause, Sydney J. "Whitman, Music and 'Proud Music of the Storm,' " *PMLA*, LXXII (1957), 705–21.

Krogvig, Kjell. "Till Whitman gjennem Wergeland." *Samtiden* (Oslo), 57, Heft 3, pp. 196–202 (1948).

Kroll, Ernest, *et al.* "Walt Whitman: A Centennial Celebration," *Beloit Poetry Journal*, 1954. (Special Whitman number.)

Kwiat, J. J. "Robert Henri and the Emerson-Whitman Tradition," *PMLA*, LXXI (September 1956), 617–36.

Lacote, René. "Le Chemin de Whitman," *Lettres Françaises*, no. 610 (March 8–14, 1956), p. 2.

Lars, Claudia. "Septimo en cuento con Chile," *Repertorio Americano*, XLI (May 20, 1945), 280–88.

Lauter, Paul. "Walt Whitman: Lover and Companion," *American Image*, XVI (1959), 407–35.

Leach, Nancy R. "Edith Wharton's Interest in Walt Whitman," *Yale University Library Gazette*, XXXIII (1958), 63–66.

Leidecker, Kurt F. "Walt Whitman—American Sādhu," *Visvabharati Quarterly*, XXII (1956), 39–68.

Lewis, R. W. B. "The Danger of Innocence: Adam as Hero in American Literature," *Yale Review*, XXIX (Spring 1950), 473–90.

Lovell, John, Jr. "Appreciating Whitman: 'Passage to India,'" *Modern Language Quarterly*, XXI (June 1960), 131–41.

Lowenfels, Walter. "Walt Whitman's Civil War," *Walt Whitman Review*, VI (1960), 52–53.

Lucchese, Romeo. "Dopo Whitman la vera Poesia Americana," *La Fiera Letteraria* (Italy), no. 43 (October 23, 1949), p. 5.

Mabbott, T. O. "Walt Whitman and Catullus," *Notes and Queries*, CXCVI (1951), 500.

———. "Whitman's 'Song of Myself,' XXIV, 19," *Explicator*, V (April 1947), 43.

Maxwell, J. C. "Swinburne and 'The Cult of the Calamus,'" *Notes and Queries*, n.s., VI (December 1960), 72–73.

McCormick, James P. "Walt Whitman in Japan," *Walt Whitman Newsletter*, III (1957), 11–13.

McCullough, John M. "Walt Whitman Bridge—Philadelphia, 1957," *Walt Whitman Newsletter*, III (1957), 42–44.

———. "Whitman in Bronze," *Walt Whitman Review*, V (1959), 74.

McDermott, John Francis. "Whitman and the Partons:

Glimpses from the Diary of Thomas Butler Gunn, 1856–1860," *American Literature*, XXIX (1957), 316–19.

McElderry, B. R., Jr. "Hamlin Garland's View of Whitman." *Personalist*, XXXVI (1955), 369–78.

———. "Inception of Passage to India," *PMLA*, LXXI (September 1956), 837–39.

McWilliams, David Jackson. " 'Leaves of Grass': Whitman en la Universidad," *El Mundo* (San Juan, P. R.), November 19, 1955.

Maiti, Mercedes. "Walt Whitman, 1819–1892," *Tribuna Libre*, July 6, 1952.

Marks, Alfred H. "Whitman's Triadic Imagery," *American Literature*, XXIII (March 1951), 99–126.

Marshall, William H. "Leigh Hunt on Walt Whitman, a New Letter," *Notes and Queries*, IV (1957), 392–93.

Martí, José. "Walt Whitman," *Bulletin of Pan American Union*, LXXIX (May 1945), 270–72.

Marx, Leo. "The Vernacular Tradition in American Literature: Walt Whitman and Mark Twain," *Die neueren Sprachen*, 1958, pp. 46–57.

Matsuhara, Iwao. "Walt Whitman in Japan: from the First Introduction to the Present," *Thought Currents in English Literature* (Tokyo), XXIX (January 1957), 5–42.

Mayer, Frederick. "Whitman's Social Philosophy," *Sociology and Social Research*, XXXIII (1948–49), 275–78.

Mayfield, John S. "Shake the Hand that Shook the Hand of Whitman," *Manuscripts*, X (1958), 50–52.

Mendelssohn, Maurice. "Leaves of Grass," *Soviet Literature* (Moscow), no. 7 (1955), pp. 161–66.

———. "Walt Whitman," *New World* (Moscow), XXII (March 1945), 183–88.

———. "Walt Whitman and the Struggle for Peace and Democracy," *Znamia*, no. 5 (1952), pp. 170–82.

———. "Walt Whitman in Russia," *Voks Bulletin*, no. 5 (1954), pp. 111–12.

———. "Walt Whitman to the 60th Year since His Death," *Ogonëk*, no. 13 (1952), p. 15.

Mercer, Dorothy F. "Walt Whitman on God and Self," *Vedanta and the West*, X (May–June 1947), 80–87.

———. "Walt Whitman on Learning and Wisdom," *Vedanta and the West*, X (March–April 1947), 57–59.

———. "Walt Whitman on Love," *Vedanta and the West*, X (July–August 1947), 107–13.

———. "Walt Whitman on Reincarnation," *Vedanta and the West*, IX (November–December 1946), 180–85.

———. "Walt Whitman on Karma Yoga," *Vedanta and the West*, X (1947), 150–53.

Merrill, Stuart, "Walt Whitman," translated from the French by John J. Espey, *Walt Whitman Newsletter*, III (1957), 55–57.

Messaien, Pierre. "Walt Whitman, Poète des États-Unis et la Démocratie," *Le Croix*, March 24, 1956, p. 3.

Miller, Edwin H., and Miller, Rosalind S. "Preparing a Checklist of Walt Whitman's Correspondence," *Bulletin of New York Public Library*, LXI (1957), 113–16.

Miller, Edwin H. "Whitman's First Letter to Anne Gilchrist: A Few Cautionary Remarks," *Walt Whitman Newsletter*, IV (1958), 92–93.

Miller, F. DeWolfe. "Before 'The Good Gray Poet,'" *Tennessee Studies in Literature*, III (1958), 89–98.

———. "Known Copies of Drum-Taps," *Walt Whitman Newsletter*, III (1957), 25–26.

———. "Lincoln and Whitman: The Author's Rejoinder," *Lincoln Herald*, LIX (summer 1957), 16, 24.

———. "The Battle of a Book," *Walt Whitman Newsletter*, IV (1958), 79–80.

————. "The First Advertisement of Drum-Taps," *Walt Whitman Review*, V (1959), 15.

————. "The 'Long Foreground' of Whitman's Elegies on Lincoln," *Lincoln Herald*, LVIII (Spring–Summer 1956), 3–7.

Miller, James E., Jr. "Four Cosmic Poets," *University of Kansas City Review*, XXIII (1957), 312–20.

————. " 'Song of Myself' as Inverted Mystical Experience," *PMLA*, LXX (1955), 636–61.

————. "Whitman and Eliot: The Poetry of Mysticism," *Southwest Review*, XLIII (1958), 113–23.

————. "Walt Whitman and the Secret of History," *Centennial Review of Arts and Sciences* (Michigan State University), III (1959), 321–36.

————. "Whitman and the Province of Poetry," *Arizona Quarterly*, XIV (1958), 5–19.

————. "Whitman in Italy," *Walt Whitman Review*, V (1959), 28–30.

————. "Whitman the Mystic Vagabond," *Walt Whitman Review*, VI (1960), 14–15.

————. "Whitman's 'Calamus': The Leaf and the Root," *PMLA*, LII (1957), 244–71.

Miller, Perry. "The Shaping of American Character," *New England Quarterly*, XXVIII (1955), 435–54.

————. "The Common Law Codification in Jacksonian America," *Proceedings of the American Philosophical Society*, CIII (1959), 463–68.

Millet, Fred B. "[Whitman] Man—Liberator—Visionary," *Nocturne* (Brooklyn College), VII (Spring 1955), 12.

Milne, W. Gordon. "William Douglas O'Connor and the Authorship of *The Good Gray Poet*," *American Literature*, XXV (March 1953), 31–42.

Miner, Earl R. "The Background, Date, and Composition of Whitman's 'A Broadway Pageant,' " *American Literature*, XXVII (1955), 403–5.

Miranda, Hernany. "Walt Whitman," *Tribuna Libre*, July 6, 1952.

Montalvo, Antonio. "Estampa de Walt Whitman," *Repertorio Americano*, XLIII (1948), 124.

Morgan, Claude. "Walt Whitman et Howard Fast," *Parallèle*, vol. 50, no. 108 (October 15, 1948), p. 5.

Morgan, Paul. "New Significance to Whitman's 'Song of the Exposition,'" *University of Texas Library Chronicle*, IV (Summer 1952), 137–50.

Morley, Christopher. "The Astral Lamp," *New York Times Book Review*, January 25, 1953.

———. "Rude Brief Recitatives for Walt Whitman's 134th Birthday," *Saturday Review of Literature*, XXXVI (August 22, 1953), 30.

Morris, Lawrence. "Walt Whitman, o Poeta da Identidade," *Kriterion*, XL–XLI (1958), 438–52.

Moyne, Ernest J. "Walt Whitman and Folger McKinsey or Walt Whitman in Elkton, Maryland, a Study of Public Taste in the 1880's," *Delaware Notes*, 29th series (1956), pp. 103–17.

Murciaux, Christian. "El Genio Puritano en el Siglo XIX," *Sur*, nos. 215–216 (September–October 1952). (Whitman, pp. 88–108.)

Murry, J. Middleton. "Walt Whitman: The Prophet of Democracy," *Pacific Spectator*, IX (Winter 1955), 32–57.

Nag, M. "Hamsun og Hamsun—Tradisjonen" (influence of Whitman, Ibsen, and Dostoyevsky on Hamsun's style), *Vin*, X, 187–91.

Nakado, Shozo. "On the Complete Translation of 'Leaves of Grass' into Japanese," *Walt Whitman Foundation Bulletin*, IV (April 1951), 8–9.

Narita, Narihisa. "Whitman and Science," *English Study and Teaching* (Japan), no. 1 (1947?).

Neilson, Kenneth P. "Bella C. Landauer, an Appreciation," *Walt Whitman Birthplace Bulletin*, III (July 1960), 20.

———. "Calamus: Search and Discovery," *Walt Whitman Birthplace Bulletin*, IV (October 1960), 13–19.

———. "Lilacs for Lincoln," *Walt Whitman Birthplace Bulletin*, III (July 1960), 12–15.

Neilson, Shaw. "Free Verse Old and New," *Southerly* (Sydney, Australia), XVII (1956), 38.

Nuhn, Ferner. "Leaves of Grass Viewed as an Epic," *Arizona Quarterly*, VII (winter 1951), 324–38.

Oakes, Frances. "The Philatelic Whitman," *Walt Whitman Newsletter*, III (1957), 34.

———. "Toward Destroying a Myth [Whitman's homosexuality]," *Walt Whitman Newsletter*, II (1956), 19–21.

———. "Whitman and Dixon: A Strange Case of Borrowing," *Georgia Review*, XI (1957), 333–40.

Oliver, Egbert S. " 'The Seas Are All Crossed': Whitman on America and World Freedom," *Western Humanities Review*, IX (1955), 303–12.

———. "Walt Whitman's 'Passage to India,' " *Journal of University of Poona* (India), no. 5 (1955), pp. 84–85.

———. "Whitman on World Freedom," *American Review* (New Delhi), I (1956), 18–29.

Ota, Sabura. "Walt Whitman and Japanese Literature," *Asia and the Humanities*, XI (1959), 62–69.

———. "Whitman Influences Japanese Literature," *Asian Student*, VII (1959), 3.

———. "An Outline of the Translation of American Literature in Japan," *Japan Science Review and Humanistic Studies*, XI (1960), 38–41.

Palandri, Angela Chih-Ying Jung. "Whitman in Red China," *Walt Whitman Newsletter*, IV (1958), 94–97.

Paris, L. "He Glorified the Common-Place," *Senior Scholastic* (Teacher's Ed.), XI (January 10, 1958), 13.

Parke, R. A. "Walt Whitman's Long Island," *Ford Times*, April 1955, pp. 14–15.

Parks, Edd Winfield. "The Public and the Private Poet," *South Atlantic Quarterly*, LVI (1957), 480–85.

Pearce, Roy Harvey. "Ezra Pound's Appraisal of Walt Whitman: Addendum," *Modern Language Notes*, LXXIV (1959), 23–28.

————. "On the Continuity of American Poetry," *Hudson Review*, X (1957), 518–39.

Peek, George A., Jr. "Walt Whitman and Politics," *Michigan Alumnus Quarterly Review*, LXII (1956), 254–61.

Penuelas, Marcelino C. "Walt Whitman y Chocanu," *Cuadernos Americanos*, XV (1956), 223–31.

Pollak, Georgiana. "The Relationship of Music to 'Leaves of Grass,' " *College English*, XV (April 1954), 384–94.

Pongs, H. "Walt Whitman und Stefan George," *Comparative Literature*, IV (fall 1952), 289–322. (Translated in G. W. Allen, ed., *Walt Whitman Abroad*—see under Books.)

Pound, Louise. "Two Curious Words: Whitman's *Carlacue*," *American Speech*, XXX (May 1955), 95–96.

Praz, Mario. "Whitman e Proust," *Il Mondo*, March 24, 1951.

Pucciani, Oreste F. "Walt Whitman and the XIX Century," *Twice a Year*, 1948, pp. 245–58.

Pulos, C. E. "Whitman and Epictetus: The Stoical Element in Leaves of Grass," *Journal of English and Germanic Philology*, LV (January 1956), 75–84.

Rabassa, Gregory. "Walt Whitman Visto por José Martí," *La Nueva Democracia* (New York), XXXIX (1959), 88–93.

Randel, William. "Walt Whitman and American Myths," *South Atlantic Quarterly*, LIX (1960), 103–13.

Redman, B. R. "Separating Poet from Pretender," *Satur-*

day Review of Literature, **XXXIII** (February 18, 1950), 17.

Remords, G. "Les Lettres Americanes et la Critique Universitaire Française," *Bulletin de la Faculté des Lettres de Strassbourg*, January 1957.

Resnick, Nathan. "Whitman, Democracy and the Rolling Earth," *Walt Whitman Birthplace Bulletin*, **III** (April 1960), 6–11.

Ridley, Hilda M. "The Good Gray Poet," *Dalhousie Review*, **XXXV** (1956), 370–73.

Riese, Teut. "Walt Whitman als Politischer Dichter," *Jahrbuch für Amerika-Studien*, **III** (1958), 136–50.

Ringe, Donald A. "Bryant and Whitman: A Study in Artistic Affinities," *Boston University Studies in English*, **II** (1956), 85–94.

Roddier, Henri. "Pierre Leroux, George Sand et Walt Whitman, ou l'éveil d'un poète," *Revue Litératur Comparée*, **XXXI** (1957), 5–33.

Rodgers, Cleveland. "Lincoln . . . Walt Whitman Kinship," *Walt Whitman Birthplace Bulletin*, **I** (1958), 3–6.

———. "The Good Gray House Builder," *Walt Whitman Review*, **V** (1959), 63–69.

———. "Walt Whitman and Marshal Smuts," *Walt Whitman Foundation Bulletin*, **IV** (April 1951), 4–8.

Romig, Edna. "More Roots for Leaves of Grass" in *Elizabethan Studies: University of Colorado Studies in the Humanities*, **II**, no. 4 (1945), pp. 322–27.

Rosenberry, Edward H. "Walt Whitman's All-American Poet," *Delaware Notes*, **XXXII** (1959), 1–2.

Roundtree, T. J. "Whitman's Indirect Expression and Its Application to 'Song of Myself,'" *PMLA*, **LXXIII** (December 1958), 549–55.

Roy, G. R. "Walt Whitman, George Sand and Certain French Socialists," *Revue Litératur Comparée*, **XXIX** (1955), 550–61.

Ruohuma, Kosti. "The Paths Whitman Walked, Photographed for *Life*," *Life*, June 20, 1955, pp. 38; 113–21.

Saito, Takeshi. "Whitman and His Democratic View," *American Study* (Japan), January [1948?].

Sarenkov, V. "Uolt Uitman—Poet na Demokracijata." *Septemvri* (Sofia), VIII (1955), 154–57.

Schiffman, Joseph. "Walt Whitman and the People Across the Street," *Nassau County Historical Journal*, XIX (1958), 17–25.

Schiller, Andrew. "Thoreau and Whitman: The Record of a Pilgrimage," *New England Quarterly*, XXVIII (1955), 186–97.

Schlesinger, A. M., Jr. "Jackson and Literature," *New Republic*, CXIV (May 27, 1946), 765–68.

Schneps, Maurice. "Walt Whitman and His Critics," *Today's Japan* (Tokyo), IV (March 1959), 54–58.

Semans, Mary Biddle Trent. "Josiah Charles Trent as a Collector," *Library Notes: A Bulletin Issued for Friends of Duke University*, December 1956, pp. 1–5.

Sengfelder, Bernhard. "Walt Whitman," *Deutsche Rundschau*, CXX (November 1947), 108–14.

Shapiro, Karl. "The First White Aboriginal," *The Rising Generation* (Tokyo), CIII (1957), 608–10, 669–71; CIV (1958), 74–77, 133–36. Reprinted in *Walt Whitman Review*, V (1959), 43–52.

Shephard, Esther. "An Inquiry into Whitman's Method of Turning Prose into Poetry," *Modern Language Quarterly*, XIV (March 1953), 43–59.

———. "Possible Sources of Some of Whitman's Ideas and Symbols in 'Hermes Mercurius Trismegistus' and Other Works," *Modern Language Quarterly*, XIV (March 1953), 60–81.

———. "Photoduplicates of Whitman's Cardboard Butterfly," *PMLA*, LXX (September 1955), 876.

———. "Whitman's Whereabouts in the Winter of 1842–1843," *American Literature*, XXIX (1957), 289–96.

Sherman, Paul. "Walt Whitman, Thinker and Artist," *Journal of English and Germanic Philology*, LII (1953), 278–79.

Sherrinsky, Harald. "Walt Whitman in modernen deutschen Übersetzung," *Neu Philologische Zeitschrift*, III (1950), 189–91.

Shimizu, Haruo. "A Study of Whitman's Imagery," *Walt Whitman Review*, V (1959), 26–28.

Sillen, Samuel. "Walt Whitman poète de la démocratie américaine," *La Pensée* (1956) ; no. 69, pp. 77–91 ; no. 70, pp. 69–82.

Silver, Rollo G. "Sir Edwin Arnold and Walt Whitman," *Notes and Queries*, CXCIII (August 21, 1948), 366.

Slonin, Ruth. "Walt Whitman's 'Open Road,' " *Research Studies of the State College of Washington*, XXV (1957), 69–74.

Slote, Bernice, and Miller, James E., Jr. "Of Monkeys, Nudes, and the Good Gray Poet: Dylan Thomas and Walt Whitman," *Western Humanities Review*, XIII (1959), 339–53.

———. "The Structure of Hart Crane's 'The Bridge,' " *University of Kansas City Review*, XXIV (1958), 225–38.

Smith, Henry Nash. "Walt Whitman and Manifest Destiny," *Huntington Library Quarterly*, X (August 1947), 373–89.

Smith, Ray. "Whitman: The Leaves of Grass Bicentennial 2055," *Approach*, XVIII (1955–56), 7–12.

Spaeth, Duncan. "Backward Glance O'er Traveled Roads with 'Leaves of Grass,' " *Philadelphia Forum*, XXVII (June 1948), 13–14, 32.

———. "Geopoetics vs. Geopolitics," *Walt Whitman Foundation Bulletin*, VI (April 1953), 8–11.

Spector, Robert D. "The Reality of War in Whitman's *Specimen Days*," *Notes and Queries*, CXCVI (June 9, 1951), 254–55.

Spitz, Leon. "Walt Whitman and Judaism," *Chicago Jewish Forum*, XIII (1955), 174–77.

Spitzer, Leo. "Explication de Texte Applied to Walt Whitman's 'Out of the Cradle Endlessly Rocking,'" *Journal of English Literary History*, XVI (September 1949), 229–49.

Sprague, Harriet. "Whitman and Poe," *American Notes and Queries*, V (August 1945), 75.

————. "Whitman Exhibition Catalogue," *Papers of the Bibliographical Society of America*, XL (1946), 245–46.

Stauffer, Ruth. "Whitman's 'A Passage to India,'" *Explicator*, IX (May 1951), 50.

Steadman, John M. "Whitman and the King James Bible," *Notes and Queries*, n.s. III (1956), 538–39.

Stebner, Gerhard. "Whitman—Lilencron—W. H. Auden: Betrachtung und Vergleich Motivähnlicher Gedichte," *Die Neueren Sprachen*, IX (March 1960), 105–18.

Stepanchev, Stephen. "*Leaves of Grass* in the Soviet Camp," *Walt Whitman Newsletter*, II (1956), 3–4.

Stevenson, Lionel. "An English Admirer of Walt Whitman," *American Literature*, XXIX (January 1958), 470–73.

Stovall, Floyd. "Leaves of Grass," *University of North Carolina Extension Bulletin*, XXXV (1956), 19–29.

————. "Notes on Whitman's Reading," *American Literature*, XXVI (November 1954), 337–62.

————. "Walt Whitman and the Dramatic Stage," *Studies in Philology*, L (July 1953), 513–39.

————. "Whitman, Shakespeare and the Baconians," *Philological Quarterly*, XXXI (January 1952), 27–38.

————. "Whitman, Shakespeare and Democracy," *Journal of English and Germanic Philology*, LI (October 1952), 457–72.

————. "Whitman's Knowledge of Shakespeare," *Studies in Philology*, XLIX (October 1952), 643–64.

————. "Walt Whitman and the American Tradition," *Virginia Quarterly Review*, XXXI (1955), 540–57.

————. "Walt Whitman: The Man and the Myth," *South Atlantic Quarterly*, LIV (1955), 538–51.

Straumann, Heinrich. "Hundert Jahre 'Leaves of Grass' zu Walt Whitmans Ersten Gedichtband," *Literatur und Kunst*, December 4, 1955, p. 8.

Suckling, Norman. "Walt Whitman in English Music," *The Listener* (London, BBC), August 22, 1946, p. 257.

Sutton, Walter. "The Analysis of Free Verse Form, Illustrated by a Reading of Whitman," *Journal of Aesthetics and Art Criticism*, XVIII (December 1959), 241–54.

Takano, Fumi. "Whitman's Spiritual Pilgrimage," *Studies in English Literature* (Tokyo), XXXIV (1957), 59–75.

Templeman, William Darby. "Hopkins and Whitman: Evidence of Influence and Echoes," *Philological Quarterly*, XXXIII (1954), 48–65.

————. "On Whitman's Apple-Peelings [in *Leaves of Grass*], *Philological Quarterly*, XXXV (April 1956), 200–202.

Thorp, Williard. "Walt Whitman Without Apology," *Saturday Review of Literature*, XXIX (August 17, 1946), 10.

Todd, Edgeley. "Indian Pictures and Two Whitman Poems," *Huntington Library Quarterly*, XIX (1955), 1–11.

Tolles, Frederick B. "A Quaker Reaction to 'Leaves of Grass,'" *American Literature*, XIX (May 1947), 170–71.

Topen, P. "Gordye pesni Uitmena," *Ogonek* (Moscow), XXXII (1954), 25.

Traubel, Gertrude. "The Second Hundred Years," *Walt Whitman Newsletter*, II (1956), 4–5.

Trilling, Lionel. "Sermon on a Text from Whitman," *Nation*, CLX (February 24, 1945), 215–16.

Turner, Katharine. "American Literature in China," *Colorado Quarterly*, VI (1958), 418–28.

Turner, Lorenzo D. "Walt Whitman and the Negro," *Chicago Jewish Forum*, XV (1956), 5–11.

Undurraga, Antonio de. "Walt Whitman y el Hombre Total," *Cuadernos del Congreso por la Libertad de la Cultura*, no. 32, pp. 37–42.

Untermeyer, Louis. "Faith of a Failure," New York *Herald Tribune Magazine Section*, March 21, 1948, p. 2.

Van Horne, John. "Leopardi y Whitman," *Italica*, XXXIII (1946), 161–69.

Vanson, F. "Edward Carpenter: The English Whitman," *Contemporary Review*, CXCIII (June 1958), 314–16.

Vittorini, Elo. "Nascita della Letteratura Americana," *Prospetti* (Florence), no. 8 (1954).

Wain, John. "Disguises of Walt Whitman," *Spectator*, CXCIV (November 1955), 802–3.

Walcutt, Charles C. "Whitman's 'Out of the Cradle Endlessly Rocking,'" *College English*, X (February 1949), 277–79.

Walker, R. J. "Controversial Walt Whitman," *Hobbies*, LXI (April 1956), 108–9.

Warfel, Harry R. "'Out of the Cradle Endlessly Rocking!" *Tennessee Studies in Literature*, III (1958), 83–88.

————. "The Structure of 'Eidólons,'" *Walt Whitman Newsletter*, IV (1958), 103–5.

————. "Whitman's 'Salut au Monde': The Ideal of Human Brotherhood," *Phylon*, Second Quarter 1958, pp. 154–56.

————. "Whitman's Structural Principles in 'Spontaneous Me,'" *College English*, XVIII (1957), 190–95.

Weathers, W. T. "Whitman's Poetic Translations of His

1855 Preface," *American Literature,* XIX (March 1947), 21–40.

Wescott, Ralph. "A Great Letter . . . to Van Wyck Brooks," *Walt Whitman Birthplace Bulletin,* I (April 1958), 8–10.

Westerfield, Hargis. "A Whitman-John Pierpont Parallel," *Walt Whitman Review,* V (1954), 17.

Wheatley, Elwood A. "Walt Whitman and the Bridge: An Unsuccessful Campaign to Change a Name," *Churchman,* CLXXI (1957), 6–7, 9–10.

Whicher, Edward G. " 'Pioneers! O Pioneers!' " *American Literature,* XIX (November 1947), 259–61.

Whicher, Stephen E. "Whitman's 'Out of the Cradle Endlessly Rocking,' " *Explicator,* V (February 1947), 28.

White, Courtland Y. "A Whitman Ornithology," *Cassinia: Proceedings of the Delaware Valley Ornithological Club,* XXXV (1945), 12–22.

White, Frederick C. "Whites and Negroes: Literary testimonies," *American Notes and Queries,* IV (January 1945), 153–54.

White, William. "A Walt Whitman Poster [facsimile]," *American Book Collector,* X (1959), 5–6.

———. "Lincoln and Whitman: A Note on the 'Van Rensellaer' Letter," *Lincoln Herald,* LIX (Summer 1957), 16–24.

———. "Mary Whitall Smith's Letters to Walt Whitman," *Smith Alumnae Quarterly,* XLIX (1958), 86–88.

———. "Mr. Comstock as Cato the Censor," *Walt Whitman Review,* V (1959), 54–56.

———. "More about the 'Publication' of the First *Leaves of Grass,*" *American Literature,* XXVIII (1957), 516–17.

———. "Sir Edmund Gosse on Walt Whitman," *Victorian Studies* (Indiana University), I (1957), 180–82.

———. "The Walt Whitman Fellowship: An Account of

Its Organization and a Checklist of Its Papers," *Papers of the Bibliographical Society of America*, LI (1957), 67–84.

―――. "The Walt Whitman Fellowship: Additions and Corrections," *Papers of the Bibliographical Society of America*, LI (1957), 167–69.

―――. "Walt Whitman on New England Writers," *New England Quarterly*, XXVII (September 1954), 395–96.

―――. "Whitman on Newspaper Practices in the 1870's," *Journalism Quarterly*, XXXVII (Summer 1960), 438–39.

Willard, Charles B. "Ezra Pound and the Whitman Message," *Revue de Litératur Comparée*, XXXI (1957), 94–98.

―――. "Ezra Pound's Appraisal of Walt Whitman," *Modern Language Notes*, LXXII (1957), 19–26.

―――. "Ezra Pound's Debt to Walt Whitman," *Studies in Philology*, LIV (October 1957), 573–81.

―――. "The Saunders Collection of Whitmania in the Brown University Library," *Books at Brown*, XVIII (1956), 14–22.

―――. "Whitman and Tennyson's 'Ulysses,' " *Walt Whitman Newsletter*, II (1956), 9–10.

Williams, Mentor L. "Whitman Today," *University of Kansas City Review*, XIV (summer 1948), 267–76.

Willingham, John R. "Whitman's Centennial," *Nation*, CLXXX (May 14, 1955), 426–28.

―――. "Words of the Poet." *Nation*, CLXXXII (January 7, 1956), 15.

Wilson, Lawrence. "The 'Body Electric' Meets the Genteel Tradition," *New Mexico Quarterly*, XXVI (1956), 369–86.

Winwar, Frances. "Fern Leaves and Leaves of Grass," *New York Times Book Review*, April 22, 1945, p. 7.

Wirzberger, Karl-Heinz. "Einhundert Jahre Leaves of

Grass," *Zeitschrift für Anglistik und Amerikanistik* (East Berlin), IV (1956), 77–87.

Wood, Frank. "Three Poems on Whitman [Lorca, S. V. Benet, Hart Crane]," *Comparative Literature,* IV (winter 1952), 44–53.

Woodward, Robert H. "Davy Crockett: Whitman's 'Friendly and Flowing Savage,'" *Walt Whitman Review,* VI (1960), 48–49.

———. "Journey Motif in Whitman and Tennyson," *Modern Language Notes,* LXXII (January 1957), 26–27.

Workman, Mims Thornburgh. "The Whitman-Twain Enigma," *Mark Twain Quarterly,* VIII (1948), 12–13.

Zardoya, Concha. "Walt Whitman y Espana," *Indice* (Madrid), nos. 86–87 (1956), 27.

Zarsurski, Ja. "Uitmen na Stranicaen 'Ordine nuovo,'" *Ogonek* (Moscow), XXXIII (1955), 23.

Zeiger, Arthur. "In Defense of Whitman," *Tomorrow,* IX (June 1950), 54–56.

Anonymous. "Discoverer [Rena V. Grant] of Whitman Papers," *New York Times,* December 13, 1960, p. 30.

———. "The Long Islander and Walt Whitman," *Long Islander,* July 2, 1959, Section 3, p. 1.

———. "Poets Are Travelers," *Scholastic,* XLVIII (February 15, 1946), 15.

———. "Walt Whitman's Vision of Lincoln Square," *Promenade Magazine,* XXVI (1959), 40–41.

———. "Walt Whitman's Morals." *Newsweek,* XLVII (January 2, 1956), 39.

———. "Walt Whitman: Yesterday and Today," *Literary Cavalcade,* March 1958, pp. 18–22.

THESES ON WHITMAN

Brasher, Thomas Lowber. "To All the People of Brooklyn: Whitman as Editor of the Brooklyn Eagle, 1846–

1848," *Dissertation Abstracts*, XVI (Louisiana State, 1955), 1681–82.

Carr, Harry L. "The Comparison of Poetry and Painting: Whitman's 'Out of the Cradle Endlessly Rocking' and Some Paintings of Albert Pinkham Ryder," *Dissertation Abstracts*, XX (Southern California, 1959), 665–66.

Cobb, Robert P. "Society versus Solitude: Studies in Emerson, Thoreau, Hawthorne and Whitman," *Dissertation Abstracts*, XV (Michigan State, 1955), 1396.

Gibbons, Robert F. " 'Ocean' Poem: A Study of Marine Symbolism in *Leaves of Grass*," *Dissertation Abstracts*, XIX (Tulane, 1959), 2344–45.

Kanes, Martin. "La Fortune de Walt Whitman en France," summary by Roger Asselineau of an unpublished thesis for the doctorat d'Université, Paris, 1953.

Nicholson, Homer K., Jr. "O Altitudo: A Comparison of the Writings of Walt Whitman, D. H. Lawrence and Henry Miller," *Dissertation Abstracts*, XVII (Vanderbilt, 1957), 2614.

Oakes, Frances E. "The Whitman Controversy in France," *Dissertation Abstracts*, XV (Florida State, 1955), 1621.

Ogilvie, John Thayer. "The Art of Leaves of Grass: A Critical Analysis of the Final Text with Particular Attention to Imagery, Symbolism, and Structure," *Dissertation Abstracts*, XIX (Indiana, 1959), 2339–40.

Davidson, Loren K. "Whitman's 'Song of Myself,' " *Dissertation Abstracts*, XX (Duke, 1959), 4097–98.

Sanderlin, Wallace S., Jr. "The Growth of Leaves of Grass, 1856–1860: An Analysis of the Relationship of the Valentine-Barrett Manuscripts to the Third Edition," *Dissertation Abstracts*, XV (Virginia, 1955), 1857–58.

Westerfield, Hargis. "Walt Whitman's Reading," *Dissertation Abstracts*, XIV (Indiana, 1954), 2353–54.

WHITMAN IN ART

MUSIC AND DANCE

Bacon, Ernst. *The Commonplace (Walt Whitman).* New York: Associated Music Publishers, 1946. 5 pp.

Dello, Joio Norman. *The Mystic Trumpeter: For Full Chorus of Mixed Voices* . . . Text adapted from Walt Whitman, New York: Schirmer, 1945. 36 pp.

Hindemith, Paul. *When Lilacs Last in the Dooryard Bloom'd.* A Requiem for mezzo soprano and baritone, solo, chorus and orchestra; on the poem by Walt Whitman. New York: Associated Music Publishers, 1948. 153 pp.

Lockwood, Normand. *I Hear America Singing.* For mixed voices, poems by Walt Whitman. Delaware Water Gap, Pa.: Shawnee Press, 1954. 30 pp.

Shawn, Ted. "Whitman: His Immortal Leaves." Selections from *Dance We Must* (The Peabody Lectures), by Ted Shawn. Selections from Photographic Records of the Art [of Ted Shawn's] Dancers. Linden Dahlberg, Editorial Director. Kent, Washington: John Victor, Ltd., 1948. 84 pp.

RADIO AND STAGE DRAMA

Anonymous. "The Legend of the Mountain." (Eternal Light Series.) Presented by the National Broadcasting Company, December 16, 1951. New York: The Jewish Theological Seminary, 1951. 10 pp.

Goodman, Randolph. *I, Walt Whitman* [words of Whitman arranged in a drama]. Brooklyn: Library Associates of Brooklyn College, 1955. 88 pp.

POEMS ABOUT WHITMAN

Angoff, Charles. "Walt Whitman Contemplates His Biographers," *American Mercury*, LX (March 1945), 340.

Dell, Floyd. "To a Poet Once Resident in Washington," *Walt Whitman Newsletter*, III (1957), 39.

Garret, F. R. "To Walt Whitman," *Saturday Review of Literature*, XXXII, (June 11, 1949), 24.

Ginsberg, Allen. "A Supermarket in California" in *Howl and Other Poems*. San Francisco: City Lights Bookshop, 1958.

Honig, Edwin. "Walt Whitman," in *The Gazabos: 41 Poems*. New York: Clarke & Way, 1959.

Ignatow, D. "Walt Whitman in the Civil War Hospitals," *Saturday Review of Literature*, XL (December 14, 1957), 42.

Lorca, Garcia F. "Ode to Walt Whitman" in *Poet in New York* [Spanish text with translation into English by Ben Belitt. New York: Grove Press, 1955, pp. 119–27. Belitt's translation also in *Poetry* (Chicago), LXXXV (January 1955), 187–92.

Ninck, Roger. "Ode à Walt Whitman" in *Les Couteaux du Destin*. Paris: Caractères (Collection Ariane), 1956, pp. 58–62.

Pessoa, Fernando [pseudonym of Álvaro de Campos]. "Saudação a Walt Whitman," in *Poesias: Obras Completas de Fernando Pessoa* (Lisbon: Edições Ática), 1958, pp. 202–12. [Translated into French by] Guibert, Armand, "Salutation à Walt Whitman," in *Ode Triomphale et Autres Poèmes de Alvaro de Campos* (Paris: Pierre Jean Oswald, 1960), pp. 27–37.

Simpson, Louis. "Walt Whitman at Bear Mountain," *Paris Review*, Spring 1960, 26–27.

Squires, Fred D. L. "Rendezvous: With Message to Whitman Comrades Everywhere." Privately printed, 1959. 8 pp.

Tuarello, Margaret. "Poem for Walt Whitman," *Books Abroad*, XXX (1956), 31.

FICTION

Aronin, Ben. *Walt Whitman's Secret.* Chicago: Argus Books, 1955. 374 pp.

NOTES

1. Introduction, *Walt Whitman: Complete Poetry and Prose* (New York, 1948).

2. *The Solitary Singer: A Critical Biography of Walt Whitman* (New York, 1955); see especially the discussions of the second and third editions of *Leaves of Grass.*

3. *Reminiscences* (New York, 1899), I, 225–27.

4. *The Good Gray Poet* (New York, 1866), p. 6.

5. *Three Tales* (Boston, 1891), p. 211–320.

6. From holograph in Berg Collection, New York Public Library; printed by Louis Untermeyer (ed.), *The Poetry and Prose of Walt Whitman* (New York, 1949), 930–32.

7. Sholom J. Kahn, in *Walt Whitman Abroad,* ed. G. W. Allen (Syracuse, N. Y., 1955), p. 250.

8. R. M. Bucke, *Walt Whitman* (Philadelphia, 1883), p. 136.

9. See *The Solitary Singer,* p. 103.

10. *Ibid.,* p. 425.

11. Horace Traubel, *With Walt Whitman in Camden* (Philadelphia, 1953), p. 313; Traubel's account of Whitman's reaction has been rearranged as dramatic dialogue.

12. *The Solitary Singer,* p. 440.

13. *Ibid.,* p. 492.

14. J. Johnston and J. W. Wallace, *Visits to Walt Whitman in 1890–1891* (London, 1917), p. 186.

15. Bucke, *Walt Whitman,* p. 56.

16. *Days with Walt Whitman* (London, 1906), p. 38.

17. *Critical Kit-Kats* (New York, 1896), p. 106; Gosse slightly misquotes "Stanzas Written in Dejection Near Naples."

18. *Whitman: A Study* (Boston, 1896), p. 53.

19. *Walt Whitman, His Life and Work* (New York, 1906), pp. 307–8.

THE POET: *Cosmos Inspired*

1.   Lazare Saminsky, *Music of Our Day* (New York, 1939), 105–6; The quotation is from James's *Varieties of Religious Experience* (New York, 1902), p. 84.

2.   Imogene Holst, *Gustav Holst* (London, 1923), p. 45.

3.   Eric Fenby, *Delius as I Knew Him* (London, 1936), p. 36.

4.   Laurence Gilman's Preface to John Alden Carpenter's *Sea-Drift, Symphonic Poem* (New York, 1936).

5.   The whole section of poems called "Inscriptions" is composed of short pieces stating Whitman's poetic themes and purposes.

6.   Quoted in *Complete Writings of Walt Whitman* (New York, 1902), V, 217.

7.   *The Background of Modern French Poetry* (London, 1951), p. 78.

8.   A. G. Lehmann, *The Symbolist Aesthetic in France: 1885–1895* (Oxford, 1950), p. 151.

9.   For discussion of Whitman's esthetic theory and practice see G. W. Allen and Charles T. Davis (eds.), *Walt Whitman's Poems* (New York, 1955), pp. 1–51.

10.   Quoted from *Geschichte der Religion und Philosophie in Deutschland* by Kuno Francke, *A History of German Literature* (New York, 1903), pp. 521–22.

11.   The 1882 revised version of the 1855 Preface.

12.   Cf. "The 'Long Journey' Motif."

13.   Not collected by Whitman; edited by Edward Grier, *The Eighteenth Presidency!* (Lawrence, Kansas, 1956).

14.   Quoted from the 1882 version.

15.   Herbert Bergman, "Ezra Pound and Walt Whitman," *American Literature,* XXVII (March, 1955), 56–61; R. H. Pearce, "Ezra Pound's Appraisal of Walt Whitman: Addendum," *Modern Language Notes,* LXXIV (January, 1959), 23–28.

16.   *The Nation & Athenaeum,* XLI (June 4, 1927), 302.

17.   "Modern Poetry," written by Hart Crane for Oliver M. Sayler's Symposium, *Revolt in the Arts* (New York, 1929); reprinted in *The Collected Poems of Hart Crane* (New York, 1933), pp. 175–79.

THE POET: *Mutations in Whitman's Art.*

1. I have discussed some of these differences in *The Solitary Singer* (New York, 1955), but nowhere as a specific subject.

2. See Mark Van Doren's "The Poet," in *Walt Whitman: Man, Poet, and Philosopher: Three Lectures* . . . (Washington, 1955).

3. In London *Critic;* whole review reprinted in *Leaves of Grass Imprints* (Boston, 1860), pp. 43–45.

4. In the 1855 edition Whitman used periods (usually, though not consistently, four) to indicate a rhetorical pause, or caesura.

5. See Sister M. Bernetta Quinn, *The Metamorphic Tradition in Modern Poetry* (New Brunswick, N. J., 1955).

6. See Malcolm Cowley's Introduction to *Walt Whitman's Leaves of Grass: The First (1855) Edition* (New York: Viking Press, 1959).

7. See *The Solitary Singer,* pp. 179 ff.

8. In a very late poem, "To Soar in Freedom and Fulness of Power," Whitman specifically stated the theory on which he created such symbolical music: "I have not so much emulated the birds that musically sing, /I have abandoned myself to flights, broad circles . . ."

9. See P. Jannaccone, *La Poesia di Walt Whitman e L'Evoluzione delle Forme Ritmiche* (Torino, 1898), pp. 65 ff.

10. *Introduction to Poetry* (New York, 1951), p. 43.

THE POET: *The "Long Journey" Motif*

1. Richard M. Bucke (ed.), *Notes and Fragments* (London, Ont., 1899), p. 124; Bucke's work furnishes the main evidence for this plan.

2. Other projected poems on kindred themes: "Poems of the Ancient Earth to the Ancient Heavens," "Poem of the Universalities. Poem of the Universal likenesses of all men—humanity. Though the times, climes, differ, men do not so much differ." See also the "Poem of existence." A great deal of the "Shorter Notes" (Part IV) published by Bucke are concerned with historical names, facts, and comments which indicate Whitman's interest in world history and speculations on prehistorical ages. Characteristically, however, as in *The*

American Primer, he seldom gets beyond the names—a fact which plainly indicates that he was capable of treating historical material only in a poetic manner. Bucke, *Notes and Fragments,* pp. 10, 13, 21, 22, 77, 134, 142, 151–92.

3. Bucke, *Notes and Fragments,* pp. 140–41, 144. See also Frederik Schyberg, *Walt Whitman,* trans. Evie A. Allen (New York, 1951), pp. 170–71, and Johannes V. Jensen, *The Long Journey,* trans. A. G. Chater (New York, 1945).

4. The term is used in "Song of Myself," "Song of the Open Road," and "Pioneers! O Pioneers!" and in "I Sing the Body Electric" the poet declares that "All is a procession, / The Universe is a procession with measured and perfect motion."

5. In a footnote to *American Criticism* (Boston, 1928— p. 164) Norman Foerster mentioned "Whitman's idea of life as a pilgrimage, for which he was indebted mainly to Bunyan and to Hawthorne" ("The Celestial Railroad"). But the "Long Journey" seems to be fundamentally different from these Christian allegories. As early as 1840 Whitman was also thinking about life as a "long journey by steamboat, stagecoach, and railroad" (*Uncollected Poetry and Prose of Walt Whitman,* ed. Emory Holloway—New York, 1932—I, 38). This trite sort of allegory, too, is far removed from the "journey" motif in *Notes and Fragments* and *Leaves of Grass,* which was probably inspired chiefly by Whitman's readings in popular works on astronomy and evolution. See Eugene Dugdale, "Whitman's Knowledge of Astronomy, *University of Texas Studies in English,* No. 16 (July, 1936), pp. 125–37.

6. Bucke, *Notes and Fragments,* p. 144.

7. *Ibid.,* pp. 124–25; see Arthur O. Lovejoy, *The Great Chain of Being* (Cambridge, Mass., 1935), especially Chap. IX and pp. 259, 265: Leibnitz converted "the once immutable Chain of Being into the program of an endless Becoming." Leibnitz also held a theory of "cosmic evolution" to which Whitman was undoubtedly at least indirectly indebted.

8. *Leaves of Grass,* 1855 edition, p. 68. At times his evolution doctrine sounds almost like oriental transmigration. Concerning the animals, in "Song of Myself" he wonders "where they got those tokens, Did I pass that way huge times ago and negligently drop them?" He also claims he has "died ten thousand times before."

9. "Crossing Brooklyn Ferry"; Mody C. Boatright has studied Whitman's relation to Hegel in "Whitman and Hegel," *University of Texas Studies in English,* No. 9 (July, 1929), pp. 134–50.

10. Bucke, *Notes and Fragments,* p. 85; and "Thoughts" (p. 230 in Holloway ed. of *Leaves of Grass*).

11. Cf. Schyberg, *Walt Whitman,* pp. 90–91.

12. Clifton J. Furness (ed.), *Walt Whitman Workshop* (Cambridge, Mass., 1928), p. 44.

13. For a thorough analysis of Whitman's religious intentions see George L. Sixbey, " 'Chanting the Square Deific' —A Study in Whitman's Religion," *American Literature,* IX (May, 1937), 171–95.

14. Bucke, *Notes and Fragments,* p. 45; "Song of the Open Road"; and Lovejoy, *Great Chain of Being,* p. 255 and *passim.*

15. See the index of Holloway's *Uncollected Poetry and Prose,* also Bucke, *Notes and Fragments,* pp. 38, 43, 48, and Section 49 of "Song of Myself"; for the opposite view see Floyd Stovall's "Main Currents in Whitman's Poetry," *American Literature,* IV (March, 1932), 3–21.

16. *Wilhelm Meister* was largely responsible for the popularity of the wander motif in romantic literature, and Nietzsche actually wrote *Thus Spake Zarathustra* on a walking trip. Mme de Staël, exiled by Napoleon, also contributed greatly to the use of the wander theme, though the *émigré* literature tended to be nostalgic, only faintly Whitmanesque in tone.

17. Horace Traubel (ed.), *With Walt Whitman in Camden* (Boston, 1906–14), II, 5, 21.

18. Cf. Henri Bergson, *Creative Evolution* (1911), p. 27: Life is a "current passing from germ to germ . . . the continuous progress indefinitely pursued." So far as I know Whitman has not been seriously studied for any relationship to "expressionism," but the characteristics of this movement, as summarized by Carl Dahlström, *Strindberg's Dramatic Expressionism* (Ann Arbor, 1930), p. 80, exactly fit *Leaves of Grass.* For Dujardin see Mary M. Colum, "Literature of To-day and Tomorrow," *Scribner's* Magazine, C (October and December, 1936), 66–69, 98–106.

19. This point of view motivates "Salut au Monde!"

20. Bucke, *Notes and Fragments,* p. 79.

21.   G. M. Gathorne-Hardy makes some interesting comparisons between Whitman, Shelley, and Wergeland in his introduction to Henrik Wergeland's *Poems*, trans. Gathorne-Hardy, Jethro Bittrell, and I. Grøndahl (Oslo and London, 1929).

22.   Schyberg, *Walt Whitman,* p. 266.

23.   Signe Toksvig, *The Life of Hans Christian Andersen* (New York, 1934), p. 127; Andersen, *Fodreise fra Holmens Canal til Ostepynten af Amager, i Aarene 1828 og* in *Samlede Skrifter* (København, n.d.), pp. 208, 210.

24.   Recently a critic in Norway has argued that Wergeland provides a bridge for Norwegian understanding of Whitman: Kjell Krogvig in G. W. Allen (ed.), *Walt Whitman Abroad* (Syracuse, N. Y., 1955), pp. 137–42.

25.   *Skabelsen Mennesket og Messias* (Kristiana, 1921); the Gathorne-Hardy translation, *Poems,* has selections from this epic.

26.   Gathorne-Hardy translation, pp. 172–73, 175, 176, 178; "Song of Myself," Sections 47 and 48.

27.   Translated by E. A. Allen from *Skabelsen . . . ,* p. 130.

28.   Gerhard Gran, *Norsk Aandsliv i 100 Aar* [Norse Spiritual Life for 100 Years], I, 7–8. Quoted by Schyberg, *Walt Whitman* (Allen translation), p. 260.

29.   Translated by E. A. Allen from *Skabelsen . . . ,* pp. 186–87.

30.   See Gathorne-Hardy's introduction to Wergeland's *Poems,* and Just Bing, *Litteraturens Indre Udvikling i det Nittende Aarhundrede* (København, 1926), pp. 46–47.

31.   "There is a paradox and an irony about the fact that Henrik Wergeland should have established a reputation for an exclusive . . . nationalism when in fact, of all Norwegian writers, he . . . was . . . the most cosmopolitan in his interests and his disposition," wrote Gathorne-Hardy in the introduction to *Poems,* p. xvi.

32.   The translations are mainly in Chap. II of *Hjulet* (København, 1920); the hero is a Whitmanesque poet, the villain is homosexually inclined and also illustrates the absurdity of Whitman's belief that he could incorporate all religions. "The Wheel" motif is also Whitmanesque, celebrating the machine age in America. The setting of the novel is Chicago.

33. Compare Whitman's "I see a great round wonder roll-ing through space" ("Salut au Monde!") and his poet (1855 Preface) who stands high up "turning a concentrated light."

THE POET: *Translations of Whitman Since World War II*

1. See Chap. VI of G. W. Allen's *Walt Whitman Hand-book* (Chicago, 1946), and introductions to countries repre-sented in *Walt Whitman Abroad* (Syracuse, N. Y., 1955). See also Part III of the present volume.

2. In 1860 and later editions this poem closed *Leaves of Grass,* exclusive of the "annexes" after 1881.

3. Roger Asselineau, reviewing Jamati's book in *Les Langues Modernes,* XLII (1948), 447, remarked: "Certes, la traduction de Bazalgette a ses mérites. . . . Mais elle con-tient des gaucheries tout à fait inutiles et même des contre-sens caractérisés qu'il aurait été facile de corriger discrète-ment." He then cites some of the errors of Jamati and Sibon.

4. See W. T. Weathers, "Whitman's Poetic Translations of his 1855 Preface," *American Literature,* XIX (March, 1947), 21–40.

5. *Indiana University Conference on Oriental-Western Literary Relations,* eds. Horst Frenz and G. L. Anderson. University of North Carolina Studies in Comparative Litera-ture—Chapel Hill: 1955—pp. 177–89.

6. In an interview published in the New York *Herald Tribune Book Review,* March 26, 1950.

7. See G. W. Allen, "Biblical Analogies for Walt Whit-man's Prosody," *Revue Anglo-Américaine,* X (August, 1933), 490–507.

THE LEGEND: *Whitman's Image in the Twentieth Century*

1. Bliss Perry, *Walt Whitman, His Life and Work* (New York, 1906), p. 286, used this phrase to characterize the Whitman fanatics. He did not apply it to the poet's well known friends, though others have done so.

2. *Interpretations of Poetry and Religion* (New York, 1957), p. 178; first published in 1900. See also reply by

Henry Alonzo Myers, "Whitman's Conception of the Spiritual Democracy, 1855–1856," *American Literature,* VI (Nov., 1934), 239–63.

3.   Santayana, *Interpretations,* p. 178.

4.   *The Pluralistic Philosophies of England and America,* trans. Fred Rothwell (London, 1925), p. 31 and *passim.*

5.   *The Varieties of Religious Experience* (New York: Modern Library), p. 84.

6.   See index of *Walt Whitman Abroad.*

7.   *Varieties of Religious Experience,* p. 84.

8.   *Der Yankee-Heiland: Ein Beitrag zur Modernen Religions-Geschichte* (Dresden, 1906), pp. 228–29.

9.   *Walt Whitman, A Study* (London, 1893), p. 93.

10.   All of Edward Carpenter's books show his affinity for Whitman, but one of the strongest evidences of Whitman's influence is Carpenter's book of poems *Toward Democracy* (New York and London, 1912).

11.   Quoted by Isaac Goldberg, *Havelock Ellis: A Biographical and Critical Study* (New York, 1926), p. 75.

12.   Havelock Ellis, *My Life: An Autobiography* (Boston, 1939), p. 308.

13.   Havelock Ellis, *The New Spirit* (New York: Modern Library), p. 106.

14.   Quoted by Goldberg, *Havelock Ellis,* p. 220.

15.   This seems to have been Emory Holloway's view in "Whitman Pursued," *American Literature,* XXVII (March, 1955), 1–11, and has probably motivated his diligent search for children of Whitman. A major theme in his *Free and Lonesome Heart: The Secret of Walt Whitman* (New York, 1960) is Whitman's heterosexuality.

16.   "La Vie Anecdotique: 'Un témoin des funérailles de Walt Whitman,' " *Mercure de France,* CIII (1913), 658–59.

17.   Roger Shattuck, in *The Banquet Years* (New York, 1955), p. 220, refers to Apollinaire's "facetious chronicle," and remarks that, "The international polemic he provoked over Whitman's respectability and sexual mores spiced the pages of the *Mercure* for a year to come and tended to replace one misapprehension for another."

18.   *Mercure de France,* CIV, 204–10; CV, 221–22, 654–55; CVI, 219; CVII, 222–23; CIX, 864.

19.   Rufus Jones, *Some Exponents of Mystical Religion* (Nashville, 1930), chap. VI.

20. *A Life of Walt Whitman* (London, 1905), p. 55.

21. Vol. IV, edited by Sculley Bradley, was published in 1953 by the University of Pennsylvania Press and reprinted in 1959 by Southern Illinois University Press.

22. *Walt Whitman,* trans. Evie Allison Allen (New York, 1951), p. 300.

23. *Walt Whitman: L'Homme et Son Oeuvre* (Paris, 1908); trans. Ellen Fitzgerald (Garden City, 1920), p. 5.

24. Fernando Alegría, "The Whitman Myth in Latin America," *Américas,* VI (Feb., 1954), 9. This article was based on Alegría's book, *Walt Whitman en Hispanoamerica* (Mexico, 1954).

25. Quoted by Edwin Honig, *García Lorca* (Norfolk, Conn., 1944), p. 90. Quotation and translation used by special permission of *New Directions.*

26. *Ibid.,* p. 92.

27. Abridged translation of Gilberto Freyre's *O Camarada Whitman* (Rio de Janeiró, 1948), in *Walt Whitman Abroad,* p. 229.

28. *Ibid.,* pp. 146–47.

29. *Ibid.,* p. 147.

30. Most important: Samuel Sillen (ed.), *Walt Whitman, Poet of American Dream: Selections From His Poetry and Prose* (New York, 1944).

31. *Walt Whitman Abroad,* pp. 168, 169, 175, 177, 182.

32. *Walt Whitman: Oeuvres choisies, Poèmes et Proses,* (Paris, 1914); quotations are as translated by Roger Asselineau in *Walt Whitman Abroad,* pp. 72–73. On the Hegel question, see *Walt Whitman Handbook,* pp. 455–57.

33. From translation by Horst Frenz in *Walt Whitman Abroad,* pp. 7, 14.

34. *Ibid.,* p. 16.

35. From translation by E. A. Allen in *Walt Whitman Abroad,* p. 127.

36. *Studies in Classic American Literature* (Garden City, 1953), p. 183.

37. *Ibid.,* p. 190.

38. *Ibid.,* p. 191.

39. James E. Miller, Jr., Karl Shapiro, and Bernice Slote, *Start with the Sun: Studies in Cosmic Poetry* (Lincoln, Neb., 1960), pp. 133–34.

40. *Three Essays on America* (New York, 1934), pp. 79, 85.

41. See Frederick J. Hoffman, *The Twenties: American Writing in the Postwar Decade* (New York, 1955), pp. 124–27.

42. See Crane's letter to Allen Tate, *The Letters of Hart Crane: 1916–1933,* ed. Brom Weber (New York, 1952), pp. 352–54; also Philip Horton, *Hart Crane: The Life of an American Poet* (New York, 1957), pp. 262 ff.

43. *Defense of Reason* (New York, 1947), pp. 577, 590.

44. *The Man of Letters in the Modern World: Selected Essays: 1928–1955* (New York, 1955), pp. 296 ff.

45. Quoted by Hoffman, *The Twenties,* p. 126, from *American Mercury,* Dec., 1925.

46. "Alias Walt Whitman," *Harper's Magazine,* CLVII (May, 1929), 698–707.

47. See Herbert Bergman, "Ezra Pound and Walt Whitman," *American Literature,* XXVII, 56–61 (March, 1955); R. H. Pearce, "Ezra Pound's Appraisal of Walt Whitman: Addendum," *Modern Language Notes,* LXXIV, 23–28 (Jan., 1959); Babette Deutsch, *This Modern Poetry* (New York, 1935), pp. 125–26.

48. *T. S. Eliot and Walt Whitman* (Wellington, New Zealand, 1952), p. 15.

49. *Pictures: An Unpublished Poem by Walt Whitman* (New York, 1928); *I Sit and Look Out: Editorials from the Brooklyn Daily Times* (New York, 1932); *New York Dissected . . .* (New York, 1936).

50. See *The Solitary Singer,* pp. 221 ff.

51. Schyberg, *Walt Whitman* (translation), p. 342, note 77.

52. *Ibid.,* p. 252.

53. *Some Notes on Whitman's Family* (Brooklyn: privately printed, 1941), p. 5.

54. After Furness's death his papers came into my hands, and I used his bibliography and his transcriptions of Whitman manuscripts in preparing my biography.

55. *Walt Whitman, an American* (Boston, 1943), pp. 2, 3, 93.

56. A reference to a diary note of 1870 (now in Library of Congress)—see *The Solitary Singer,* p. 421.

57. *The Problem of Style* (Oxford, 1922).

58. "Whitman—Poesia del far poesia," *La Letteratura Americana e Altri Saggi* Turin, 1951); translated by Roger Asselineau, *Walt Whitman Abroad,* pp. 189, 193.

59. New York University Press, 1955; reprinted 1958 by Grove Press in Evergreen Editions.

60. *Howl and Other Poems* (San Francisco, 1956), pp. 23–24. Quoted by permission of Lawrence Ferlinghetti, publisher of City Lights Books.

61. "Notes Written on Finally Recording Howl," *Evergreen Review,* III (Nov.–Dec., 1959), 133.

62. *Walt Whitman's Leaves of Grass: The First (1855) Edition* (New York, 1959).

63. " 'Song of Myself' as Inverted Mystical Experience," *PMLA,* LXX (Sept., 1955), 636–61.

64. "Walt Whitman: Passage to India," *Indian Literature,* II (April–Sept., 1959), 38–43.

THE LEGEND: *Some Letters Concerning Whitman*

1. Benjamin not identified.

2. The residence of George Whitman, Walt's brother, with whom he lived after his paralytic stroke in 1873.

3. The sketch looks much more like a conventional image of Christ than any of the photographs of Whitman except possibly the frontispiece of the 1855 edition of *Leaves of Grass.* It plainly shows Carpenter's idealization of the poet.

4. Mrs. Anne Gilchrist came to the United States in the spring of 1876 with the intention of marrying Whitman. She rented a house in Philadelphia at 1929 North 22nd Street for herself, two daughters, Beatrice and Grace, and her son Herbert (one son remained in England). She furnished one room for Walt to use, and occasionally he did use it.

5. "Job" (the reading may not be correct because Carpenter's handwriting is very difficult to decipher) and the "genius" are probably children of the unidentified "Benjamin."

6. "A Woman's Estimate of Walt Whitman," Boston *Radical,* May, 1870.

7. The Gilchrists left America on June 7, 1879.

8. A pseudonym by which Carpenter was known to his friends.

9. Evidently the manuscript note books kept by J. W. Wallace on his visit to Whitman a few months before the poet's death and finally published by J. Johnston and J. W. Wallace as *Visits to Walt Whitman in 1890–1891* (London, 1917).

10. *Walt Whitman, A Study* (London and New York, 1893).

11. *The Life of Michelangelo Buonarroti* (London, 1892).

12. The name (something like Labaechere's) is practically illegible, and the newspaper notice has not been located.

13. Dr. John Johnston, see note 9 above.

14. Roden Noel (1834–94), British poet, whose *Essays Upon Poetry and Poets* (London, 1886) contains an essay on Whitman.

15. Horace L. Traubel, "Round Table with Walt Whitman," *In Re Walt Whitman* (Philadelphia, 1893), p. 303.

16. I do not find this title in Symonds's bibliography, though *A Problem in Modern Ethics* was published in London in 1896 by Leonard Smithers. Had he sent Carpenter a manuscript copy?

17. Edward Carpenter, *Civilization: Its Cause and Cure* (London, 1889).

18. Thomas Harned, an attorney in Camden, N. J., who with Horace L. Traubel and Dr. R. M. Bucke became Whitman's literary executor.

19. Dr. R. M. Bucke, a Canadian psychiatrist and author of a biography, *Walt Whitman*.

20. A magazine edited by Horace Traubel, devoted mainly to discussion of Whitman.

21. The "grandson" was probably the son of the widow of Walt Whitman's brother, Andrew; see review of Emory Holloway's *Free and Lonesome Heart: The Secret of Walt Whitman* (New York, 1960) by C. Carroll Hollis in *Walt Whitman Review*, VI (June 1960) 36–37. A letter presumably referring to this visit was reproduced in facsimile by John Ciardi in his review of Holloway's book, *Saturday Review*, June 25, 1960, p. 36. Holloway identifies the visitor as probably Walt Whitman's own son. Evidence against this identification is the letter quoted by Hollis and Ciardi. It is dated Dec. 7, 1892 (after Whitman's death), but Charles E. Feinberg owns a check list of letters received by Whitman prepared by Horace Traubel before the division of the poet's

papers in the summer of 1892, and this letter is listed. Evidently the letter was written Dec. 7, 1891.

22. The firm of Thayer and Eldridge published the third edition of *Leaves of Grass.*

23. Carpenter knew only the facts in the biographies of Whitman by John Burroughs (1871, 1896) and Dr. R. M. Bucke (1883). These did, indeed, give "only the barest outline" of Whitman's early life, but of course in 1902 many who had known Whitman were still living.

24. Eldridge seems to have confused two events: in 1840 Whitman campaigned for Van Buren on Long Island, in the region of Jamaica, and on July 30, 1841, he gave a speech at a Democratic rally in New York City.

25. The commonplace book in which Whitman made these entries is now owned by Mr. Charles E. Feinberg, of Detroit. It has never been published in whole although Edward Naumburg, Jr., quoted this letter in his article, "A Whitman Collector Looks at Walt Whitman," *The Princeton Library Chronicle,* III (November, 1941), 1–18.

26. "H. S." was indeed Harry Stafford, the teen-age son of Mr. and Mrs. George Stafford, who owned a small farm at Timber Creek, near White Horse, N. J., where Whitman partly regained his health during long summer vacations. The poet took a fatherly interest in the boy, though sometimes they quarrelled about money Whitman had loaned him, and a ring that Whitman had loaned or given him. (These details come mainly from conversations with Mr. Feinberg, who is almost the only person to have read through the commonplace book.)

27. During and after the Civil War many soldiers addressed Whitman as "father." Mr. Feinberg's collection contains many letters with this salutation.

28. Binns's brackets.

29. E. H. Griggs was a professional lecturer on literary subjects who was interested in Whitman.

30. This letter is in the Feinberg collection. I quoted it from a copy in the Lion Collection of the New York Public Library in *The Solitary Singer,* pp. 279–80. See also C. Carroll Hollis, "Whitman's 'Ellen Eyre,' " *Walt Whitman Newsletter,* II (1956), 24–26.

31. Laurens Maynard was a Boston publisher who published several Whitman books, including *Calamus: A Series*

of *Letters Written during the Years 1868–1880 by Walt Whitman to a Young Friend (Peter Doyle)*, ed. Dr. R. M. Bucke (Boston, 1897). Later he was a partner in the firm of Small, Maynard and Company, which also published Whitman books.

32. Peter Doyle gave a different impression of Whitman's relations with women in an interview with Horace Traubel and Dr. Bucke published in *Calamus* . . . (see note above), p. 25.

33. Henry Bryan Binns published *A Life of Walt Whitman* (London, 1905).

34. Whitman believed that the Negro should be educated and given time to attain a sense of civic responsibility (most were then completely illiterate) before receiving the franchise.

35. *A Life of Walt Whitman*, pp. 51 ff.